A HISTORY OF THE DEVIL

A HISTORY

William Woods

OF THE DEVIL

G. P. Putnam's Sons, New York

Here are hobbits,
hobgoblins and hobbyhorses
for my splendid
Alison, Jonathan and Jason
to read about when they are older.

Illustrations between pages 96 and 97

A prehistoric painting, the man-animal dancer, in the cave *Les Trois Frères* (in Ariège, France).

The ecstasy of the Bacchanalia painted on a Greek amphora; despite fantastic elements, this would seem to be a depiction of a real event.

A more controlled and "civilized" view of the horned god Pan, in a Roman sculpture; he is depicted teaching Daphnis to play the syrinx.

The head of a young girl, victim of a ritual sacrifice in the Danish Windeby bog.

A detail from the Gundestrup Cauldron, showing the method of sacrifice.

St Hildegarde of Bingen (1098–1180).

The devil embracing a young woman, in a woodcut dated 1489. For three centuries the devil appeared to many a young country girl.

The anti-establishment impression of the devil, as depicted in the confessions of many witches—and clearly it was important to the establishment that he look as reprehensible as possible.

A most comprehensive depiction of the activities of witches, from a sixteenth-century engraving.

Urbain Grandier, the priest of St Peter's Church in Loudun, burned at the stake for his part in the now-famous events that took place there.

Illustrations between pages 160 and 161

The exorcism of people "possessed by devils" was much described and depicted in the middle ages and even later, suggesting that the possession itself was by no means un-common—or at least thought to be so.

A cross-section of a witch's house, presumably for the instruction of the ignorant (1579). The conventions of witches' behaviour were firmly fixed in people's minds.

The trial by water of a suspected witch; the devil often resided in the body of a pig—as in the Gadarene Swine.

A seventeenth-century Dutch print of witches. The artist seems more interested in his own drawing than in the subject he is depicting—as though he no longer believed in it.

A renaissance Italian view of Hell from Orvieto Cathedral.

A witches' sabbath by Gillot.

Two of the devil's many guises. Herne the Hunter is only the English version of a very general legend of malicious woodland demons—an image both widespread and powerful, perhaps owing much to the frightening dark-ness of northern forests.

Le Lupeux, a night-phantom of Norman marshes; though it is described as having bird-like aspects, the artist has still felt constrained to give it horns.

The pattern of witchcraft continued into the eighteenth-century; all these drawings of the interiors of witches' houses are worth studying for their detail.

. . . but Poussin's age increasingly romanticized Pan and his followers, who in an earlier time would have been seen as the devil and his witches, and, earlier still, the god and his priests and priestesses.

This pacified, sophisticated Pan is a long remove from the fierce horned god of the old religion—and yet Burne-Jones's image retains elements that have shown a most particular durability.

Preface

The only unfortunate things about this book (to me) are the stories I have had to leave out: the diabolical and fascinating Johannine heresy, certain ideas about the cathartic function of the ballad, the rationale of blood sacrifice in Hartmann von Aue, mermaids, Hermes Trismegistus, the Rev. H. J. Prince, the Pied Piper, the story of Phrixus and Helle, the eye-biting witches of Ireland, my private miracle of Delphi that will comfort me if I am conscious in my own eternal bonfire, and a hundred other stories every bit as living as the ones I have set down. It could easily have been three or four times as long and, like the human race, have had an adolescence so protracted that it merged into senility.

I want to thank Kit for having remained unnaturally patient and my children for having tiptoed past my door and many others for having pointed out sources I should never have found without them. Philip and Nancy Vellacott offered help and encouragement beyond the call of friendship. My daughter, Pamela Thomas, has prepared the index.

w.w.

I

In one of his little *contes* Borges tells us that misery invariably uses the thought of a lost paradise to console itself, and any of us can summon up the memory of some sunlit, uneventful afternoon, translucent with innocence. The past may be dead, but it smells sweet (so Edward Thomas said); it acts as a counterpoise to the present, and even if that past is no more than some rheumatic old woman's memory of having looked up the chimney as a girl and been able to see the sky, it lends both nostalgia and a dimension of innocence to whatever part of life comes after it.

Indeed, our subliminal memory of paradise, of the garden of pomegranates, is perhaps the oldest in human history. Hesiod's Golden Age, Rousseau's noble savage, most of our greatest poetry, our music, our finest flights of the imagination, they all grew out of it. To pensioners sitting in the sun, the past was always purer. Old soldiers remember with advantages. Lost loves are savoury with hopes never to be realized. We began as angels, and here we are, "hung up like a box by a thread", as Jung says, with the cosmos, the ultimate reality gone out of sight. Whoever wrote the Egyptian *Book of the Dead* bemoaned that the stories had already been written, and Sir Thomas

Browne reminded us in the seventeenth century that the best was over. The night of time already far surpassed the day, and who knew when was the equinox? Burton, his near contemporary, complained, almost in the very words of the old Egyptian, that "We can say nothing but what hath been said". Like so many oarsmen, he tells us, we spend our lives rowing in one direction while we look backward in another.

Now, to explain this longing for the past is an essential part of my purpose, for whether that past was really akin to a golden age or only anybody's half-memory of the womb, we are going to discover that the devil, who is said to have caused the rot, to have killed paradise by creeping like a weevil into the uncorrupted wheat, did nothing of the sort. He was there, part of us from the beginning, for divinities, both gods and devils, are of course simply different facets of man, made as large as our imaginations can make them. It was not a devil who killed innocence, but the interrogative and acquisitive instincts in men, and we long most poignantly of all for that in us which we have ourselves betrayed. God walked in the garden, we are told, and the wheat was orient and immortal. But the devil was already inside; he was simply the material and thus frightening face of God, the face without which God (or man) would have been incomplete and unmanlike. Chekhov calls him the principle of the forces of matter, and William James, just as pertinently, the negative or tragic principle.

But Jung, in a mere two sentences, goes deeper. "Sexuality," he wrote, "is of the greatest importance as the expression of the chthonic spirit. That spirit is 'the other face of God,' the dark side of the God-image."[1] We shall see, I think, that either sexuality or a flight from sexuality is at the root of all western religion. Much in paganism exemplifies the one, much in Christianity the other. And the ultimate inadequacy of both lies in the fact that the parts of men's minds to which they appeal are complementary, but have generally been thought mutually exclusive.

For the moment, however, we are looking not at the wider picture, but at the devil. From the very start, human beings

[1] Jung, C. G., *Memories, Dreams, Reflections*. London, 1965.

needed—and created—not an infinite dimension to adore, but divinities with strengths and weaknesses similar to their own. Long before he was more than half understood, the devil became an identifiable protagonist, a tragic actor-in-man during an innocent, safe and irrecoverable yesterday. He was not only Satan. He was also, as the earliest prophets were perceptive enough to understand, Lucifer, the bearer of light, the spur to curiosity and thus to knowledge.

In time people built and lived in various established and evolving societies, based not only on the possession of material goods, but on customs and rituals of many sorts. Whoever rebelled against that evolution, whoever yearned after earlier gods, was said to be worshipping the devil, until some of the rebels actually began to believe it themselves. The more primitive is by definition uncouth and savage when it faces the contemporary. And we shall meet these rebels later when we talk about *la vecchia religione*, the primitive religion that had survived into a mordantly Catholic Europe.

Whoever in the face of spiritual disciplinarians cried out for tangible and immediate pleasures was anathematized as evil. He used an old, pragmatically efficient magic, not as a means of worship, but to gain an advantage. In Rome these people were *scelerosi* and *venefici*, and the *lex Cornelia* was promulgated during the republic to put them down. *Venefici* were poisoners. Indeed, under the Empire the use of aconite as a poison became so widespread that even its cultivation was made a capital offence. *Scelerosi* were slanderers. Both were destroyers in the devil's name of body or reputation. In later centuries they were called witches, and like the members of the Christian *agape*, or love feast, like the disciples, like various primitive groups before them who had gathered in the largest possible units able to maintain a certain psychic bond, they were organized in covens of thirteen. They worshipped and copulated with their leaders, whom they called devils, and used charms to create anything from storms at sea to sickness in their detractors, and that great minatory text of the Inquisition, *Malleus Maleficarum*, was written in what we might call medieval cooking Latin to explain, to identify, to examine and eventually to crush them. The attempt cost a good many lives, but in the end it failed.

People we would today think psychopathic personalities, or those whose behaviour looked to be perversely at odds with that of their neighbours, used a generation or two ago to be known as moral defectives. But three or four centuries earlier, such "moral defection" was taken as evidence that the sufferer had chosen deliberately to follow the devil's lead. So the history of the devil is in another sense the history of our continually shifting concepts of morality. Eve, after the Fall, whether a remnant of the mythology of Ur or not, covered her loins with fig leaves because the serpent had taught her to recognize her own desires—and because her history was written by a Hebraic moralist who wanted her to go out and eventually crush the serpent's head. Pandora, after she, too, brought evil into the world, was crowned by the Graces with flowers and new-grown herbs because hers was not.

But the story is of course more than that, more than desire. In time, the devil became the creature of whoever used God for his own purposes, whether political, legal, philosophical or economic, and invariably such men anathematized their opponents as heretics. God became the guiding light of establishments, and thus, if only by implication, the devil the leader of those who opposed them. We shall see this happening more and more frequently in the future as our own economic and environmental problems become more pressing.

Thus, to illustrate, when three thousand years ago Moses was brought before Pharaoh and turned Aaron's rod into a serpent, according to the authors of Exodus it was the work of God. When Pharaoh's servants showed that they could perform similar magic it was the work of sorcerers or witches. And did not Mosaic law, in an effort to keep spiritual matters in the hands of its own priesthood, decree that "thou shalt not suffer a witch to live"? And later, by the same token, "a man also or a woman that hath a familiar spirit, or that is a wizard, shall surely be put to death".[1]

[1] Exodus, xxii. 18 and Leviticus, xx. 27.

Yet 1,800 years afterwards, by the time Mahomet caused the *Koran* to be written down, Moses had in Moslem eyes been turned into a witch himself, for he was not only a theological but also a political opponent. Was not in fact a whole diabolical hierarchy invented by the medieval church to account for the continued and widespread evidence of heresies, some of which were heretical only if seen through the eyes of the momentarily established power? Johann Wier (1515–1588), a physician to the Duke of Cleves and in many ways a most remarkable man, worked out the number of devils exactly. There were 7,409,127, and they were led by 79 princes. The numbers are not actually divisible, one by another, and anyway there seems to have been a wide dispersion of the blood royal.

In a case of heresy, moreover, the evidence was always and only evidence for the prosecution. Kittredge makes it plain that at least in later centuries, prosecutions for witchcraft were generally not so much the work of any court as of the witch's neighbours. To that extent hobgoblins to frighten children are created by parents safe in front of their own fires. The idea of evil incarnate has long been familiar, not only to those who were afraid of their own unconscious urges, but also to politicians anxious to discredit the opposition.

So the devil was a poisoner—*veneficus*—the devil was a worker of spells, a witch, a sorcerer, the heir to conjurative mystery and incantation whose secrets are as old as the longing for magic itself. He lay at the root of our secret and uneasy pleasures and fed on our universal appetite for miracles. The devil was a heretic. And the devil was an alien god, worshipped at primitive or outmoded rites. Ovid and Apuleius, the lesser known Iamblichus of Chalcis, Porphyry and Plotinus and that great paganist, Proclus, give us many examples. More and more as the Christian church acquired its dominant position in western thought, the devil became known as the only formidable adversary to God himself, for Christian theology is a great exponent of the Newtonian law that every force is opposed by an equal and opposite force. Satan actually worked evil (there was no other way to account for it) as part of Almighty policy, and whereas in more primitive times the devil simply offered his followers pleasure as a bribe, when the struggle began to be exacerbated by the realities of temporal power, he came more and more frequently to offer that pleasure only in exchange for the delivery of an immortal soul, as though there were an undisclosed plan afoot to organize some vast electoral resolution at the time of the Last Trump.

But there is still more to it, of course. Just as the Christian devil, being more recognizably human than the Hebrew or Christian God, became easier to imagine and identify (because of course he lay inside us all), so the concept of hell was always more readily imagined than that of heaven. Preachers could pile on the agony of eternal torment; hell was vivid enough, for pain is translatable into every language. But heaven had to be left vague, for not only does its nature vary with every individual; the prospect of an excess of pleasure—no matter of what sort— was unquestionably bad for the character. And on the simplest level, no theologian in his right mind could offer in return for a virtuous life on earth a promise of endless drunkenness, fighting and fornication.

I have listed three categories of those damned with the devil. There is a fourth, that of the insane. When by reason of severe neurosis or perhaps unbearable stress the evil in a man burst out —in blasphemy, in whirling, incongruous words or actions, he was said to be devil-possessed, one of the wild and lonely ones battered by spirits that worked uncontrollably in their bodies. St Hildegarde of Bingen had her thighs and belly slashed by devils that dwelt in her. Illiterate peasants have spoken Greek, Latin and even Hebrew. Jews in Russia and Poland were possessed by the dibbuk that spoke out of their mouths in quite unfamiliar tongues. I have seen black professional dancers so utterly possessed that they could control neither their voices nor their movements, and through them have been able to touch that terror of the intangible which saints and psychopaths have tried to express. The casebooks of modern psychiatry are crowded with the victims' stories, with accounts of the tormented and hysterically possessed. When Christ cast out devils, it was either these devils he cast out, or, in several cases, those of epileptics.

A sub-category is that of the contagious hysterics, the flagellants, for example, whose mania swept western Europe until the Pope decreed that a penitent might only be whipped by a priest. Or there were the hordes that marched singing toward the sea in the Children's Crusade, or the wild groups like that of Lambert, the stammerer. These were not heretics, nor were they possessed. They were hunters after heaven, devil-driven into a wild, contagious and quite irrational spirit of self-destruction. They were hanged, burned, drowned, decapitated, murdered in one way or another by each other or by the establishment, for the church had great faith in punishment for the body as a cure for rebellion in the spirit. One medieval German army of the infected taught doctrines remarkably like those of the Nazis. Their hold on western Europe was almost as bloody, as brief, and every bit as suddenly ended. Or there were the devils of Loudun, who in the past few years have been palmed off on us almost *ad nauseam* as entertainment. But we are not often aware that there were roughly twenty-seven contemporary outbreaks of the same disease in various convents and orphanages.

Over fifty years ago, in spite of what many of us consider her later scholarly aberrations, Margaret Murray effected something of a revolution in the study of anthropology by demonstrating that all through the Catholic Middle Ages and the Puritan seventeenth century, those who were said to have sold their souls to Satan were by no means simply credulous or hysterics or victims of hallucination. And this we suspected. Most of them, she maintained—and here was the great discovery—were adherents of *la vecchia religione*, a religion better thought of as magic that had lain deep in human consciousness since neolithic times. So their diabolism had depended largely on when they had been born or in what milieu they had lived. To illustrate: the obscure, heretical and mostly illiterate followers of Peter Waldo, the Waldenses, were sent to the stake for doing that which caused St Francis to be canonized; and, many a half-savage Briton had his cottage burned down round his ears for not having been converted at the same time as the king.

To confuse matters even more, judges and witnesses in the many well documented trials seldom said what was really in their minds. Thus a man like Gilles de Rais, hanged in 1440, perhaps really had slaughtered hundreds of children (as witnesses alleged) in the exercise of barbaric ritual. He was the original Bluebeard. But he was not charged with murder. He was charged with witchcraft, Satanism, heresy, sacrilege and apostasy. Yet within two years of his death not only had a statue of him been erected at the place of his execution, not only had the king granted his loving family letters of rehabilitation, stating that he had without cause been condemned and put to death, but, oddly for a killer of children, he had begun to be venerated at the place of his execution by nursing mothers.

According to Professor Murray, Joan of Arc was in fact guilty as charged, but only in the sense that she was a worshipper of the primitive. To be sure, Alphonse Constant (who called himself Eliphas Lévi) had said the same thing a hundred years earlier, that she was "rather of the fairy family, than the hierarchy of holy women".[1] For in Joan's case, to be a witch meant to be a country girl from Lorraine, imbued like many of her neighbours with a pagan faith, with an animistic sense of nature and with powers of clairvoyance that stood in mute and stubborn rebellion against a hierarchy which ascribed all magic and all clairvoyance to one individually-named God or to itself. *Menteresse, pernicieuse, divinesse, superstitieuse, blasphemeresse de Dieux, ydolatre, invocateresse de déables, apostate, scismatique et heretique* was how they phrased the charge. Rather an unusual burden to be borne by a straightforward country girl of twenty.

But looked at in the light of Margaret Murray's evidence— and if I may digress here for a moment—it is interesting to note that like her escort and protector, Gilles de Rais, and like most later "devils", she rode a black horse (she was known for it all over France), and if we consider even for a moment that she may actually have been a "devil", then not only this, but the record

[1] Lévi, Éliphas, *The History of Magic*, trans. A. E. Waite, London, 1971.

of her trial provides illuminating reading. Thus she spoke of having seen the angels who were her Voices "even among Christians, they themselves unseen". At one point she admitted that she now and then signed letters to her friends with a cross "so that they not do as the letters said".

"My king and many others," she told the court, "have also heard and seen the Voices which came to me". Or, on another occasion, "Those of my party know well that the Voice had been sent to me from God. They have seen and known this Voice". Many a later witch made clear in front of her judges that she and her companions were accustomed to address the master of their coven as God.

Similarly, a certain Pierronne, a follower of Joan's who was burned in 1430, stated on oath that she had seen God in the shape of a man, and that when she had last met him he had been wearing a scarlet cap and a long white gown. Two hundred years afterward to Bessie Henderson he was to seem "a bonny young lad in a blue bonnet," to Elspeth Reoch a man in a green tartan plaid, to Rebecca Jones a very handsome young man who came to the door and asked how she did. Who but an hysteric or a follower of some *vecchia religione* could have made such a statement? And surely these women who gave the same evidence over and over again about what they had seen were not all hysterical in the same way, all suffering from the same aberration.

Never once like the treasonable Bishop of Beauvais and his priests who judged her did Joan refer to "our Lord", or "Christ", or "our Saviour".[1] And it was only when, twenty-five years after her death, it became desirable to rehabilitate her, so that her mother and brothers might lay hands on the fortune that had been amassed in her name, that Pope Calixtus III appointed a commission to re-open the case. And then, and only then was a witness found who would swear that he had heard her call on Jesus at the stake.

It is surely not unpleasant to remember (now that Joan is a heroine) that the bishop who had originally condemned her died suddenly a few years afterward, and that his body was thrown

[1] Murray, Margaret, *The God of the Witches*. London, 1952.

into the common sewer. And Charles VII, incidentally, who had abandoned her, died miserably by starving himself, for he had lived in perpetual terror of being poisoned by his son, who cannot, however, be accused of anything except an eager expectation of his death.

But none of us sees except with his own light, and Joan has been studied by certain twentieth-century psychiatrists as an archetypal case-history. For what it is worth, they have diagnosed her both as a victim of repressed sexuality and as an hallucinatory schizophrenic. And they tick off the bits of evidence with wonderful facility on their fingers. Schizophrenics, they say, rarely refer to Christ, but (like Joan) often to God. Most hallucinations, it seems, are auditory. Few are visible. Schizophrenics are totally without volition. If "voices" command them to act, it is quite beyond their power to disobey. Her well-attested clairvoyance, her unquestionable skill as a soldier and her fine flair for political management have, it seems, nothing to do with the case. They see only an introverted peasant girl at war with inward urges, who communed much with herself, heard voices commanding her to do certain things, ended (as she had to) by obeying, and doomed herself inevitably to the stake.

But if Professor Murray is right and Joan was an adherent to a religion (to a magic, if you like) older than Jesus, if we believe her statement, like Pierrone's, that the angels actually appeared to her and were thus not angels as we imagine them, but people she had known in the flesh, then the psychiatrists' case falls apart. We have to remember that even a hundred and fifty years afterward Remigius (Nicholas Remy) found the peasants of Lorraine so infected with witchcraft that with the best will in the world he could not avoid having several hundred of them put to death.

If in a word Joan was the "maiden" of what we might loosely call a witch's coven, we would have at least one possible explanation for the universal acceptance of her cognomen, *pucelle*. If none of what she heard and saw was a figment of the imagination (and in most of her words and actions she seems to have been both cautious and eminently sane) then we are no longer forced to think her courage, single-mindedness and intense devotion to France symptomatic of mental disease. She knew almost from the start what the end would be (she gave herself a year, and lasted fifteen months). And the prospect of being burned alive in the midst of a pile of brushwood no doubt frightened a twenty-year-old girl as much as it would any of us. Presumably the psychiatric criterion of healthy-mindedness is that it knows when to stop. But if that is true, some of the best of us are very ill indeed. Socrates heard voices too, and although one of the most healthy-minded of men, knew after his trial what the end would be, was offered the chance to escape, yet went voluntarily to his death.

In a word, as we shall gradually be made aware, the subject is very complex indeed, and as wide as the human imagination. Thus, as I pointed out earlier, sickness and death are supposed to have been born in the smiling and inquisitive face of Eve when she succumbed to the phallic serpent. And for her, of course, bitter experience made that phallus evil, although later, with Lamia and Dionysus and a host of others it had been turned into an object of worship. By the same token, graceful Pandora, made by order of Zeus as the first woman, and endowed by various deities with all delightful qualities, loosed evils into a once lovely world when she was unable to restrain her curiosity. That they were both women is part of the story's complexity, as is the fact that most of the redeemers and benefactors—Prometheus, Bran, Asclepios, Attis, Osiris, Wotan, Dis, Christ—should have been men, for later myth-makers resented the fact that many primitive societies had been matriarchal. With a host of others—Pan, Dionysus, Artemis, Isis, Lucifer, Belial, Beelzebub (or Baal), Apollo and Jahweh himself, they have almost all at different periods been both gods and devils, depending on the observer's point of view.

Only two things more remain to be said before starting on this voyage along what we might call the coasts of ascertainable fact. The first is that we shall not be concerned with the deliberate deviants, the more modern hunters after incantation and magic, who hunt because they are dissatisfied with actuality. We are not primarily concerned either with those occultists, indeed Satanists, who derived a fearful pleasure out of the pursuit of evil. They form a very unimportant category indeed.

No, our devil, the creature with horns and hoofs, may be so old as actually to be a fragment of racial memory, but he was never a flight from reality. He was part of far more interesting, more complicated, more vital and contradictory concepts of the world itself, part of the vast democracy of the dead on which without knowing it we still depend. For our purposes he was the god of the heretic, the hysteric, the sorcerer witch, the possessed, and of the atavistic religion that we all dimly remember. These are the subject of our story.

Two things more, I said. The other must be an apology. I am restricting myself largely to the devil in European civilization, and if I were to tell even that much history with any pretence at completeness, I should tax the patience of any but Satan himself. Thus, what someone has called the dark, voluptuous culture of Egypt, wherein so many of our ideas about magic were germinated, must be left as though it had hardly existed. Nor can the magic and demonology of Africa be included (though this too had its genesis in Egypt), or of Polynesia, of India, China and the West Indies. There are sometimes fascinating parallels to be found there with our own beliefs and superstitions. There are rites and practices in all these societies that fill gaps in the anthropological history of Europe and the Middle East.

The subject is simply too large for one book, or perhaps for any one man to do it justice. So I have had to draw what are in fact arbitrary limits, and within those limits simply set down as much of the story as I can.

2

The Pan-god who wore horns and hoofs like the later devil, the
goat god suckled by the nymph or she-goat Amalthea, was born
with palaeolithic man some thirty or forty thousand years ago.
Then and in his later Mediterranean incarnation he was a vigorous fellow with so hearty an appetite that when he had to be
weaned the milk spurted fiercely out of the nymph's breasts and
flooded the sky to become the milky way. He had all the devil's
strength, capriciousness and violence, as well as a very long
history indeed. So at first you will have to bear with me, because
it is absolutely essential to my purpose that I set him and his
origins into perspective. Let us therefore put him out of mind
for a moment while we talk about a number of things that will at
first seem irrelevant. They are not, but it is meaningless to talk
of the devil until we have first talked about worship, and thus
have some idea what the devil either lusted after or opposed.

Now, gods and demons were both born out of man's relationship with—his need of—the earth and of the powers he dreads
and appeases. And it can be shown that almost every one of our
beliefs about a communion with invisible and suprahuman mysteries, almost every one of our basic fears and superstitions
comes to us nearly intact out of palaeolithic or neolithic times.

A good many things we keep doing or believing long after we have forgotten the reasons. Some magic we still dimly apprehend, like the virtues of salt and iron, the ability of a dog or a horse to smell fear, the power the new, horned moon has to grant us our wishes. A forlorn faith in Magi who could foretell the future lives on in a hundred million readers of newspaper astrologers, and most of us believe in that sort of future memory called female intuition, the dumb knowledge that comes from a deeper level than ideas.

All of these superstitions have a basis in fact; all of them were once as real as daylight. For example, Marcel Mauss points out that "women are particularly disposed to hysteria, and their nervous crises make them particularly susceptible to superhuman forces which endow them with special powers". They are the "butt of superstition . . . which marks them off as a special class in society".[1] It is this psychic difference, not muscular weakness or the handicap of childbearing, that has set them apart and turned them at various times into lawgivers and chattels, into prophetesses and objects of worship, then into inferior beings and again into pure spirits which, to justify man's uneasy sense of superiority, have to be defiled. It is no accident that a woman's virginity—or a wife's fidelity—has always and in all societies been more important than a man's.

But to understand these things we have to start at the beginning. The Eskimo, the Australian aborigine, a few Filipinos like the Tasaday people of southern Mindanao and some Bushmen in Africa are the only remnants left of palaeolithic civilization today. Until only a little over a hundred years ago there were people painting animals on the walls of South African caves very like those painted 25,000 years ago in the caves of the Auvergne. But if we take a small step forward, the Orochon of northern Siberia, a few Gilyaks roaming the lower reaches of the Amur and the dwindling tribes at the northern end of Sakhalin Island are still migrant hunters who travel with the seasons and the game. And these people seem even today to possess an almost

[1] Mauss, Marcel, *A General Theory of Magic,* trans. by Robert Brain. London, 1972.

overpowering awareness, a vivid and animistic sense of collusion with the physical world that houses, feeds and in the end destroys them. It is such things, the animism, the intrinsic awareness, that are the roots and foundations of magic.

The Orochon is an essential part of his surroundings, equally functional with and neither more nor less important than the sticks, stones, trees and running water among which he lives. He and his world have struck a balance in ways that can only make us nostalgic for lost innocence, for an innocence destroyed by our dependence on a different causality and on our knowledge of the good and evil in ourselves. It is a balance, incidentally, not unrelated to that of the Greeks, who taught that all things, both in nature and in human relationships, are governed by an equilibrium which must not only be sought for, but which, when found, it is perilous to disturb. And if collusion is the beginning of magic, that equilibrium and the struggle to attain it are the origins both of what we call religion and what we call superstition, which is simply religion that we are not able to believe in.

But before we so much as look at this animistic Orochon, one fact has to be made perfectly clear. His primitive thinking or reasoning or even his perceptions are in no way whatever like ours. We must never for a moment try to imagine how we would think in his place, for his thoughts are not simply elementary or more banal versions of our own. They are radically different. For him there is no distinction between what is to us the real and the unreal, the factual and the imaginary. He never asks how a thing happens, or why. He does not deduce from evidence. But all anthropologists agree that in place of—indeed, in the virtual absence of—any power of practical reasoning, he has instead the equally important ability to remember selectively that which seems to pertain to the matter in hand, and to do so in vivid and complex detail. Among us this power is given only to some children, and now and then to the illiterate. Caesar tells us in *de bello Gallico* that the Druids did not write down sacred matters, partly for fear of allowing them to be vulgarized, but also because to do so might impair the memories of their priests.

And not only this. The primitive's world is populated, indeed crowded with spirits and invisible forces for both good and evil, spirits more numerous and quite as actual as the things he can see. We look first for natural causes, he for supernatural. We understand, let us say, that people die for certain reasons. But he, seeing children perish and old men survive, the injured man recover and the healthy man of middle age drop in his tracks, is just as certain that death cannot be explained in any rational manner. It is due, not to reasonable but to mystically ordained causes, perhaps to the malignancy of an absent enemy, perhaps to a victim's own failure to propitiate the gods. In a word, nothing ever happens purely by accident or misfortune, and neither illness nor a wild beast nor a spear in the side is the actual cause of death. These are merely the agents of the occult power which willed the death, and which might equally have chosen any other instrument to bring it about.[1]

And since this is true, the more an event looks to us like an accident, the more significant, the more malign it will look to a primitive man, and the more likely it will seem to him that the perhaps innocent instrument of accident or death was, all unknown to itself, possessed by the devil. There is in fact an even more complicated possibility. The tiger, the falling tree, the lightning that struck may actually be the property, the familiar as it were, of an enemy. And it is that unknown enemy, not the tiger or the tree, that must be destroyed or avoided.

Some Orochon campfire talk has been set down, and in this case it illustrates not his religion, but his sense of the vividness and individuality in all things.[2] "Old shadows look tired. Creeping slowly this evening behind branches, under trees, on the ground. Evening come not very fast. Tomorrow cold."

Or he talks to the fire as if for all the world it could hear him. A wicked woman, he calls her, and scolds her playfully. Old on the outside, with flying white hair and many tongues. But inside she is as young as a girl, with red blood in her veins, and terribly strong. The fire is always hungry, little greedy-guts. So you must

[1] Lévy-Bruhl, Lucien, *Primitive Mentality.* Boston, Mass., 1966.
[2] Lissner, Ivar, *Man, God and Magic.* London, 1961.

throw her a bit of bear fat now and then. Look how she laughs! And never leave her alone, for a woman is jealous and wants company. Turn your back on her and it makes her angry. Give her no fat or wood—no sacrifice to her needs—and she goes wandering and burns a forest.

That Orochon was on intimate terms with whatever part of the world he inhabited. Even inanimate things in the forest were alive, and that was the whole point. Water was temperamental. It laughed, it shouted or wept. Clouds played like the bears, tucked in their heads and rolled delightedly over the mountains. Every stick of wood in the fire spoke a different language, depending on the character and experience of the tree it came from. The very stones had souls. We shall see how true this is later, in a tale about the Venerable Bede. A stone was glad to be a stone, and could not for the life of him imagine being anything else.

So this man who lived in the midst of nature had a knack of talking familiarly to the thousands of things and creatures he saw around him. Hours were segments of an animate day, no two minutes of which looked alike. That is, if one had eyes. Days were parts of seasons. Seasons were visible stages in your life. To find shelter you adjusted yourself to the terrain. You used the friendly and familiar qualities of fire and water to cook food, and when your family was hungry you apologized to the bear before you killed him. But to do this you had first to establish a relationship, intimate and remarkable, with him, and he with you.

This you did partly with the help—perhaps with the incantations—of the shaman, or priest, who according to Bastian entered while conducting his ceremonies into a state of possession so intense that he could with impunity clutch a red hot iron in his hands or slide hot knives over his tongue until the hut was filled with the smell of burning flesh.

"According to the Tungures of Turukhansk," wrote Mikhailovsky, "the man destined to become a sorcerer sees the devil in a dream. . . . Among the Yakut the incipient shaman raves like a madman. He mutters incoherent words, loses consciousness, throws himself into fire or water, wounds himself with whatever weapons lie handy." He is taken to an old shaman to be taught where spirits live in the air or underground, and "the old man leads his pupil up a high mountain, clothes him in shaman's robes, gives him the tambourine and drumstick . . . and above all commands that the candidate abjure God and devote his whole life to the demon who in turn will do as he asks".[1]

It hardly needs pointing out that Christ too was led up into a mountain by the devil, and indeed we shall meet this shaman-like state of possession by spirits not one's own again and again. So intense was the emotional strain among those professionally possessed that, like the prophetesses at Delphi and the inspired priests of the Bataks, they often died while still very young. As a matter of fact, a Russian neurologist, Dr W. W. Karelin, reported in 1909 that he had observed a shaman whose rate of respiration rose while in a state of possession from twenty to thirty-six a minute, and whose pulse-rate rose from 80 to 200.

We have learned so much about our own palaeolithic ancestor thirty or forty thousand years ago, that like the Orochon he was a small, dark-haired, swiftly moving hunter. That he lived very often in caves to shelter from the cold of the last Ice Age. That he dressed in skins, for he was neither a herdsman who sheared wool (and in any case there were no sheep or goats in Europe), nor a farmer who could grow flax or cotton for cloth. That although he was not quite as tall as we are, he seems to have been every bit as intelligent and in appearance as manlike, with a mind (as with primitive peoples today) probably not as given to reason, but far more retentive than ours. That his brain was as large, in some cases larger. That he lived in tribes or family groups, if for no other reason than that a man who hunted alone in that barbarous climate would have been helpless. That his need for being part of a group established physical and indeed

[1] V. M. Mikhailovsky's report in the *Transactions* of the Russian Royal Society of Natural History, Anthropology and Ethnography (1892) was translated and republished in the *Journal* of the Anthropological Institute of Great Britain in 1895.

psychic bonds between him and his fellows as strong as those of instinct-ridden animals that hunt in packs, or of those highly organized insects such as ants or bees who invariably die if they become separated from the community.

But most important of all to our enquiry is the fact that his way of thinking unquestionably corresponded to that of the modern Orochon or Bushman, Dyak or Melanesian, first in that he was radically conservative and unwilling to change or experiment (and thus release heaven alone knew what hitherto unknown spirits), and second in that, as Lévy-Bruhl says, "Not a single being or object or natural phenomenon . . . is what it appears to be to our minds. Almost everything we perceive in it escapes their attention or is a matter of indifference to them. On the other hand, they see many things of which we are unconscious".[1]

Equally important, at least for our purposes, is the fact that there was very likely no marriage or giving in marriage, but that girls and women enjoyed (if that is the word) a polyandrous relationship with several or even many of the men in their family or tribe. This meant of course that fatherhood did not exist as an institution, paternity being both uncertain and irrelevant, and wherever this has been true the society has been matriarchal. Most of our myths and many of our religions can be demonstrated to have originated in matriarchal societies. Perhaps, incidentally, this is the reason for the later marriages of various ancient kings with their sisters—to preserve the primal stock. Cinyras, king of Paphos, begat the god Adonis in intercourse with his daughter, Myrrha. But it would be interesting to know when and why the taboo against incest among ordinary people originated, for it exists in most (though not all) primitive societies that have been studied, in some of which is a capital offence, and in many others is supposed to blast the crops and bring pestilence to the people themselves.

Death came early to those ancestors of ours. Examinations of Stone Age skeletons reveal that their average expectation of life

[1] From his *Les Fonctions Mentales dans les Sociétes Inférieures* (1910) which so far as I know has not yet been published in English.

was probably about fourteen years, for of mesolithic bones that have been uncovered 86·3% were of people who had died before they were thirty, 95·5% before they had reached the age of forty.[1] Most, of course, perished in infancy or childhood, and indeed, of a hundred and seventy-three skeletons examined, only three proved to be those of people who had reached the age of fifty.

With so many deaths before puberty their birth-rate was dangerously low, and on the basis of these facts, as well as on estimates of the amount of game that could feed on the subarctic vegetation, it has been computed by De Laet in his *L'Archéologie et ses problèmes* that the average population of Belgium during the last Ice Age was about four hundred for each generation, while that of England (according to an estimate of Sir J. G. B. Clark) was hardly more than two hundred and fifty.

But because palaeolithic man lived almost entirely on meat, there is evidence that he never suffered from rickets, and rarely from dental caries. He seems to have known the arts of trepanning and (in the Magdalenian culture) of circumcision, of amputation and the setting of broken bones. Indeed, a knowledge of bone-setting was necessary if he was to survive, for it was a bloody, dangerous, terrible time wherein for a space of perhaps three hundred centuries and during well over a thousand generations, only the fittest and most agile could survive. Müller-Christensen examined the skull of a man aged forty or forty-five who had over a period of several years suffered four separate cranial fractures, caused probably by blows from a stone axe.[2] All of them seem to have healed, although one had actually cost him the use of his left eye. (it is interesting to note, by the way, that even in the twentieth century a dying Breton peasant could ask of his fellow villagers that his skull be smashed with a stone axe). Near Ofnet in Bavaria the members of an entire tribe have been found murdered in their cave. This seems likely to have been a rare occurrence, however, for war grows out of a desire

[1] Janssens, Paul A., *Palaeopathology*, trans. Ida Dequeeker, London, 1970.
[2] Quoted by Janssens, op. cit.

for territory or material goods, and these men had plenty of one and none of the other.

Palaeolithic man was adaptable and good with his hands. He not only made arrow heads out of flint, out of horn and bone he made points for harpoons, awls, pins, and needles with well-formed eyes. Out of shells and animals' teeth he made bracelets and necklaces. Out of reindeer horn he made a curious wand that has been called by differing anthropologists an arrow straightener and a *baton de commandement* and lately has been identified by Alexander Marshak, on the basis of microscopic examinations (and with far greater probability), as a primitive calendar.

He may in times of hunger have practiced cannibalism (although authorities disagree about this), and when there were too many mouths to feed was probably guilty of infanticide. He had not yet domesticated the horse or even the dog, for horses as we know them did not exist in that climate, and dogs, which were then largely wolves, would have been little use to him. With his spears and stone-tipped arrows he hunted the musk ox, the reindeer, the bison and the hairy mammoth, and the miracle is that, in spite of conditions not unlike those of modern Greenland, in spite of bloody and incessant dangers, in spite of sporadic hunger, sometimes for months on end, in spite of sickness (without even herbal remedies for help) and almost invariably early death, the race actually managed to continue in some sort of natural equilibrium, with no increase, but with no real depletion of numbers either, for thirty or forty thousand years.

A bloody, terrible time indeed, yet man survived. And it is probably true to say that he did so principally because he possessed powers both of endurance and clairvoyance, powers of memory, of acute observation and resistance to pain similar to those of primitive people still alive today. Those who did not simply went to the wall.

"No arts, no letters, no society," says Hobbes in a famous passage in his *Leviathan*, "and which is worst of all, continual fear and danger of violent death; and the life of man, solitary, poor, nasty, brutish and short." Well, that was only part, and probably an inessential part of the truth. Man was certainly not solitary and not without arts, as we shall see in a moment. Hobbes makes the more important mistake of looking at that alien environment through the eyes of a cultivated seventeenth-century Englishman, instead of understanding that it could only be evaluated properly by those who grew up and lived in it. Like Hobbes, we who are able to read, nevertheless look without seeing, listen without hearing, are told without remembering more than a small particle of both things and seasons laid out like a map in front of us. On the other hand, it has been reported of tribes living in neolithic conditions even in the twentieth century that they possess what can only be described as a supranormal ability to communicate without visible or audible signals over enormous distances.[1] In other words, they are capable of accurate thought-transference. A good many modern observers have testified to the ability of people as advanced as the Tibetans to run journeys approaching two hundred miles a day, which any coach of athletics will tell you is a physical impossibility. But tales both of endurance and of complete indifference to pain among primitive people are not merely common but commonplace.

Much of the evidence, to be sure, the exhumed shreds of palaeolithic life, is evidence not of ideas but of things. Seashells from both the Atlantic and the Mediterranean coasts have been found in Pyrenean caves, so it seems likely that trade or traffic was carried on between reindeer hunters in the hills and fishermen on the still unharvested sea. What can only be described as factories for the manufacture of tools and weapons have been found in northern England, and implements made in these factories turn up as far away as Devon and Cornwall. All over Britain there are neolithic trackways. Boats, nets, jewels, weapons, bones, pitfall traps, whole dwelling places and the debris of temporarily settled communities have been uncovered with ashes from their fires still lying in the middle of the floor.

These are physical manifestations, primary evidence. There is

[1] Klaatsch, Hermann, *The Evolution and Progress of Mankind*, trans. Joseph McCabe. London, 1923.

secondary evidence, partly inferential, to be sure, but none the less valid and important, that this society, preoccupied with the need for food, warmth, sexual gratification and the preservation of the species, lived a communal existence (as I pointed out above) more intense than any industrialized man can reasonably understand. Yet to see it in practice one need only think of animals in front of our very eyes, of birds in flocks, of fish in their shoals which not only travel enormous distances with an almost infallible accuracy, but which are alert the whole time to all but invisible and inaudible signals, and which act in moments of danger with a unanimity and cohesiveness of which men are no longer capable except at moments of quite overpowering emotion.

In his superbly lucid study of prehistoric times, *Ancient Europe*, Stuart Piggott does indeed point out that "there is a past in itself which we can never grasp". And in this journey of ours, this setting out to discover truths whose origins are ultimately undiscoverable, we must beware of drawing unwarranted inferences. But a certain distance we may go. If from what we have already discovered we adduce that people could hardly have survived without intra-tribal bonds, intense but not needing to be spoken, we shall probably be very near the truth.

Now, such intensity, such almost hypnotic union is close to possession and comes very near the borders of magic. And if we add to this near magic what we know of the Orochon, with his animistic awareness of the world he uses and is used by, we are very close to perceiving how suprahuman divinities could grow at one's very fingertips.

Not only can the Orochon (and by inference our palaeolithic ancestor) smell out, so to speak, things to which we are insensitive, not only can he, like the gypsy, talk intelligibly to horses, not only can he receive and send out signals to which we are blind; his world—and here is the essential point—is quite in balance. The tribe is a unit, and it is surrounded by darkness, by silence, by an infinity of which it is not even aware. Good and bad are both within reach and complementary, and there is for the individual no causality. There is no why. He is adjusted, not only to his society but to his environment. Nothing for which he can be held responsible either increases or diminishes him. And this state of balance, this having the ultimate within one's grasp, no matter what privation attends it, what suffering or death it carries with it as facets of its normality, is surely the fundamental, the prerequisite of a golden age. For it lacks that kind of rationalized forward striving which in the past few thousand years we have come to think idiosyncratic to man himself.

To be sure, we usually equate a golden age with some idyllic place to inhabit, a South Sea island perhaps, drugged with idleness, a perpetual afternoon wherein men can make love, drink and lie swathed in flowers while fruit falls into their laps. In fact we soon tire of not having to struggle; there is no lasting equilibrium in ease. The foetus struggles to be free of the womb. Circe's lovers were turned into swine. But the thought that we lived in palaeolithic Europe for tens of thousands of years when the struggle was exactly adequate, when from century to century nothing really changed, when we wanted no more than we had (for we could imagine no other), that we made the tools we needed and nothing else, that for all the pain and early death we were sufficient, both to ourselves and to our surroundings, that in a word we had not yet eaten the fruit of the knowledge of good and evil—these things argue not only a certain truth in the simplification of Genesis, they argue that the racial memory of a time not necessarily golden, but at least in equilibrium, is not without foundation, and I shall have much to say about that Greek equilibrium when we come to it. It is in fact the fundamental prerequisite for human happiness.

Like the Orochi or the aborigine, these people were not agriculturists, but hunters. The hunter undoubtedly mimed the hunt in telling about it when he came home at night—his modern counterpart does the same. That he mimed what he would do in the next hunt, what valley he would follow, what ambush employ, what weapons carry, seems equally clear. And of course the individual mime, being only part of a communal expression, became a dance that not only gave expression and delight; it was an evocation of reality, of material fact out of thin air, and to make facts out of thin air is always a pleasurable and an intensely emotional business.

The dance, being often repeated, would evolve into a form of sympathetic magic. Like produces like; the image produces the object of which it is a picture. Dancing, he would come to believe utterly in a quasi-sensible wizardry for which he had no proof that there were consequences (except that consequences seemed manifest), in actions which could have no real influence on anything but the mind of the actor. He had none of what we would call logical reasons for the things he was doing, and yet as far as he could ascertain they worked, because they satisfied needs in himself as vivid and important as the hunt for which they were designed. What is more, these dances—naked, of course, because clothing was worn only as a protection against the cold—the masks they wore (and representations can be found over and over in cave drawings), the chanting, the incantation would now and then have seemed even to us not only frightening (for raw, physical force is always frightening), but wildly beautiful, just as the drawings they made and their very concept of magic were beautiful, and that, because both were effective.

This dancing would tend to become a necessary inward experience and probably a sexual excitant as well, for in many of the drawings the phallus seems unnaturally prominent. It evolved into a kind of contagious hysteria which expressed the tribe's sense of community, of continuity and of its relationship with exterior reality. It was the precursor of the Pict's tattooing, the demoniac frenzy of the Voodoo worshipper, the trance-like state of possession known to both saints and psychotics. The individual abandoned his individuality and made himself part of the larger tribal consciousness. Indeed it can be maintained that as with our famous equilibrium, a ritual approach to life that gives each one his part to play is essential to human happiness. In any case, it was the beginning of religion, a religion which must have been peculiarly satisfying and needful, for it grew, not superimposed, but in the very muscles of the mind, and made its worshipper part of the larger unseen order to which he had subjugated himself.

But there was a material side to it too. As modern Hungarians produce a wine they call *egri bikaver*, or Bull's Blood,[1] and scores of companies manufacture beef broths and essences supposed to restore the convalescent, to give him the strength of the bull on the label (sympathetic magic again), as many a gullible housewife thinks a fish diet good for the intelligence, no doubt because it looks like brain, so palaeolithic man drank the blood of his victim to acquire the victim's courage and agility, and wore the skin and horns of the stag wherein to act out the hunt and acquire an even stronger affinity with the beast he was about to kill. So, incidentally, did Dionysiac revellers much later. In *The Bacchae*, Euripides described their costumes in detail. So did witches in seventeenth-century Lincolnshire, not in imitation, for they knew nothing about their ancestors, but because all through history similar urges have been expressed in similar ways. Thracian orgiasts danced and then copulated on the hillside with their companions, and thus not only assured the fertility of their crops by the use of sympathetic magic, but achieved that purgation of the emotions which according to Aristotle was the beginning of drama. So, incidentally, did witches with a leader they called the devil, but that is another matter, and we shall be looking into it.

Now, no dance, no ritual ever remains spontaneous for long. There must be leaders, either particularly vigorous men possessed of much empathy, or perhaps old and experienced hunters who remember which cries and dances have in the past seemed particularly effective. And with these one would have the beginnings of a priesthood, a religious as opposed to a secular leadership. When that leadership began to employ ritual too consciously as a trick, when the animism became a device to

---

[1] It is worthy of note that according to Robert Graves in *The White Goddess*, "Bull's blood was most potent magic, and was used, diluted with enormous quantities of water, to fertilize fruit trees in Crete and Greece. Taken neat, it was regarded as a poison deadly to anyone but a Sybil or a priest of mother earth". Actually, as any horticulturist knows, dried blood is rich in nitrogen and would be particularly nourishing for plums.

sustain personal power, when in a word religion began to be used for alien purposes, then the quondam equilibrium had been lost. Eve had eaten the apple, and neither she nor Adam would ever be innocent again.

3

So far I have been talking about our ancestor's physical environment. But strangely enough, in spite of the seeming lack of evidence, a good deal can be deduced of what he knew (or imagined) about a supernatural world as well. For the evidence is there, more than one might suspect.

First, it is something of a truism that to a primitive man, as to a child, the representation of a thing is the thing itself. Mauss writes that in magic the image is to the object as the part is to the whole, not because the image is a portrait, but because whatever shape it takes, it is meant to represent the object, just as a knot represents love. But the symbolism can be even more complex. The "V" sign represented victory, not only because it was the word's initial, and, if made with the fingers, a symbol of defiance. The magic was perhaps reinforced when it was discovered that the Morse code for "V" is beaten out by the first four notes in a Beethoven symphony. Some of Henry Moore's sculptures do not look like women. They are ideograms, implying more than they say. Or to take an equally simply example, I can very well remember going to my first film at the age of six or seven, seeing the representation of a railway train on the screen and being puzzled because I knew perfectly well that there were no tracks anywhere in that part of town.

Second, primitive man had not made (any more than have the Siberian tribes with their shaman leaders) the simple step from a personal to an institutionalized religion. It was all of it intensely personal (the only sort of religion that carries weight), and if we may take the beliefs of our contemporary primitives as any sort of guide, the world was densely populated with invisible forces and with the souls of the lonely, vindictive and forsaken dead, against whom one had to be perpetually on guard, for they were both subtle and malevolent. What was worse, when at the moment of crisis, one perceived that they were at work, the damage had already been done.

There is evidence that palaeolithic man worshipped his ancestors as some of us do today, for in a world as crowded with demon spirits as a summer night with gnats, one would expect those of one's forebears to be more clearly aware of one's needs, more sympathetic, perhaps, than any anonymous ghosts. And of course in dealing with a mother or grandmother one started with the huge advantage of knowing the most private and secret thing about her, which was her name. Even in modern Melanesia magicians derive their power from the souls of dead relations, and mediaeval European blood pacts with the devil were of this genre.

It is probable that just as food was buried or burned with the dead to nourish them when they could no longer sit on their hams with the family, so offerings of food or whatever else they might need were made long after they had died. As long as anyone could remember them they were not really dead; they were part of the community. But like the rest of the living they required not only justice; they wanted affection. And they were crotchety and demanding. As Lévy-Bruhl points out in speaking of modern primitives, "Of all the complex feelings which ancestors inspire, fear is the predominating one. They are exacting, and one can never be sure of having satisfied them. In order that the prayers addressed to them may be heard, they must be supplemented by liberal offerings. Everything is done as if their good will were purchaseable . . . Junod has clearly set forth the nature of the unvarying relations subsisting between the tribe and its ancestors. These rest upon the principle of *do ut des*, allied with the feeling that a higher power rests in the ancestors. They may be entreated, supplicated, cajoled, but they cannot effectively be compelled."[1]

We may with all the more assurance infer that palaeolithic man had a relationship something like this with the ancestors he worshipped, first because it is a relationship more or less common to all the primitive societies we have been able to study, and second because it is almost precisely the same as that which was extended to the later European gods and demons of whom we actually have record. One worshipped, not out of love but out of fear, and the French missionary Junod's statement (he had worked for many years among the Ba-Ronga of South-East Africa) would apply equally to deities and demons as diverse as Jahweh and Herakles. They too required burnt offerings. They too demanded concrete evidence that they were remembered. Then, as now, the living needed the dead, and without the living the dead would no longer exist.

But for a moment we must go back to the beginnings and picture a cave in the Pyrenees (our case does not depend on the supposition), a cave wherein five or ten sweating figures are gyrating, crying out, quite possessed in the light of a smoky fire. By accident the head and shoulders of a dancer throw a shadow that looks remarkably like a reindeer on the wall. He turns, sees what he has done, picks up a bit of burnt stick and redraws the shadow he had made, for the shadow is most potent magic.

It is not his first attempt at drawing. On other nights he has already dipped his hand in red or black or ochre dye and pressed it against the wall to leave an imprint of the palm. Such imprints (sometimes they are negative prints) have so far been found in about fifteen caves. It was his signature, his individual protective magic, something like the initials we draw in soot at the back of a chimney or cut into the bark of a tree. He almost always used the left hand, incidentally, and the prints often show

[1] *Primitive Mentality*, p. 88.

one or two of the fingers missing. These one would normally imagine to have been lost by accident, but, curiously enough, it is rarely the thumb he has lost. If fingers were deliberately sacrificed, as some pygmies and Hottentots sacrifice them today, the hunter was at least careful not to deprive himself of a thumb.

But I said that the representation of a thing was the thing itself. And palaeolithic man left such representations in well over a hundred caves that he inhabited. We have all seen reproductions of the wall paintings in Altamira, Lascaux, the Cueva Remigia or in the Caverne des Trois Frères in Ariège. These are of hunters and animals in movement, in several instances of men and women dancing (one at Cogul wherein women dance round a man who wears garters; we shall presently see why), some masked, wearing horns or the heads of birds, and almost all of them displaying a sharpness of eye and memory in the draughtsman quite equal to that of a Renaissance artist.

The pictures are alive, for the painters are not only acutely observant; they are bound by a deeply-felt, animistic awareness to the reality of what they were setting down. The animals' legs, for example, the hock, fetlock and shank of deer and bison, the curve of the neck, are drawn with marvellous exactitude. In a word, the animal—or indeed the hunter himself, running, throwing the spear—is so vividly realized that it becomes almost a hallucination. The drawing is quite obviously not done for mere love of decoration; some of the figures are actually hidden, in remote parts of the cave, places that must have been difficult of access. They were in all probability magic-inducing representations, as were those of the horned dancer. They were remembered passion that had gone out into the night beyond reason, but was here made tactile and permanent. It was not only the figure that interested the artist, perfectly as it may have been realized. It was the movement of living bodies, the vitality behind that movement, and thus the magical power over those bodies that he hoped to attain.

No less was this true in drawings of animals jumping, falling feet uppermost into a pit, even giving birth. These were representations of acts either seen or wished for—and the fertility of the beast was no less important than its capture. This can equally well be said about the remarkable engravings on ivory or stone, of fish (for of course these men became fishermen, too, as the ice retreated), of rivers flówing or the outlines of human beings. There is nothing primitive about these works of art, nothing stylized, either, for real magic, as we shall see later, has no use for the extraneous.

Less easily explicable are the tiny stone or ivory sculptures, generally only a few inches high, of female bodies (they have been called Venus figurines), generally steatopygous, with enormous buttocks, but sometimes as graceful and slender as the more familiar paintings of medieval women in England and France. Della Santa has put forward several suppositions to account for them.[1] But the fact that two such figurines seem to be wearing horns, and that others have been found in a niche in a cave during excavations in Siberia, would seem to indicate that they were fertility symbols and household goddesses. We remember too that the hunter's penis was exaggerated in drawings, and that this was very likely a form of sympathetic magic to increase his physical potency, that is his potency in both fecundation and in the kill. In primitive societies, as in our own, the female pudenda are generally taboo because they are considered both private to the individual and unclean. But secondary sexual characteristics, breasts and buttocks, can be represented instead to increase her fertility.

The witch who later made a wax image of some enemy in order to destroy him was doing the same thing in reverse. Then, as now, like a spear or an arrowhead, a human figure was made for its utility, not for its power to give aesthetic pleasure. Indeed, the idea of aesthetic pleasure may not originally even have existed. A farmer buys a cow, after all, not for her pretty face, but for her power to produce healthy calves. Twentieth-century Eskimos have more than thirty words for various types and conditions of snow, but no satisfactory word for art. James Houston wrote that "Like most other hunting societies, they

[1] Saccasyn-Della Santa, E., *Les Figures humaine de Paléolithique supérieure Eurasiatique.* Anvers, 1947.

have considered living in harmony with nature as their art. The objects they carve or decorate are to them merely reflections of their total art of living". And later he adds, "Hunters are of necessity butchers, and this gives them a fine knowledge of anatomy. They judge a good carving by the sense of life the carver imparts to the stone. A good carving should reveal the weight of a walrus, the agility of a bear, the sleekness of a fish, the closeness of a mother and child, the terrifying gaze of the moon spirit."[1]

Incidentally, the idea of art as collective magic, magic belonging to society as a whole, no matter by whom created, is still with us. If a man buys an acre of land or puts money into a bank the income will accrue to his descendants in perpetuity. But if he writes a book or a piece of music the copyright will after a certain number of years revert to the community.

In any case, we have come a long way forward from the simple magic of the horned dancer, and with the Venus figurines we have an inanimate representation, distinct from that of the artist and intended to serve an animate function which he cannot himself perform. To be sure, these people had probably not yet formed any idea (as we have) of cosmic forces too vast for comprehension. They made magic, but so far it was made only to affect the happenings of the day.

There was an even more potent magic in dreams, which in all primitive societies are understood to be tokens of warning or advice that must invariably be heeded. For quite obviously, in a dream your own spirit has either walked abroad and given you notice of what was about to happen, or else the spirits of friends, enemies (perhaps hitherto unknown as such) or ancestors have revealed themselves. In sleep, it was maintained, one's spirit enters into a spirit world, and by doing so confers on its owner advantages that it would be foolish or even dangerous to ignore. What a primitive man sees while dreaming is as true, as real as the things he sees while awake. The dead have made their wishes known to the living. The tiger, the tree about to fall, have given warning of their evil intent.

[1] *The Observer*, 1 October, 1972.

In *An Experiment with Time*, J. W. Dunne presented a good deal of data to confirm a theory that time, like space, looked consecutive only if seen from a fixed position, the here and now, but, just as a vast area of land can be looked at all at once from a balloon, so events past and to come can be seen as simultaneous when we have escaped the restricting evidence of our senses. Thus, in dreams, he maintained, we can sometimes see before and after, and this is of course what for three thousand years the prophetess at Delphi purported to do. Our ignorance about primitive clairvoyance is profound, except that there seems to be more than a presumption that it exists.

"And Joseph dreamed a dream, and he told it his brethren, and they hated him yet the more."[1] In Egypt, of course, Joseph acquired political power by interpreting Pharaoh's dreams, for to the more subtle it early became clear that dreams were not always the literal records of future events, but had to be divined before their inner meanings could be understood.

Lévy-Bruhl tells us that "What it behoves the primitive to understand above all is the agency of the mystic forces by which he feels himself surrounded. These forces, by their very nature, are invisible and imperceptible. They only reveal themselves by more or less explicit manifestations. . . . When these manifestations are not forthcoming of themselves, the primitive mind exercises its ingenuity to induce them; it invents methods of procuring them (such as dreams which are instigated, processes of divination, ordeals, and so on). . . . Thus the dream brings to primitives data which in their eyes are equal to, perhaps even more valuable than, the perceptions of the preceding day."[2]

In a word, then, and to sum up what we have so far discovered even with only shadowy evidence to go on, it seems at least highly probable that before men and women had so much as built settled communities, witchcraft, magic, contagious hysteria and what later became thought of as religious possession had become integral parts of their experience. Certainly no one can point to a time when these things were not already old.

---

[1] Genesis, xxxvii. 5.
[2] *Primitive Mentality*, pp. 98–99.

But now, with the gradual evolution of an easier environment, the imagination of primitive man was about to take a great leap forward. For a little after 10,000 BC the ice began to melt and drift away northward, and during a period that lasted several dozen generations men began to find around them a vegetation which, at least as far as they knew, had never grown before. The land bridge between Britain and the continent still existed. The Thames and Rhine were branches of a single river, and indeed it seems a man could have walked on dry land all the way from Italy to Iceland. Kiel Bay and the Kattegat did not exist, and the Baltic was nothing but a fresh-water lake. But the Mediterranean grew wider with the melting of glaciers, and there was a positive explosion of population, for not only did life become easier, but its average span lengthened to about twenty-five years, so of course far greater numbers lived beyond puberty and were able to bear children. Thus an estimated population per generation of 400 in Belgium during the last (Würm) glaciation grew to 10,000.

For the first time Europeans were able to stop roaming, leave their winter caves, form rude villages with thatched houses built to last more than a season, and explore the possibilities of the land itself, instead only of the game. About 8000 BC dogs that looked rather like our modern chows were domesticated. The hunters learned the advantages of becoming herdsmen, driving their deer and wild cattle into corrals around the hutments. Then for the first time grain was sown broadcast as they had seen the wind doing it, first of all wheat and barley. As the climate continued to improve, other grasses which had originally seemed weeds—varieties like oats and rye—established themselves, turned out to be edible and began to be sown as crops in their own right. In fact, many plants now once again thought of as weeds—knotweed and bristle grass—were then parts of the staple diet.

Bliss was it in that dawn to be alive.

But a new prosperity brought new problems too. We read in Genesis, for example, that Abel was a keeper of sheep, Cain a tiller of the ground. And the antagonism born of conflicting interests between arable farmer and cattleman has been perpetuated all through agricultural history. And even though herdsman and sower of seed have made common cause against forces that threatened them both, it was in fact out of their opposition and out of the divergence between past and present in the emerging communities that the devil as we know him was originally conceived. Man, no longer tightly knit into a community, but working for the first time as an individual and being in competition with other men, began to have something to lose.

By 3000 BC they had begun cultivating apples in England. By 2900 BC they had constructed a plough, castrated their bulls and turned them into oxen to pull it. But it was not until the eighteenth century—so conservative is the farmer's thinking—that Jethro Tull first formulated the idea of sowing seeds in drills so that land could be cultivated even when the crops were growing.

Gradually walls and ditches were built round the villages, first as protection against marauding animals, then against one's neighbours. They started to grow flax for its oil, and it seems to have taken people some time before they realized that, like the nettle, it could be dried and spun into cloth. Sheep, and thus wool, came in from the Middle East. With the increase in personal comfort, jewellery began to be fashioned out of copper, gold, silver and semi-precious stones. The first musical instruments that we know of were invented, the flute, the drum, the tambourine and the *lurs*, a splendid bronze pipe capable of a wider melodic range than any before.

Over what had been tundra, growing nothing but coarse grasses, birch appeared, then pine, oak (oaks of far greater size than afterwards) and at last beech. At an elevation of five hundred feet in Lanarkshire seventy-foot oak logs as thick at one end as at the other have been dug out of peat bogs. Pines, too, were remarkable for their size.[1] In the course of a comparatively short number of centuries much of Europe became covered with dense forest, a forest like a thick animal pelt, like the fur of a bear or a musk ox, across the whole, once-naked body of

[1] Geikie, James, *Prehistoric Europe, a Geological sketch*. London, 1881.

the continent. And the people themselves, with the addition of carbohydrates to their diets, grew taller, stronger and healthier. They discovered the joys of alcohol; they brewed strong mead and myrtle beer, though cider not at all—there was no cider until about eight hundred years ago. And having now something to lose, they began that "brutal suppression of man by man, village by village, class by class, sex by sex"[1] that has continued ever since. But now the battles were fought with terrible new metal weapons.

Not only this. With the advent of wheels, of carts and oxen, trade increased from one end of the continent to the other, and with it travel, whole migrations of peoples, bringing new crafts, arts, languages and ideas, bringing unfamiliar gods, demons and ways of worship. There is not half enough space in so brief a history to list the multitude of mutually fructifying ideas that grew up, lingered in various parts of Europe and ultimately disappeared; the worship of trees, of bears, bulls, cats, wolves, monkeys and even fish, the worship of fire, which has not died out even today, and the varying concepts of transmigration and life after death. I said these religions disappeared, and so they did—as religions. But the Christmas tree, the teddy bear, the bullfight, the witch's black cat, the werewolf and even fish on Friday are records of our unconscious memories that once these things were gods. In certain parts of the world the fires in a house are still put out when someone dies.

Such evidence as we have of the great migrations is really no more than scraps and tatters on which it would be unwise even to base conjectures. One thing we do know, however, and that, for our present purposes, is the most important of all. The dark, neolithic hunter saw the arrival in the west of what was to him a new, fair-haired race, possibly from the northern shores of the Caspian, and therewith a whole new chapter begins.

"The hunter commands," someone has said, "but the farmer entreats". And in that fact lay a revolution different from any that had gone before. For this time it was not only a cultural revolution. It was a revolution which depended on forces

[1] Heichelheim, F. M., *An Ancient Economic History*, I. London, 1938.

beyond its control—drought, cold, the hot sun, defences against marauding beasts, cure for diseases in crops—a revolution whose outcome hung in the balance until society could learn methods of work which had hitherto not been imagined. It was a revolution, moreover, in new communities wherein the old, gradually superseded magic was still being practised. And as in all anthropological history, the new world, the world of the invaders, felt an inexplicable dread of the mystery and ritual of its predecessors, of the hunting communities that were gradually being forced away into the forests and uplands. Then for the first time the devil long afterwards known to *la vecchia religione*, was made manifest, because like many a devil since he had been the god of the opposition, of the dark men, the hunter whom the fair-haired farmer feared now to allow into his villages.

All over the known world, towns, the unification of peoples, attainments of various kinds—in a word—civilization developed in similar ways, but of course at speeds that varied enormously. Jericho was a fortified city with a wall, and watchtowers thirty feet high, when the last cave paintings were being made in the Pyrenees. Brilliant Minoan and Mycenean cultures were flourishing in tiny states not long after the beaker folk built their barrows in England. The Bog People of Denmark (and we shall hear more of them in a moment) were practising their savage and satisfying sacrifices when Pliny was writing his urbanely elegant epistles in Rome.

But in general, all over Europe and the Middle East the progression was similar, and the chief factors in that forward movement were the discovery of smelting and the establishment of agricultural communities. With the advent, first of bronze, then of iron, a fresh and potent magic came into being. With the advent of agriculture, with the advent of the "farmer who entreats", the whole corpus of what we should call organized and recognizable religion first took shape. And with organized religion organized heresy took shape, and a manifestation, not physically, but intellectually justified—and that was the point— of what Baudelaire called the eternal and incorrigible barbarity of man.

4

To a farmer the seasons are everything; they cause the annual miracle of reincarnation, the seed, dead as a grain of sand, that nevertheless springs wonderfully to life. But he is beset by almost innumerable dangers, the cattle murrain, burrowing insects, diseases of crops, rains, winds, unseasonable cold, too hot a sun, even at times a failure of germination that can dribble a whole year's work, turned back into sand between his fingers. And not only these. The greatest danger of all is that he is no longer part of a group. He is alone.

For the farmer, therefore, aware that he is at the mercy of natural phenomena, and that all natural phenomena are controlled by spirits, the propitiation of these powers is quite literally a matter of starvation or survival. And in the course of thousands of years the forms and rituals of that propitiation, varying though they did from place to place, became established beyond any one man's power to evade or contradict.

To be sure there had always been other gods that had nothing to do with harvest. Ever since it had grown up like some muscular giant in the midst of birch and pine, the oak had been venerated. Who has not felt a certain aboriginal awe in the midst of a forest? Indeed, trees and their fruit had always been sacred and miracle working spirits. The rowan or mountain ash, was the tree of life, a guardian against witches and lightning. A beating with a rowan switch, so the Druids believed, would make even the devil answer questions. The yew was the tree of death (it still does duty in our churchyards), the ash sacred to Wotan, highest of Teutonic gods. Ygdrasil, the great ash of Norse mythology, symbolized the universe itself. The alder, according to Homer, was the tree of resurrection. The willow was sacred to Hecate, the witch goddess, and the sixteenth-century witches of Berwick confessed that they rode out to sea in willow baskets. The huge oak was not only venerable; it was sacred alike to Zeus, Thor, Jahweh, all three, and the vestal fires in Rome were fed with oaken logs. Druids, of course, worshipped the oak, and all over Europe men made their doors of it on account of its hardness (the words door and durable are thought by some to come from the same root). The hazel was the tree of wisdom. In the south the silver fir was sacred to Artemis, the moon goddess, patronness of childbearing; in the north it was dedicated to women in childbed. Attis was said to have been turned into a fir by Cybele before his resurrection, and even today we honour Attis with the Norway spruce we carry into our houses at Christmas. The list is almost as long, indeed, as the number of our indigenous trees.

As for fruit, apples grew in the gardens of the Hesperides, and the apples Herakles long afterward gathered from that dragon-guarded tree at the world's end were *mala aurea Veneri consecrata*, golden apples consecrated to love, to Aphrodite, and by later extension to the Virgin Mary herself. Atalanta, the immoral huntress, succumbed to her lover, Melanion, only after he had thrown three apples in front of her to tempt her. "Comfort me with apples," sings the *Song of Solomon*, "for I am sick of love". Avalon, where Arthur went to be healed of his grievous wound, was an island of apple trees. As late as two or three centuries ago, Snow White choked on a poisoned apple.

It is no coincidence that the fruit of a forbidden tree brought about the downfall of Adam and Eve, though it was long called an apple only because the Latin word *malum*, or apple, is a homonym of *malus* which means evil. Several millenia later Merlin was locked by magic into a tree, and Christ's cross was called a tree until comparatively recent times.

In fact Bronze Age Europe saw the birth not only of a great diversity of gods. Almost from the beginning there had been a vast and basic schism within that very diversity, and it had been nourished not only by differing forms of agriculture, differing climates and social customs, but by different principles of behaviour that reflected a fundamental dichotomy in human temperament.

In Germany they grew barley. Along the Mediterranean they planted vineyards. In northern Europe, ice and deep snows bred hardy people, for only hardy people could possible survive, and both the Rhine and the Danube were frequently frozen so deeply that they would carry enormous weights, not only whole armies, but cavalry and heavy wagons. Along the Mediterranean one could afford a certain languidness in life. In the south the sea was a high road from city to city, in the north a turbulent and dangerous enemy that led nowhere.

So the deities of the north became gods of thunder and battle, gods that demanded obedience, for life was a perpetual struggle, more full of roughness than pleasure. As Tacitus tells us in his *Germania*, the northerners were not only violent warriors, they were possessed of an intense morality in matters of sex, money and hospitality. A man who seduced a girl before she was twenty-one was considered a scoundrel, and when the northerner drank, he drank to get drunk. In the south, however, they dreamed of nymphs and satyrs; they drank the warm, watered wine with Dionysus; they danced with the Bacchantes or crept out at twilight into the stubble fields, aching in mingled terror and delight to smell the sweat and body of the goat-god Pan. Zeus, their very god of thunder, dallied with innumerable maidens. He was a swan; he was a bull, and any man who was man enough could emulate him.

But if it be objected that the stern Jahweh, like Zeus, came out of that gentler Mediterranean world, one has to point out that unlike his contemporaries, Jahweh was born of nomadic tribes basically homeless, evolved by a people in bondage, and that he grew more intolerant and fiercer to the imagination during decades of hard wandering in Sinai. He was a god of opposition, perpetually fending off the claims of other gods, and indeed the very idea of monotheism, although it had always been the religion of primitive and isolated peoples, had been almost impossible to maintain so soon as any group inter-married, fought or simply tried to reach some *modus vivendi* with other groups. But the Jews of the exodus, and later of the diaspora, succeeded, stiffnecked and ruthless, in holding to isolation. Like the wind-driven northerner, battered by adver-sity, they clung to the law and to a stern morality, and found in cohesion their chief salvation.

Even so, as the prophets continually remind us, whenever they stumbled into a period of comparative ease they went whoring after gentler masters, just as one would have expected. Like all the rest of us they longed for the past. Moses came thundering down from Sinai with the tablets of the law in his arms, found his followers worshipping the golden calf, and what was that but the primitive horned god, the savage and dis-carded totem of their ancestors? In his rage he broke the tablets, and with his loyal Levites ranging beside him, slew three thousand of the idolaters. So Jahweh was avenged, although incidentally no other god had ever demanded vengeance for himself in all of western religious history. It was the same stiff-necked answer that the church was to make to heretics two thousand years afterwards. But I shall have more to say about the dichotomy when we come to the early Christians, and more still when we look at the Reformation. It echoes almost as loudly even today.

The ploughman, the sower of grain, was not only engaged in an historically new enterprise, he was formed by his occupation into a different sort of man, a conservative, and necessarily a man of habit, a settled man who lived by barns and byres, by winds and seasons, a man above all who stored food instead of sharing it out as it came. In dress, in diet, in the very style of his thinking, the turn of his mind, he was something new under the sun. For him the prime human enemy was the small, swarthy, autochthonous inhabitant of the forest, the ancestor who had not yet made the great leap forward, who still hunted the red deer (was an outlaw like the later Robin Hood), who used flint implements and lived in subterranean mounds which he built like wombs, merged into the surrounding vegetation; who moved through the underbrush as swiftly and silently as he had always done when on the track of game. As Dr Murray pointed out, it is today a commonplace of anthropology that our tales of fairies and elves preserve the tradition of the dwarf race that once inhabited northern and western Europe.[1] Fairies were fierce and untrustworthy, plunderers and thieves. The gentle creatures we think of as fairies were Shakespeare's invention, but Cernunnos, the horned, Gaulic god, the fierce original who was discarded and betrayed, reflects a memory of that discarded ancestor—in time, if not genetically—by the very fact of his betrayal. Even today in popular mythology the cuckolded husband is given a pair of horns.

This forest dweller became the savage (from *silvaticus*), the goblin who soured the cream, the elf who drove cattle mad, the imp, the dwarf, the dark enemy, the devil who plotted evil. He was the original worshipper of *la vecchia religione*, so at night the village farmer untied his dogs, for being a settled landowner, he had a vested interest in the status quo.

This landowner differed from his neolithic predecessor too in that he had both time and occasion to learn about the powers of various plants. Far to the south the Romans were already celebrating their *rosaliae*, their festivals of roses, and garlanding the legions' battle standards. The northerner more dourly searched out herbs for their utility, and uncovered a whole witch's cauldron of both poisons and cures. Aconite root contained 0.4% of alkaloid, and fifteen grains was a lethal dose. Valerian, on the other hand, cured colic in man and beast. Elder was good for burns. Vervain root, worn round the neck, eased rashes of the skin. Whitethorn and blackthorn were unlucky in all things.

[1] Murray, Margaret Alice, *The Witch-cult in Western Europe*. Oxford, 1921.

Haws made a potent liquor, and garlic hung over the door kept out evil spirits. Cinquefoil was a specific against the ague. The willow—*salix*—produced salicylic acid, our modern aspirin. Belladonna, thorn apple, hemlock, henbane; here he had sleep and death in the palm of his hand. Without knowing the chemistry of it, he had discovered St Ignatius's Bean, which is one of the origins of strychnine, and in orpiment he had found trisulphide of arsenic. Mandrake screamed when you pulled it out of the ground, but it cured barrenness in women. Foxglove—digitalis—is famous as an old wives' remedy, but curiously enough, I have found no reference to confirm that primitive man knew anything about it. But the flesh plant, *asclepias accidia*, was for 5,000 years the consecrated host of Asia.

With many plants a great deal depended on when they were gathered, for the magic of times and seasons was most potent. Thus mistletoe and the sacred myrtle had to be plucked at night, springwort only on Midsummer Eve. Orpine or fernseed gathered at Midsummer had the power of rendering you invisible. Dandelion was good for pains about the heart, and both camomile and vervain were guardians against thunder, sorcerers and thieves.

The list was almost endless, but so was the number of ailments and evil spirits that flitted through the air. And not only flying spirits, the ancestors of our angels. There were places too, of good and evil omen. Crossroads were dangerous; an enemy might come at you from several directions, and until very recent times criminals were buried there. A lefthanded man was to be avoided, and indeed modern neurology knows the reason. For lefthanded children receive stimuli in both cranial hemispheres, as opposed to the rest of us who receive them only in one. So they are frequently awkward, and sometimes turn stammerers until they have learned to adjust. Of course the left, being generally the weaker hand, has always been considered unlucky anyway. Demons lurk to one's left, and for that reason we still throw salt over our left shoulders.

Not even a friend could be allowed to step on your shadow or take away hair cut off your head. An axe buried blade uppermost under the floor kept away fire, and hawthorn in the house warded off the bogey (it has frequently been pointed out in this connection that the Slavonic *bog* signifies god); without it, the bogey crept in at night, for it was the ancestor of the seventeenth-century vampire, and drank your children's blood.

In other words, long before Europeans had even become literate the whole of the Germanic witch's paraphernalia had, often with very good reason behind it, been evolved. It was perhaps inevitable that witchcraft and the persecution of witches should eventually be in the main a north European phenomenon.

Not only in the north but all over Europe salt might never be eaten before one sowed, for salt was a preservative and kept the seed from germinating. Yet salt already in a field lent a particular sanctity to the soil, and by the same token a compact made over salt was inviolable. The Romans went so far as to pay both officers and legionaries away from barracks salt money, or *salarium*; indeed it was salt that made possible the huge trade in salted meat that came down from Gaul into Rome. So great in fact was the slaughter that centuries later the Saxons still called November *blotmonat* from the rivers of blood that flowed when grazing was finished and the killing had to start. Tacitus tells us in the thirteenth book of his *Annales* that the Germans actually waged war for saline streams. Down in Egypt, on the other hand, priests would eat no salt for fear of the sea. In northern Europe bread and salt sanctified a meal as was done in the south by bread and wine. When millennia later, Satanists mocked the communion by substituting black wafers and urine, they were unwittingly mocking not only the church, but sacraments older than history.

So much magic we can understand, if only because salt has always been a necessity of life, as bread and (in some climates) wine are necessities. But when iron first came to be used its magical properties were even more profound. It contained fire, for any man could see that it was capable of striking sparks out of a stone. It had the power of attraction, for it was often magnetic. And the very gods used it for their missiles; many a farmer had dug thunderbolts up out of his fields.

So far, its magic. But iron had a practical purpose, too. I said earlier that the villager both hated and feared the old, swarthy hunter, that master of a primitive religion which the new age thought of as diabolic, just as the villager's religion was to be thought diabolic by the Christian church that came after. For centuries the remnants of neolithic tribes had been retreating, as I have pointed out, either deeper into the forests, or else to the great upland plains, where their talent for camouflage or their swiftness could protect them. But iron was the gunpowder of the time, and now a whole series of savage battles was waged to exterminate the last of the aboriginal tribes. That they very nearly succeeded is clear, for gradually villagers penetrated both forest and plain. Mound dwellings ceased to be built, and stone age artifacts to be manufactured. But they could not kill or assimilate them all, for we have records of small, dark and isolated peoples surviving until as late as the seventeenth century, moving stealthily on the outskirts of settled hamlets, sometimes trading food for manufactured goods, sometimes abducting a girl that one of them fancied (many a man claimed an elf for father or mother), never staying long in one place. Even then they had a reputation for knowing forgotten secrets and for being in league with the devil.

There is evidence from all over Europe and the Middle East of the dread men felt of the new thunderbolt. Plutarch informs us that iron was never allowed to be brought into a Greek sanctuary, and iron nails were avoided when they built the Temple at Jerusalem.[1] The Archon of Plataea was never allowed to touch iron. According to the *Saturnalia* of Macrobius, Roman and Sabine priests could only be shorn or shaved with bronze, never with iron, and the Etruscans used only bronze ploughs at the ceremony of the foundation of cities. In Poland, Frazer tells us, as late as the seventeenth century a series of bad harvests cast discredit on the iron ploughshares that had recently been introduced, and in a curious mixture of superstition and Christianity, Scottish Highlanders believed until only recently that iron must never be put into the ground on a Good Friday. According to

[1] I Kings, vi. 7. Exodus, xx. 25.

Pliny, mistletoe had to be cut from the oak without the use of iron. The druids used golden sickles. And conversely, all over the world even today, iron rings are worn as amulets against disease. But to our northern European farmer in the first centuries before Christ, iron was chiefly valuable because the dark man of the forest was afraid of it. So he nailed a bar of it over his door to keep him away, and to make assurance doubly sure, remembering also the gods of his ancestors, bent the ends upward to resemble a horned moon—or a horseshoe.

For every month the moon grew horns to remind men of her divinity. Sun, moon (considered two of the seven planets), seasons, birds, winds, leaves, blossoms, the wicks of lamps, even the entrails of animals were full of natural auguries. With their help men partly understood the annual miracle of sowing and generation. In a word, remembering as we must with what intensity men love and fear the mysterious, thinking back into any individual childhood to recall what terrifying powers there were in unfamiliar sounds or places or merely in the dark, we may acquire some sense of the dread any Iron Age man felt, merchant or farmer, in his beleaguered hamlet surrounded by the night.

One of the most powerful weapons he could use in his eternal supplication was to sacrifice whatever he most valued, as though there had to be some rough justice or balance in the eternal scheme of things.

Now, before I set down what I have to say about sacrifice I must acknowledge a debt to Hubert and Mauss,[1] for if the selections of fact are mine, my interpretation of them rests in part on the profound scholarship and its pellucidly clear exposition by these much neglected students. They do not in fact deal with the instances of sacrifice I shall here be describing. But they have set down the psychically satisfying laws by which all sacrifice is governed.

We have already seen how it seems likely that palaeolithic

[1] Hubert, Henri and Mauss, Marcel, *Sacrifice, its Nature and Function*, trans. W. D. Halls. London, 1968.

man sacrificed his fingers. Abraham thought it a natural idea to sacrifice his only begotten son. In fulfilment of a vow, Jephtha, Judge of Israel, sacrificed his daughter;[1] the writer of that story actually ends it by saying, "And it was a custom in Israel". Indeed Frazer suggests that it may not have been the firstborn of Egypt who were slaughtered on the night of the Passover, for that would have run counter to anthropologically understood custom, but the firstborn of Israel,[2] and that the story was later amended to wipe out the shame of so hideous a price that had had to be paid for freedom. He points out elsewhere that of course Christ himself was sacrificed on the eve of Passover. And indeed sacrifice was a custom, not only in Israel, but almost everywhere else as well. Agamemnon offered up his child, Iphigenia, on the side of a hill that overlooked the windless sea near what is now the hamlet of Avlidos, and like the author of *Exodus*, Euripides could not (if only for dramatic reasons) stomach so crude an immolation, but used a version of the story that others had invented and brought the girl back to life.

Some years ago on that very hillside I asked a small shepherd girl if she could tell me who Iphigenia had been. "Yes," came the answer quickly, "a very brave girl who died for Greece". Perhaps in that answer lies a clue to the feelings of the victim.

And incidentally, two thousand years later Nicholas Remy (Remigius) did the same for Jephtha's daughter. For we believe what we need to believe. "Josephus," he writes in his *Demonolatry*, "considers that she was put to the knife, Zonaras that she was burned, and Sabellicus that she was immolated as a victim upon the altar. Yet there are not wanting those who interpret certain of the Hebrew authorities to the effect that she was only shut away for a time among the virgins dedicated to God." For to make her a genuine sacrifice, he affirms, would not have been pleasing or in conformity with God's justice.

But whether or no, jewellery, bracelets and torques (neck rings), human hair, bronze and silver coins (silver was frequently more precious than gold), cattle, beasts killed in the hunt, prisoners, priests, pubescent girls, the very king himself when

[1] Judges, xii. 39. [2] *The Golden Bough*, iv. 176.

he showed signs of waning powers, all were burned, buried, thrown off clifftops, stabbed, drowned or decapitated in that never-ending seasonal supplication. The Germans drowned reindeer (their most valuable game). The Egyptians sacrificed donkeys and redheaded men by throwing them off cliffs, for donkeys and the colour red had been sacred to Set. The Prince of Wales's feathers are a relic of the ass's ears, and in Apuleius we read of a virgin who to ride in triumph climbed upon an ass. But after Set, or Setekh, was discovered to have murdered Isis, and fell from being adored to being execrated, it was decided that he had been violent, lustful and murderous. (This would explain the superstition current even today that redheaded women are both randy and hot-tempered. My wife points out—and she is a redhead herself—that wicked ogres in children's books seem often to have red hair, and Dr Alex Comfort has lately propounded a theory that redheaded men give off what he calls a pheronomal odour that causes other men to feel antagonistic, by which same token, he says, redheaded women attract us.) In any case the history of human sacrifice is so voluminous that one can only refer the reader for other examples to almost any one of the thirteen volumes of *The Golden Bough*. In historical terms, at any rate, man's unappeasable passion for destruction had begun.

Corn and wine, bread and blood, these had always had a natural affinity, for if bread was the staff, blood was the very sap of life itself, as was the juice of the vine. They fed each on the other, gave back to the earth what had been nourished by the earth. "The spirits of the dead and the gods," says Mauss, "are the real owners of the world's wealth. With them it was particularly necessary to exchange, and particularly dangerous not to; but on the other hand, with them exchange was easiest and safest. Sacrificial destruction implies giving something that is to be repaid." For "one has to buy from the gods, and . . . the gods know how to repay the price". They "give something great in return for something small".[1] And indeed what are modern funeral baked meats, the eating and drinking at a wake, the

[1] Mauss, Marcel, *The Gift*, trans. Ian Cunnison. London, 1969.

throwing of money over a wedding procession in China, our own gifts to a bride (rarely to the groom), even alms to a beggar but a propitiation of the dead, a sacrifice to induce fertility, a charm to ward off the beggar's ill fortune from ourselves? I have walked out of the casino at Monte Carlo at two in the morning with a man who had just lost £2000, which was more or less all he owned in the world. As we strolled along the front he found a hundred-franc chip in his pocket, and without a moment's hesitation, leaned back and flung it out over the sea. "It'll come back," he said.

As I said earlier, sacrifice was carried on all over the habitable world. It has been estimated that in the name of fertility and the harvest, Aztecs slaughtered more people than died of natural causes—Prescott has told the story in all its horrifying detail. In Egypt the blood of the lamb was sacred, and to have it washed over one's face was to undergo a form of communion. We remember that palaeolithic man, indeed almost all primitive peoples, drank the blood of their victims.

And certain laws, certain customs seem almost universally to have been applied to the sacrifice itself, and particularly to the victim. That they were observed in the most disparate civilizations, among Jews, Hindus, Mexican Indians, only confirms our belief that they satisfied intrinsic human needs. Thus in most of the rituals the one who was sacrificed had to go happily to his death, and by implication promise that his spirit would not return to take vengeance. Not only this, of course. Only an open-handed offering would be acceptable to the gods. This was true for Iphigenia, for Jephtha's daughter and, according to Prescott, for the Aztecs. If the victim wept, struggled or cried out his death would lose its efficacy. And indeed the man Mauss calls the sacrifier, he by whom the necessary sacrifice was instigated, had also to expiate his crime against the dead spirit. In Athens the priest at the sacrifice of the *Bouphonia* fled after the ceremony. According to Porphyry his knife was condemned and thrown into the sea. Judas took the silver and then hanged himself in the potter's field.

Except for a meal of grain on the day before the ceremony

(for he was dying to ensure the fertility of that grain), the victim had to die fasting. Sometimes he or she would be scourged to drive out any demons he might unwittingly be harbouring. He had to be shaved; he had to remain chaste; during the ceremonies that preceded his death he had to wear clean clothing. Often at the very end he would be stripped naked again to make quite certain that he was uncontaminated, for the priests of the sacrifice were as conscious as any modern surgeon of the necessity for, in their case, a spiritual asepsis. Without it the victim would be impure and the sacrifice invalid. Christ, indeed, was naked, a hundred Renaissance painters to the contrary, for we read that they parted and cast lots for his garments.

The farmer entreats, and surely no entreaty could be more potent than the deliberate killing of one's own flesh and blood. No magic could be more frightening, no offer more surely satisfying to whatever gods held in their hands the gift of germination.

Peat bogs contain certain humic acids that consume the bones but preserve the skin and hair of human beings buried in them. In the course of the past several decades some six hundred and ninety such bodies have fortuitously been uncovered. Most of them were dug up in Schleswig and Jutland, but some few have come from Holland, Ireland, Germany. A good many date back to the neolithic period, about 5000 BC, but others, according to pollen analyses of the contents of their stomachs, come from the time of the early Roman Empire. Most were of sacrificial victims. They had been imbued by purification with the divine spirit, and this in turn was released by their deaths to pour blessings on the community for which they died.

How they were chosen we do not know. If they struggled against fate or went willingly to their deaths can be no more than conjectured, though it is interesting and perhaps relevant to observe that many of them lie in the same position (left leg over right, right arm clenched to the chest) as did some of Charcot's patients when in a state of hysterical possession. There is some evidence, as we shall see in a moment, that they too were possessed, and felt within them an almost supernatural exaltation.

To look at them is to look Iron Age man and woman in the face. There they lie, tall, generally fair-haired, most of them naked but sometimes with clothing bundled up at their feet. Now and then a woman will still be wearing a horn comb in her hair or a woollen head-band, or a man his leather cap, the fur side next the skin.

Their musical instruments have been found too, the lyre, the *lurs*, the harp. Some graves (but not those of the victims), contained food for the journey, their porridge, pork, beef, mutton, their carving knives, their cups still brown with the sediment of beer or barley wine. In one child's grave they had laid the wings of six jackdaws and two crows to help carry him into the other world.

In the graves of the sacrificed there was nothing. Dead or still dying, they had simply been tumbled into the earth and left to fend for themselves, for they were no longer of any account as members of the community. They belonged to the god, had themselves become the incarnate god, and the godhead would ensure that they became sacred and were thus without any need of material baggage.

The clothing that has been preserved gives us a very clear idea how they had dressed when alive. The men wore long capes and pointed hoods, the women checked linen skirts often little longer than miniskirts, woven tartan-like in combinations of green, red, yellow and dark brown. There were kerchiefs to match, and over the upper part of the body a lamb-skin cape worn next to the skin. Their belts were of leather, their shoes of double leather, again with the fur side inward, bound with hide laces to the ankles. They had clearly developed a sense for aesthetics, a sense for style.[1] A few of the women wore their hair in plaits, a few of the men in pigtails. Without exception the men

[1] Most of this evidence will be found in Glob, P. V., *The Bog People*, trans. Rupert Bruce-Mitford, London, 1969. Professor Glob relies in part on Margrethe Hald's positively monumental work on Danish Iron Age textiles and costume.

were clean-shaven. Sometimes the women wore bracelets or bronze brooches and belt buckles.

The foundations still stand of many of their cottages, mostly (like the ones in my own village today) facing east and west along the narrow street. For hundreds of years past they would have painted their inner walls red or white, for it had been a prosperous time and they had come a long way from the forest. In the centre of the floor, a platform raised two or three inches for the hearth. At one end the kitchen utensils, cups and storage jars, sieves, scissors, mortar and pestle; in one cottage a half-finished clay pot bearing a child's fingerprints, in another a burned, forgotten cake marked on the top like a hot cross bun with a magic cross. Even among pre-Christian peoples the cross had been sacred, for it represented a tree.

They were not cut off from the great world, these rustics. Tinkers and pedlars from the Baltic, from Germany or the far south passed through every now and then, no doubt bringing news and unfamiliar tales. One wishes it were possible to know how much of a *lingua franca* there was among them, or if every small district spoke its own language, or at least dialect. This, at least, we know, that no primitive people today speaks a language less complex grammatically than our own.

In one of the cottages there seems to have lived a man who had served in the Roman legions, for he had buried his pay in silver denarii under a stone near the hearth, and then, presumably, died without telling anyone where it was hidden. From Gaul and Rome too, they would have learned about savage men who decapitated their enemies and hung the heads in rows under the eaves of their houses, or men who wore outlandish things like trousers because they habitually rode horses.

Even more important, the *Iliad*, *Finnesburgh*, *Beowulf* and the *Edda* give us, in the light of people's illiteracy, some inkling of the great lost oral tradition common to all of prehistoric Europe. The stories they told and retold of gods, warriors and vast, shadow-casting battles were not only stories out of a golden past. They were actions complicated by genealogies, like much of the pentateuch, and references to place that gave entire families and localities a part in a mythology peculiar to themselves. And there are unquestionably lyrics by the hundreds, indeed whole epics which, never having been written down, though familiar to these people as grass and air, are now irretrievably lost.

Without any question children asked, as they do now, "Is it true? Is it true?" For Iron Age man the seen and the unseen, the demons good and bad, the magic, the witchcraft and its purifications, the enormously complicated ceremonies, the omens, the powers, the chances that wracked or delighted made up a truth almost too baroque for understanding. Anyone who has travelled and taken the trouble to listen to the talk in tiny, remote hamlets all over the continent knows how almost every glade and cottage echoes its own animate past, and every spot its relationship with the demons and good spirits that once inhabited it. The idea of the sacredness of the hearth-fire has not yet died, or the builder's habit of placing a coin under a foundation stone, or indeed the almost universal custom of propitiating we hardly know what deities by throwing coins into a fountain.

But aside from all this we must think of Iron Age man as inhabiting a world intrinsically similar to our own, filled with similar laughter, mingled with apprehension and fear of the unfamiliar, similar gossip, accident, good fortune and not dissimilar dreams. They ached, they wept, they worked, they munched their suppers and stretched out in front of the fire at night. Mothers washed, cooked, baked, fetched water from the well, quarrelled, listened, smiled at secret thoughts and knitted clothing for their children. The sun rose and set as it does now. Birds sang; labourers drank beer with their bread and cheese; dogs barked in the villages, and the farmer cast shadows in the lane as he trudged homeward from the fields beside his laden wagon. It is only his animal perceptiveness, his sharp eyes and ears, his memory for detail, his sense for the mysterious that we have lost.

As I mentioned earlier, some of the sacrificed bodies have actually been subjected to a forensic examination to determine what they were given to eat for their last suppers. And always it was what we would have expected; barley, linseed, knotweed, camomile, bristle grass ground up without any meat or animal fats to form what we should think a rather unpalatable gruel. And this not only because in primitive magic, like produces like, but because, as Frazer deduced, objects which have been in contact—in this case the grain in the stomach and the grain about to be sown—continue to act on each other even after contact has been lost. The divine power in one confers divine power on the other. We are told nothing of what was eaten at Christ's last supper except that he and his disciples took bread and wine.

The age-old sense of community was very strong in these people, and the age-old sense of souls wrestling with and overcoming inward crises, when every year at the spring equinox they prepared to propitiate the gods by sacrificing at least one of their number. They did not do this perfunctorily, or without days and months of preparation. "Sacred things were considered to provide an inexhaustible source of power, capable of producing effects which were infinitely special and infinitely varied."[1] So, to ensure that the victim was sanctified, rituals had to answer to every complex sense of the fitness of things. Nothing must be wanting in the gift to prevent its being acceptable. One must be certain that the dead have not died in vain.

One such, and he may have been a priest, for his hands look unaccustomed to manual labour, still wears the torque, or neck ring, of the earth goddess Nerthus round his neck. He frowns slightly, even in death, but he has a thoughtful and intelligent face. One would recognize him if one met him again in the road.

Another, a small and innocently attractive girl of fourteen, had had the left side of her head shaved, in token of purification, shortly before she died. Without doubt she was a virgin, and this for reasons that will later become apparent. She wore the same neck ring and had the same delicate hands as the man. In spite of foreknowledge, in spite of her awe at having been chosen to become a god, she seems to have been afraid, for

[1] Hubert and Mauss, op. cit.

someone tied a narrow woollen blindfold over her eyes and knotted it at the nape of her neck. It is tied there still.

Tacitus describes such a ceremony in his *Germania*. During the days before, attendants of the goddess accompanied her on her springtime progress through village after village. Everyone kept holiday. No one made war, and weapons were laid aside, for the goddess was with them; her very robes brushed them in the street. Everywhere there was peace, an awesome quiet and happiness until after each hamlet had been visited, the chariot bearing the goddess was drawn down to a sequestered lake. Wells, springs, ponds were always holy and frightening places where spirits lurked. There the robes, the carriage, the goddess herself were washed by various attendants, and then these people were straightaway afterwards drowned in the same lake.

It is not difficult to imagine the night-time fires, the solemn dances, the untuned music, the prayers, perhaps the terrible droning of the Germanic rhombus, the whole of what would seem to us a poverty-stricken pomp as the procession wound its way past all the cottages. They were dancing a pavane to the seasons, enacting the birth, death and rebirth of a god that took its unalterable course with every turning year and could no more be changed than could the slow swing of the sun past the equinoxes. In their own lives they were miming the periodicity by which they lived. The god suffered in their names, took on his shoulders their enormous and unwitting guilt, the winter dragon.

In Tyre Melkarth died, at Carthage Dido, in Tarsus Sandon, all burned. In Athens they hanged Erigone, in Delphi Charila; in all the ceremonies priest and god were one flesh. Marduk had fought with chaos in Babylon, Perseus with the Gorgon, St George with a dragon, Herakles with Typhon, Mithras with a bull. In Mexico they kneaded the image of the god in human blood, broke it into bits, shared out the bits and ate them. Without rhythmical, seasonal sanctification the god himself would die.

It is not difficult to imagine the Danish priest or the young virgin, drugged into a state close to possession by the noise, the sense of importance, the patches of smoky light in the darkness, the confusing, half-recognized faces that used to be familiar, but

vanished as soon as they were seen, the slow, almost stately un
ravelling of a ritual long practised, like a flower visibly unfold-
ing, like a revelation of some splendid collective holiness of
which she is a part. No, she is at the heart of it. Suddenly she
realizes that she is the goddess herself in a girl's body that is no
longer her own, for it has become unaware of thirst or cold or
tiredness or hunger, only of a giddy and extraordinary lightness,
an awe at having been chosen and a terrible need to do nothing
wrong.

And to the sound of a cold March wind blowing in from the
sea they take off her clothes (perhaps here is where she totters
and is given the blindfold), and at last that fair-haired, naked
girl is walked out into the thigh-deep lake, into what is now
called the Windeby bog, then suddenly with all the force of
an unarguable law, seized by the waist and by one knee (the act
is graphically shown on the Gundestrup cauldron), flung onto
her back and held down to drown in some twenty inches of
water.

Later, to keep her body below the surface, several birch
branches and a stone were laid on top of her. Neolithic man had
decapitated his dead to prevent their spirits walking. But it is
perhaps also relevant that according to one Adam of Bremen,
writing about 1070, there was a spring in the temple precincts at
Uppsala wherein men were sacrificed, and if the victim's body
stayed down the sacrifice had been accepted by the god.

Animals have rituals and ceremonies of their own, but there
is no evidence that these ever include the sacrifice of one of their
own uncompetitive number. Professor Glob tells us that on
several occasions when peat cutters came upon one of the bodies,
stained by tannin in the bog, they cried out in terror and ran to
the nearest village, shouting that they had found the devil himself.

And perhaps in a way they had. For the devil, if we may
anthropomorphize him for a moment, had long been pregnant
with the dread of seasons and equinoxes, with un-understood
desires and unanswerable questions. As religion, and particularly the Christian religion developed, he was to find even greater

scope for his remarkably human imagination. And with the help of a fear based essentially on our inability to control an environment more complex than we suspected, he was to grow in stature until he became able to use that imagination in ways he had not yet been able to foretell.

5

If we assume the existence of an omnipotent god, we ought to
assume that in the beginning he created the world he meant to
inhabit. To us, the beneficiaries, however, it was not enough to
have been born. No, we had at once to begin asking unanswerable questions. From the very first morning we had to start
hammering at the holy ribs of heaven, clamouring at somebody
to explain. But it was no good; it looks as though after a while
our god could not for the life of him remember what had come
into his head. He kept shifting his ground. He kept turning into
something that contradicted whatever he had been before, and
even the Jahwehs of Exodus and Daniel are barely recognizable
as the same.

As a matter of fact he must in time have become singularly
bemused, so often was he repudiated or interchanged with other
gods, so often diminished by our own inept understandings. In
the first millenium before Christ he took so many forms, was
described in so many ways, that to untangle the religions of the
ancient world is by now almost certainly beyond the wit of man.
Plutarch wrote that the God of the Jews was really Dionysus
Sabazius, barley god of Phrygia and Thrace. At various times he
was incarnate in nearly every imaginable animal and plant, for a

hundred trees and flowers are called by one of his names, and the golden calf was neither the first nor the last beast to be worshipped. God's poems, his riddles, his silences, his prophecies and his revenges took every conceivable form. He expressed himself in asceticism and in the phallus, in flagellation and in prayer, in sobriety, in drunkenness, in the lust for pain and the lust for pleasure, in the four lovely winds as well as in the mephitic vapours of a hundred prophetesses. So did the devil, until it often became quite impossible to tell them apart. Divinity was expressed in plain doctrine as well as in the labyrinth, in the birth of alphabets and in the science of numbers. So was the diabolic. The symbols by which either could be recognized were not only interchangeable, but as complicated as the mysteries they concealed. "When me they fly I am the wings," said Emerson. "I am the doubter and the doubt."

So to describe this idea of an omnipotent but fallible deity, to describe the variable as background to a study of the anti-hero would be futile and all but impossible, and the only thing to be done is to restrict ourselves to such aspects of the story as will make plain the purely Christian devils of the two thousand years that followed.

It is a truism to say that gods were born to set right injustice, devils to account for it, and in company with those gods to form a larger balance without which the whole structure of moral philosophy would collapse. But we have never been able to stick to so simple a view, for when we come down to it, good and evil are both subjective things, and no matter how hard we try, the concepts attack us by way of the emotions. We, the beneficiaries of creation, are beset by confusions, then by fears and aspirations, and at last by an urge to manipulate the dice, to invent formulae for understanding, to dress up chaos, as it were, in classical hexameters.

There is, for example, a tradition running through western religious history of arcane matter hidden behind doctrine. For it early became plain that no divinely inspired text or idea could ever be so presented that it looked divine. It had to be curtained off and made into a mystery, for spirit cannot by its very nature be seen, only apprehended. Thus Moses is reputed to have spent two separate periods of forty days on Sinai, learning secrets that were later transmitted, twisted into enigmas, in the Cabala.

In the same way, Christ fasted forty days and nights in the wilderness. Only he knew what, if anything, befell him there, except that when at last he hungered, the devil came and tempted him. But many a lonely hermit in the centuries that followed took the action for the idea, tormented the flesh and withered away into a semi-catatonic sainthood, trying with the shaman-devil scrabbling away inside him to imitate Christ's example. At one time it was estimated that there were as many monks and God-dedicated virgins in the wilderness as there were inhabitants in all the towns of Egypt.

Christ, of course, wrote no gospel. He simply superimposed a most remarkable personality on many old ones. Like Moses, however, like Orpheus, Asclepios, Sarapis, Mithras, Mani and the priests of Eleusis, like everybody else he was said to have revealed deeper mysteries to the elect. But a mystery revealed is no longer a mystery. Look with impunity at Medusa's head and it is no longer Medusa's head.

Nevertheless in all religions we read about the revelation to a comparative handful of the depths and terrors of an ultimate secret, a perception of the divine given only to the religious temperament, which is the same in all religions. But in fact the secret is just that, a perception, not a revelation. As Éliphas Lévi wrote (and in this at least he was accurate), for the Cabalists, God in human shape was only a hieroglyph that denoted the intelligent, the loving, the living infinite. He is not an abstract being, nor is he philosophically definable. He is in all things. His very name is ineffable and expresses only the human idea of his divinity. And the cause of his being is, in fact, being. If the concept of him did not exist, if it were false, nature would have formulated an absurdity, for the void would affirm life. To this concept the Cabalists gave a name—JHVH—which can be spelled, but not pronounced. Its ciphers produce numbers which resolve themselves into seventy-two explicatory names, and it is this enormous Hebrew concept, not the Cabalistic interpretation of it, which caused a revolution in human thinking and perception that cannot be reversed.

St Augustine says that the essence of Christian teaching was with us from the beginning, that Christ did no more than appear in the flesh and give the essence his name. In fact he might have said that Christian parable was only a gloss on a universal mysticism which had had its finger on that undefinable and unarguable secret all the way along.

There were devils, of course, long before the crucifixion. As we saw earlier, the neolithic, horned hunter god was a devil to the fairhaired agriculturist, and it was Voltaire who first discovered, to his amusement, that the Hebrew word—cherub—signifies in Assyrian a bull. Down in Mesopotamia the horned demon, Pazuzu, rode on the south-west wind and carried malaria. Job, we are told, was tempted by Satan, but Satan, which in Hebrew simply means "adversary," was not at that time in any proper sense of the word a devil. In fact he is introduced as one of the sons of God, come from walking up and down in the earth to present himself to his father. And hearing God praise Job for his uprightness, he simply argues that Job is God-fearing because God protects him.

So it is not Satan who attacks; it is Jahweh who takes away his own protecting hand. Satan has tempted nobody except God. No, we must leave him out, and say that for our purposes the devil appears in the Old Testament and the Talmud only in the shape of a divinity belonging to some other tribe, whether as Chamos, or as Moloch, who was actually the Cronos of the Phoenicians and the "abomination of the Ammonites" to whom the Jews had sacrificed their children in Gehenna, or as Lucifer, whom no less a prophet than Isaiah calls the son of the morning, or as the sons of Belial, who are offspring of the Sumerian goddess Belili, or as Lilith, the lovely night demon, goddess of debauchery, or as Belphegor with beard and gaping mouth, from which the tongue protrudes like an enormous phallus, or as Melkarth, the sacrificed Phoenician Herakles, or Beelzebub, "lord of the flies," once called Baal, who in II Kings appears as an oracular deity of the Ekronites, and in the second chapter of

Matthew as prince of the demons. Indeed in all anthropological history when two cultures come into contact, magic (and thus diabolism) is usually attributed to the less developed.

Strangely enough even the Hebrew Jahweh was once part of that infernal crew, for in the first centuries after Christ a Jewish sect of Ophites in Phrygia worshipped the serpent that Moses had carried on his banners in the wilderness, and maintained that (all Cabalists to the contrary) the Jahweh of the post-exilic centuries had been a mere demon usurper.

But with that one exception, devils were simply adversaries to Jahweh. So if we ask what evil was, or diabolism, for the Jews it was disobedience to the will of God. The devil was heresy, a subverter, not of goodness (that was a Greek idea), but of truth, of the perfect, the inevitable. For it is only when one can be certain of the truth (as the Jews were certain) that heresy not only exists, but becomes diabolical. "If thy brother . . . or thy son or thy daughter, or the wife of thy bosom, or thy friend which is as thine own soul, entice thee secretly, saying let us go serve other gods, which thou hast not known, thou and thy father . . . the gods of the people which are round about you, nigh unto thee, or far off from thee, from the one end of the earth to the other end of the earth: thou shalt not consent unto him, nor hearken unto him; neither shall thine eye pity him: But thou shalt surely kill him; thine hand shall be first upon him to put him to death, and afterward the hand of all the people. And thou shalt stone him with stones that he die; because he hath sought to thrust thee away from the Lord thy God which brought thee out of the land of Egypt, from the house of bondage."[1]

Caiaphas, Jacob Sprenger, Nicholas Remy, Bernard of Clairvaux and a host of mean-mouthed seventeenth-century divines: only men of this calibre recognized the virtue of such obedience; only they, like the old Jewish historians, knew the devil when they saw him, for only they were certain enough that they had been made custodians of the divine and inalienable truth.

Christ, when he cast out devils, saw them simply as spirits

[1] Deuteronomy, xiii. 6–10.

that had seized and subverted the rational man. The fifteenth century authors of *Malleus Maleficarum*, the Hammer of Witchcraft, on the other hand, saw the devil as that which had subverted the divinely-revealéd teachings of the church. In the same way Eve's serpent was obviously the devil because it had tempted her to disobey the commandment of God. Joan of Arc's Bishop of Beauvais saw the devil in voices irresponsible to and subversive of the status quo. So to people in the Judaeo-Christian tradition it became a rule of thumb that the devil was that which persisted in advocating beliefs they recognized, not empirically, but dogmatically to be false.

To the Greek or Roman, who unfortunately suffered a lack of similar moral revelations, sin was both a more human and a more complex matter. In its original form it had been, as with the Jews, an offence against some ritual or god. But the concept evolved. In republican Rome the word *scelus*, perhaps the nearest Latin equivalent to sin, had often been taken to mean no more than bad luck. But luck, good or bad, often turns out to be what we have earned. Some of us are accident-prone. So to call a man *scelerosus*, prone to perpetual bad luck, was to call him accursed, and by imputation to curse even his innocent descendents. *Nefas*, on the other hand, was not so much sin as an act of such horror as to put its perpetrator beyond the bounds of social acceptibility, but it had nothing to do with the gods.

There is no concept of guilt or sin in Homer, but in the course of the next few hundred years a suspicion gradually took root that evil did exist, and that it was the breaking of an unwritten spiritual contract between an individual and his fellow men. We have to understand this Greek idea, similar to that of decent human beings today, in the context of a city-state suffering many of our modern problems, for it was ceasing to be an agricultural community and becoming industrialized. We too casually picture fifth-century Athens as the city of Sophocles, Phidias and Pericles, when in fact that golden century was also a time of enormous vulgarity and enormous industrial expansion. Down near the harbour were the stinking streets of potters, shipbuilders, weapon-makers, of brawling, ignorant people hardly half a step more free than slaves, crowded into tenements and cobbled alleys. Many of them were foreigners fresh from the country, as many of Europe's modern contract labourers are foreigners fresh from poverty-sick areas abroad. They were enjoying a prosperity they had never before thought realizable. They were building the vessels that made Athens mistress of the seas, forging the shields, the javelins, the side-arms that Athenian hoplites were to carry to Africa and the slopes of the Hindu Kush.

And these amoral dregs were the moral power, or at least the political majority in Athens. The voices of men like Socrates and Euripides were either unheard or disquieting, even to the better educated. The fine irony of their protests was quite lost on the armies of illiterate soldiery, brutally commanded. Socrates was done to death. Euripides exiled himself or was exiled. And Athens fell.

But in spite of an ignoble moral climate, and because at the top it had indeed been a golden age in which a few were perpetually learning, by the end of the century intelligent Athenians had come to understand that individual morality was an awareness of the rights of others. Sin was *hubris* or arrogance, a disregard of restraints, and Theognis of Megara went so far as to affirm that in principle it was caused by prosperity, by an unwarrantable fulness in material goods.

In the very first lines of Euripides' *Children of Herakles* Iolaus tells us that:

> *I have long held the opinion that an honest man*
> *Lives for his neighbours; while the man whose purpose drives*
> *Loose-reined for his own profit, is unprofitable*
> *To his city, harsh in dealings, and a valued friend*
> *Chiefly to himself.*[1]

Sophocles went further in the *Antigone* and said that *hubris* made one blind to moral considerations, so that what was evil actually

[1] Trans. Philip Vellacott, published by the Penguin Press.

looked to be good, and the ruin that grew out of it had in a practical sense to be visited upon one's children. The *hubris* of Agamemnon reverberates down through the action of ten or more of the great tragedies. Far from wickedness being the work of the devil, it became clear to a handful of responsible men that evil grew out of the pride and disregard for others that are the effects of either power or anger.

"Know thyself," was the phrase written up in the temple at Delphi, and it might be said to have been the message of the *daemon* that had been Socrates' good angel. Know thyself to be mortal, to be fallible, to be only part of the community. It caused him willingly to obey the laws of Athens and to die when he might have lived. For the democracy of Athens was the seed-bed of his morality, and thus of whatever law he must obey.

And these were not simply the rationalizations of philosophers, for that fifth century was a time of such casual savagery that thoughtful and perceptive citizens were gradually made aware how odious was the self-interest that governed them. They discovered in their own fates the action of moral law, for in the midst of their inane and suicidal war against Sparta, Athenians attacked the neutral and peaceful island of Melos, and, when its people refused to surrender, killed all the men and sold the women and children into slavery. Mytilene was very nearly destroyed in the same way.

And the result? A mere handful of years later the Athenians were themselves destroyed, not because they had disobeyed a god (for doing which the Jews had been banished to Babylon), but because they had been guilty of *hubris*, and because that crime, which alters the criminal's character, carries in its belly the causes of the criminal's destruction. And the devil had nothing to do with it. One had to blame, not an abstract devil, but oneself. It is all of course far more complicated, but really this is the crux of the difference between Greek and Jew, between Greek and the whole Judaeo-Christian tradition. For heirs though we may be of Hebrew and Hellene, the devil, our devil is almost entirely an invention of Hebrew moral law and the Christian church, and in the end the lovely Greek and Roman mysteries simply provided a host of fresh devils for whoever in the new faith found them attractive.

To the early Christian, surrounded by a world he was no longer able to accept, or perhaps even to understand, it must often have seemed tragic to be locked in so primitive a society. He had renounced the warm and comfortable senses, and he could not possibly have foreseen that his failure at self-realization would lead to a *hubris* and savagery greater than that of Athens. For this time his every action was to be in the service of an ultimate and thus omnipotent god. Such a concept might have bewildered even Euripides. Virgil, because he was a Roman, could see tears in mortal things. Most of the obdurate early church fathers could not.

Of course with the formalization of beliefs, with an assurance growing in both Christian and pagan of a power and beauty, infinite and infinitely desirable, there came the concept of human perfectibility too, of a grace born out of the gods one worshipped and, among Christians, a striving towards saintliness as the ultimate seal of one's dedication. And so far the idea was to many both lucid and acceptable. In time, however, any religion, any important truth becomes cryptic. Everything turns out to be more of a labyrinth than it seemed, and even the simplest of mythological stories—Jacob wrestling with the angel, the death of Baldur, the rescue of Alcestis—depends for its clarity on how perceptive the observer and on the position from which he sees.

All stories, all religious doctrines exemplify in different ways the Greek sense of balance I mentioned before, for balance is justice. Balance is at the heart of truth. Balance, exemplified in the very cosmos, is an inviolable order, without which we should have nothing but chaos. The palaeolithic hunter seems to have cut off his fingers because in his heart he sensed a balance in natural forces that would compensate his pain with a reward. The very seasons are a balance of opposites. Whatever men believe they believe because it fills up a hole in logic or continuity, or because they perceive in it a balance analogous to that in the everyday things they can observe with their own two eyes.

The gods, most of them triads, were themselves a coherence of contradictory forces, just as a good deal of divine truth is contradictory. "Give away all that thou hast," was an old Greek maxim. "Then thou shalt receive." Indeed the renaissance saw all paganism as trinitarian. Artemis was chaste and a lion among women, a virgin huntress, but also a mother goddess. She was actually presented in the shape of a trinitarian goddess—with the inscription, *Theologia*—on the tomb of Pope Sixtus IV. Dionysus, winebibber, dancer, tragedian, bull and orgiast, was reborn annually as a child in a seedbasket (a sort of portable manger) in Delphi. Passionate little Eros took to wife Psyche (but he was really a demon in disguise) and produced a child who was given the name Pleasure. And just as no one is considered complete until united with a member of the opposite sex, so Christ himself, if he lacked a mortal mother and the Holy Ghost for balance, would be unimaginable as a divinity.

Now of course men varied in their response to such contradictory ideas, but by far the greater number reacted to them only through the senses, for in fact it is sensuous concepts with which we most easily identify. At pagan Eleusis the most famous of all emotional celebrations was held annually in September and October. And to that Eleusinian initiation the common people flocked in thousands (Herodotus estimates the number at about 30,000), combining in a religious festival all the laughter and excitement of a visit to the fair, the mountebanks and sideshows, the delights of conjurors and colourful dancers, of mummers, masques, impromptu musicians. Along the dusty highway, beggars; in the taverns, argument and drinking contests, and moving amid the swindlers and cutpurses, farmers with cheeks like old leather, white-shod country wenches and scores of rootless pretty boys and girls like hippies on the road to Katmandu.

The *mystai* bathed in the sea and watched the *iakkhos*, the procession of chanting and shouting devotees who carried the "sacred objects" from Athens along the thronged and sunny roads. In the evening the mystical rites themselves were celebrated in the Telesterion (which held about 3,000 people) lighted by many torches. There were the *eumolpidai*, the beautiful singers, the "things shown" and the "things performed", though what they were can no longer be determined. In the highest rites, wherein the *mystai* were purged of the fear of death and admitted into the company of the blessed, there seems to have been a certain sexual symbolism, about which nothing is actually known, and then there was probably shown a dramatic representation of the rape of Kore-Persephone.

And while a good deal about Eleusis is thus little more than conjecture, at least a similar festivity in honour of Isis is described with great gusto in Apuleius' *Golden Ass*, and indeed marriages of hilarity and religious rite seem to have been popular all over the ancient world. Aristophanes talks about a life made happy in the underworld where the elect will be able to celebrate mysteries for ever more.

In February it was the turn of the *anthesteria*, the blessing of the wine. Everybody, adults as well as children, carried his own jug. Again there were drinking contests, and on the night of the second day, called *chutroi*, they carried pots of cooked fruit in procession to the dead and, making the occasion a kind of All Souls, shouted in happy festivity to drive wicked spirits away.

To the later Christian almost all of this seemed an aspect of diabolism, first because it appealed chiefly to the emotions, and second because no moral excuse could be found for the delights it offered. And if he had perforce to leave various pagan holidays in his calendar, he condemned the sexual licence that had for centuries accompanied them. In fact he employed considerable ingenuity in discouraging any of that sensuous enjoyment which, particularly for the emotionally illiterate, had been the real cause for celebration.

Now we saw earlier that palaeolithic man made a dance drama of the hunt. This drama became father to the Dionysia, where dramatic representations were organized to accompany the orgiastic dances and drinking that had long been common in open-air, rustic celebrations. And with the Dionysia we are in the main current, the anti-rational and anti-Christian current that has run like a strong river all through human history.

79

"The orgy was held high in the hills at dead of night," says Rohde, "amid the clashing of cymbals, the thunder of drums and the 'sounds that induced madness' of the deep-toned flutes. . . . The revellers dance with shrill cries. There is no formal song. They have no breath for singing. For this is not the measured dance with which the Greeks in Homer swung rhythmically forward in the Paean, but a mad whirling as the mob sweeps ecstatically up the rocky slopes. They wear . . . fox skins, roebuck skins and horns on their heads."[1]

One is reminded of Spanish *duende*, which Goethe called "a mysterious power that everyone feels, but that no philosopher has explained". Lorca was more specific. "All that has dark sounds has *duende*," he wrote. "It is not a matter of ability, but of living form, of blood, of ancient culture, of creative action. . . . To help us seek the *duende* there is neither map nor discipline. All one knows is that it turns the blood to powdered glass, that it exhausts, that it rejects all the sweet geometry one has learned, that it breaks with all styles."

Like the witch of our own era, the female Thracian orgiast abandoned husband, hearth and children, roamed the hills, whirled barefoot in the dances and gave herself to an ecstasy wherein she is said even to have devoured babies and animals in a sacramental dinner with the god. She was the ancient equivalent not only of the witch, but of the saved sinner at the revivalist's altar, the Voodoo worshipper, even of the dreary middle-class Satanist in her California suburb, in whom both emotion and action have dwindled until they are nothing but a blue rinse smiling hopefully at the absolute.

In the *Acharnenses* Aristophanes described such a fiesta. It opened with a procession wherein two slaves carried a phallus in a basket. There was music and no doubt laughter and riotous behaviour that grew hour by hour as the wine flowed and one happy act of licence gave inspiration to another. There was the *askoliasmos*, for example, a game wherein players tried to keep their balance while dancing on a bloated wineskin. There were buffoons and brawls; goats were roasted over open fires, and

[1] Rohde, Erwin, *Psyche*. Tübingen, 1898.

the by now half-possessed revellers flogged each other and oiled their bodies to make seizure more difficult and at the same time more sensuously delightful when it came. When we come to read about witches' revels two thousand years afterwards (though witches were not possessed), we shall find that the feasting, the dances, the excitement and the culmination were very much the same.

One modern school of thought holds that unlike the later witch, the orgiast did not in fact engage in copulation, but danced in a growing frenzy until orgasm came of itself and—like Dionysiac tragedy—purged him of the hysteria by which he had been governed.

According to Aristotle the tragedy at these festivals began as improvisation. Then the dithyramb was added, the choral song to Dionysus, joyously, drunkenly chanted, and this came to be joined with the *satyrikon*, a personation of the acts of satyrs with horns and cloven hoofs. And in the earliest Dionysia, tragedy, far from being a mere spectacle, was turned into an overriding stimulus to the emotions because the celebrant was both actor and audience, and thus it effected the famous *katharsis* of pity and fear. And whether or not the *katharsis* was of hitherto unknown, unconscious or un-understood memories, there is no question but that many a mystic woke next morning when the torches had burnt out, not only with a throbbing head, but turned into a wiser and a calmer human being.

So these festivals must not be thought of as spectator sports, or even as opportunities to enjoy an orgiastic release not normally sanctioned in the bosom of the family. Psychiatric case histories describe twentieth-century housewives who have suffered breakdowns sexual in origin, and who will without knowing it, but in a state bordering on possession, reproduce a good part of Dionysiac ritual. I have seen it happen myself, and in an age that talks with such casual self-importance about sex, we have forgotten what terrifying and irrepressible emotions it can both cause and release. The Dionysia were a fundamental expression of delights and divinely inspired lusts. The medicine had to be as powerful as the sickness it purported to cure.

But like the witch, the hysteric or the possessed, the *mystai* lacked any power of reasonable analysis. Drunkenness released inhibitions, and perhaps to that extent it was good. To a rational person, however, Eleusis and the Academy in Athens might as well have been at opposite ends of the earth. For the Eleusinian or the Dionysiac had no understanding of abstract but definable beauty, or of abstract but definable value. The initiation was nothing but an exorcism of one's fears achieved by emotional means. A Christian would have called it exorcism with the help of the devil.

Of course the more intelligent Athenian paid less heed to these mysteries than did his peasant contemporary. Diogenes, for example, never joined the tens of thousands sauntering like some vociferous football crowd to be initiated at Eleusis. "It is absurd," he said, "to think that a mere tax gatherer needs only an initiation to share the rewards of the just in the next world while Agesilaus and Epaminondas are doomed to lie in the mire."[1] Heraklitus thought mysteries fit only for the vulgar. Socrates and Anaxagoras are said to have thought roughly the same.

But confronted with Christianity, the intelligent pagan would probably have suggested that Christian morality was fallible too, for it was predicated on absolutes, and in the true sense of the word impertinent. Delight, on the other hand, makes its own absolutes, which suit themselves to the individual. Moreover it is not only attainable and perceptible here and now; delight is what most men desire, whereas the felicity of self-abnegation can be experienced only by a few. As a matter of fact, during their later trials witches often deposed that the devil had come to them and said, "Christ is dead, but I am here. I am here and can help you."

In his *de mysteriis*, Iamblichus had stated that, by its very nature, felicity ended in joyous union with a god. And one wonders if the sacrificial ceremonies in Jutland were not of this order. The seventeenth century witches who went further than

---

[1] The anecdote will be found in Diogenes Laertius, *de vitiis philosophorum*, vi. 39. For the opinion of Socrates, at least according to Lucian, see Lucian, *Demonax*, 11.

felicity and actually copulated with their masters would certainly have said the same, and not for the sake of the copulation (it was often unpleasant), but for the sake of union with the divine. In the *Enniads* Plotinus (who was very possibly pathologically unbalanced) writes at some length about a state he calls mystical hilarity. The mind, he says, loses its rational powers by getting drunk on nectar (the word *nektar* means death-overcoming), enters into a condition of love and diffuses itself entirely in delight. So to him too, physical joy went hand in hand with a god. *Entheos*, filled with god, is after all the origin of our word enthusiasm. For gods were not things of the spirit; they lived in the body, in the senses and in the mind. So when Christianity sloughed off that body as something sinful and unclean, it was not only taking up arms against several thousand years of experience to the contrary, against the bronzed and joyous athlete powdered with dust in the arena, the naked god, the laughing little slave that crept into your bed at night. It was taking a position which long afterward, in the light of empirically established psychiatric knowledge, was to prove untenable.

In the classical world, not only was the body not unclean. It was often thought to be supremely beautiful. And not only could it during a certain holy madness effect a union with the gods and give pleasure which was not always physical in origin. It was actually a repository of secret wisdom. Plato writes of having seen a whole city drunk at a Dionysiac festival, and elsewhere of Corybantian revellers who danced when they were out of their minds, or Bacchic maidens who could go so far as to feel they were drawing milk and honey out of the rivers when they were under the influence of Dionysus, but not when they were sane.[1] Indeed he goes even further in the *Phaedrus* and describes madness as a gift often given by the gods themselves. "Prophecy is madness," he writes. "The prophetess at Delphi and the priestesses at Dodona have conferred great benefits on Hellas, both in public and in private life, and they have done this when they were out of their minds. But when in their senses, they have done little or nothing."[2]

[1] *Laws*, 637b and *Ion*, 534a.   [2] *Phaedrus*, 244 a and b.

In other words he describes the oracle as possessing powers later credited to witches who were supposed to be in league with the devil. And indeed the only real difference between the oracle and the witch who was later hanged or burned at the stake are that the oracle was possessed and the witch was not. The witch was accused of being the servant of a devil, while the oracle was the servant of a god.

Now at Delphi the priestess seems, at least in Plutarch's time, not to have required any particular training. She was simply (and inevitably) a virgin born in the surrounding countryside who no doubt felt she had, or was thought by the authorities to have a vocation. So she was admitted to the priesthood, and when an oracle was required purified herself, and wearing long robes and a golden fillet about her brow, went into the Adyton, or sanctuary, seated herself on a tripod over a cleft in the rock from which rose certain vapours, and there in a state of semi-anaesthetic enthusiasm (sometimes with deep cunning) foretold the future.

Stengel describes more fully what actually took place.[1] "Under the influence of the vapours rising out of the gulf, she was thrown into an ecstasy. Then she spoke more or less coherent words which were translated by priests into bad hexameters or into other poetic metres and passed on to the questioners. Often the priestess must have been in a state precluding any ability to reason. Then the priests simply had to make what they could of her words and cries. But deliberate fraud was certainly rare. It may have occurred here and there, and one Pythoness is reported to have been dismissed because she was said to have taken a bribe to deliver a false oracle. But in the great days of the oracles, Pythoness and priests believed that the god spoke in her. . . . It would be impossible to explain the unusual regard in which the oracle was held for centuries if we accepted that she was a repeated fraud."

As Plutarch says, and as I mentioned earlier, the priestesses died young, and it seems likely that they prophesied in a hypnotic state, for according to Aristides they never knew what

[1] Stengel, Paul, *Die Griechische Kultusaltertümer*. München, 1898.

they were going to say, and when they woke did not know what they had said. Bunsen maintains that they often exhibited what can only be described as genuine foreknowledge. And indeed it would be unscientific to deny oracles the power of divination simply because it is the current fashion to think such things impossible. It would be to admit that a people whose civilization has never been equalled allowed itself to be tricked by its priests for three thousand years. This would be historically and psychologically false.

Christianity, as usual, debased and vulgarized what it could not accept. Origen writes in *Contra Celsum*, "It is said of the Pythian priestess, whose oracle seems to have been the most celebrated, that when she sat down at the mouth of the Castalian cave, the prophetic spirit of Apollo entered her private parts". Chrysostom was even more specific. "She sat with parted thighs on the tripod of Apollo, and the evil spirit entered her from below, passing through her genital organs, and plunged her into a state of frenzy, so that she began with loosened hair to foam and rage like a drunkard."

In the final analysis, of course, the teachings of philosophy would have seemed to Plato more valuable than either the teachings of a church predicated upon blind faith, or the blind exaltation of a prophetess based on possession by a god. Philosophy employed pure and geometrically beautiful logic to find what the vulgar sought either in self-abnegation or in union with powers that could not be defined.

Strangely, therefore, strong links do exist between a tolerant classic paganism and the stiffnecked Christianity that was to destroy it. For their simplest difference lay only in this, that the one yearned for a life after death with the same urgency as the other felt a longing to penetrate the teasing impenetrability of life itself.

There were no festivals to Pan, the goat-god of Arcadia. Yet that simple pastoral deity to whom the fruits of the field were dedicated has survived in the popular imagination perhaps longer than Dionysus. Horace calls him lover of fleeing nymphs, and the anonymous *Incerti ad Panem* describes him as goatish, changeable, noisy and violent. "Sharp anger ever waits upon his nostril," says Theocritus. But there is hardly any mythology attached to him; a love affair or two—with Echo and Syrinx—a small shrine under the Acropolis, a meeting with Philippides on the road from Sparta; no more. To find any resemblance between him and Christ would seem ridiculous. As well find a resemblance between the devil and god.

But because he exemplifies those rustic pleasures poets have praised for well over two thousand years, because we can so clearly imagine him drinking from his leather bottle in the shade, sleeping away the heat of noon in a little grove, running to catch a barelegged girl and laughing hoarsely as he tumbles her head over heels in a haycock, because he forms part of our oldest and most primitive memories, our golden dawn, he is in fact god and devil both, and many a fanciful soul has heard the panpipes trilling in some silent wood, or the thud of invisible goat hooves dancing in some sunstruck summer field.

I said earlier that for over two thousand years girls have walked out at twilight in the rustling corn and imagined— almost smelled—the Pan in whom they no longer rationally believed, but who was nevertheless as real as the mowers or the maypole they had seen tall on the village green. It is a strange comment on a changed morality that this god, to whom such a girl might have surrendered herself with only a moment's panic struggle, should have been turned by the Christian theologians into a devil from whom she would have run screaming.

Strange, too, the ways of the scholiast. Cornutus, tutor to Lucan, who died young but wrote the *Bellum Civile*, misnamed *Pharsalia*, and to Persius, who said of his own satires that they had the taste of bitten nails, this Cornutus decided sagely that Pan's nether body had the form of a goat, to designate the roughness of the earth, but his upper parts that of a man, to designate reason.

But Pan was anything except reasonable or spiritual, any- thing except Christian. When sixteen hundred years later, witches rode out all over Europe on their broomsticks to lie with a master who wore horns, they were lying with Pan, not because he was diabolical, but because he was the most primitive, the most nearly animal, and thus the most emotionally satisfying figure they could imagine.

The Dionysiac had proclaimed that spiritual vision was less perfect than bodily delight. Dionysius (probably Dionysius of Rhinocolura), writing about AD 370, decided with appropriate gravity that the Bacchic approach to God was through a negation of the intellect. But the medieval mystic also walked toward God through the senses, and so have many of the rest of us. The old nun in nineteenth century Brazil sews away at her shroud during the siesta, and smiles because she can feel the baby Jesus stir in her lap, and I knew an old Russian peasant woman who fainted one afternoon when she saw God. Christ and the Pan-god are more nearly related than we had thought.

To some eyes in the ancient world that relationship was very close indeed. After all, there were many who saw Jesus as a corn-god, and so in a way was Pan.

"The father of Aemilianus, the orator," Plutarch writes, "and some of you may have heard of him, was Epitherses, who lived in our town and was my teacher in grammar. He said that once upon a time in making a voyage to Italy, he embarked on a ship carrying freight and many passengers. It was already evening when, near the Echinades Islands, the wind dropped and the ship drifted near Paxi. Almost everybody was awake, and a good many had not finished their after-dinner wine.

"Suddenly from the island of Paxi there was heard the voice of someone calling Thammus, so that all were amazed. Thammus was an Egyptian pilot, not known by name even to many of those on board.

"Twice he was called and made no reply, but the third time he answered. And the caller, raising his voice, cried out, 'When you come opposite to Palodes, announce that great Pan is dead.'

"On hearing this, said Epitherses, everybody was astounded, and they argued among themselves whether it would be better to carry out the order or to refuse to meddle and let the matter go. Under the circumstances, Thammus made up his mind that if there should be a breeze, he would sail past and say nothing. But if there were no wind and a smooth sea about the place he would announce what he had heard. So when he came opposite Palodes and there was neither wind nor wave, Thammus, sitting in the stern and looking toward the land, called out the words as he had heard them. 'Great Pan is dead.'

"Even before he had finished, there was a huge cry of lamentation, not simply of one person, but of many, mingled with exclamations of amazement. And as a good many passengers were in the ship, the story was very soon spread abroad in Rome, and Thammus was sent for by Tiberius Caesar. Tiberius became in turn so convinced of the truth of the story that he caused an enquiry to be set up and an investigation to be made about Pan. The scholars who were numerous at his court, conjectured that he was probably a son born to Hermes and Penelope."[1]

Eusebius, writing three hundred years later, points out that at that very time Christ was ridding the world of demons, and that these of course included the pagan gods. But Paulus Marsus in his commentary on Ovid puts forward a different explanation.[2]

According to him it was all very simple. The voice from the island of Paxi was heard in the nineteenth year of the reign of Tiberius. At that very time Christ died, and "a voice miraculously issuing forth from the solitude of the deserted rocks was announcing that the Lord was dead".

[1] Plutarch, *de defectu oraculorum*, Loeb Classical Library, Harvard, 1957. My translation is largely based on that by F. C. Babbitt.
[2] It is quoted by Patricia Merivale in *Pan the Goat God*, Harvard, 1969. I have not been able to lay hands on the text itself.

6

But Pan was not dead, for in spite of Paulus Marsus he was to wake up as Satan, though not for several hundred years. Caesarius of Heisterbach, who was ordinarily well-informed, and a most delightful gossip and raconteur, writes that the first pact of which there is actually any record was made with the devil in 1222.

But in this Caesarius is mistaken. It is difficult to believe he had never heard the story of how St Basil in the fourth century rescued a young man who had sold his soul to the devil for love of his master's daughter. Indeed long before Caesarius was born such pacts had been in the air. Silvester II, who displayed a remarkable love for both mathematics and classical literature, and became Pope in 999, was said by Cardinal Benno to have practiced sorcery, and by William of Malmesbury in the *Gestus Regum* actually to have made a pact with the devil to acquire the papacy itself. Nor was he the only bargainer in high places. In 1301 (according to one authority—1303 according to another), the Bishop of Coventry was accused of having made a pact with Satan, and John Tannere, who claimed to be a son of Edward I, confessed before he was hanged for treason that he had made a pact with the devil in return for a promise of the crown. Indeed, to go further back, St Augustine himself writes of pacts with the devil as being not uncommon in the fifth century.

Michelet has it that the first mention of witchcraft and Sabbatic dances in the devil's honour does not occur until 1353, when certain witches were brought to trial in Toulouse.[1] And this statement too is in error unless he is referring only to France. For the English *leges Henrici* of 1114 decree that murder by witchcraft shall be punishable by death, and many a later statute forbade practices which can only be described as witch-like. The practitioners, whoever they were, must have been in a desperate state, for as Michelet makes quite plain, no peasant ever sold his soul to the devil until he had been driven to extremities by hunger or by sickness, or was in imminent danger from those by whom he was oppressed. The habit of unquestioning piety died very hard.

On the other hand, from the very beginning there had been peasants who never believed at all. There was an interregnum during the long centuries before the Middle Ages when, for many, the devil walked up and down wearing a different face. Primitivists lurked in mute and ragged rebellion in a hundred little hamlets. Only the more literate were actually heretical, and their heresy lay in trying to whip the church back toward a simplicity and purity which it had early lost. But before we can understand either primitivist or heretic we have to understand the power against which they both rebelled.

Now we have seen that human sacrifice, the balancing of a visible evil with an anticipated good, developed in two different ways. The Jew worked beyond such simple beginnings and evolved a doctrine of divinely inspired law. Almost the whole of his intellectual creativeness, as Dr Oesterreich pointed out, was

[1] Michelet, Jules, *La Sourcière*. Paris, 1862. This is in many ways a splendid if old-fashioned book, original, enthusiastic and full of irreplaceable ideas. And although the author's conclusions are sometimes not warranted by the evidence, he does have a thorough understanding, for his time, not only of sources but of the spirit of medieval France. In a word, the book is indispensable, but so far as I know it is available to the English reader only in a paperback edition, where it is called *Satanism and Witchcraft*, and where Professor Michelet's footnotes are printed in almost illegible 5½ point type.

concentrated on religion. The pagan evolved a method of emotional *katharsis* whereby in place of obedience to the god he united his body with the god's. In both camps the idea of the sacrifice itself became more complicated.

I spoke of a *visible* evil, and there were two reasons why the payment had to be visible as well. As my neighbour across the field might say, "Us don't pay nowt for nowt". And from the very start the payment had to be open; it had to be seen to be made. Hecatombs were never offered in private. The god had to be paid, of course, but circuses too were important in keeping both the social and the psychological fabric healthy.

To drown a sacrificial victim may have been efficacious. It had to satisfy not only the god, however, but the audience. In the same way, the later execution of malefactors had always to be done with proper public ceremony. And this was not only to provide suitable object lessons, but also because the victim's deserved suffering provided satisfaction to people otherwise starved of an excuse for hilarity and awe. When we stopped hanging people publicly it could have been foretold that we would very soon stop hanging them at all.

Now it became in time inevitable that instead of drowning a girl or strangling a king people would create a symbolic girl or a symbolic king for the same purpose, particularly if the symbol could be made to seem even more pertinent to the suppliant's desires. If the king could be seen to have been a god even before his immolation, the sacrifice would put no strain on credulity and the king-god's ability to reward would be greater. Not only would his death satisfy our need to be awed. He would, to put it bluntly, be capable of reincarnation as the old, visible, well-known king, and thus be able to be sacrificed over and over again.

Thus kings began to be hedged with divinity. But to be believed actually to be a god and not simply a mythological figure, there had to be some sort of miraculous evidence to convince the sceptical. Thus Attis was conceived of a virgin who had impregnated herself by thrusting a pomegranate into—they say—her bosom. Indeed such miraculous pregnancies were not even particularly uncommon. Barren women often conceived in the sanctuary of Asclepios near Epidauros. They slept in the temple at night, and if they had made the proper sacrifices dreamed that a serpent appeared and made love to them. Perhaps he did. And if later they gave birth to a child it was of course the offspring of the god.

Suetonius wrote that the great Augustus was called *divus* for that reason. His mother begot him with a serpent in the temple of Apollo. In the same way, Alexander and the elder Scipio were the sons of gods. In those days there must have been gods aplenty walking on two legs. Appolonius of Tyana, the neo-pythagorean sage and clairvoyant (many of his miracles are known to us) and Alexander of Abonuteichos were teachers thought to be literally divine.[1] Some years ago a few scraps of the prose writings of Philodemos (very possibly in his own hand) were found in the ruins of a villa in Herculaneum. "Everybody is full to the teeth," he writes (he was a great popularizer) "of people who try to fall into a divinely inspired temple sleep, to feel the ecstasy of the holy spirit, to lay grateful offerings at the feet of naked statues and to shake their tambourines in front of all the available gods."

But it was not only Greek and Roman matrons who were divinely impregnated. Manoah's wife, the mother of Samson, conceived him, it seems, by an angel of the Lord who appeared to her in a field when her husband was not there. The later church, being less naive and more practical, would have called this conception by means of an incubus, a devil in disguise. Even so, as late as the adolescence of our grandparents, many a young girl lay on her back with hands clasped doggedly behind her head on St Agnes' Eve because she hoped to catch a miraculous glimpse that night of her future husband. In the second century the stoicist, Aelianus, reported that in the time of Herod there had been a serpent who made love to a Judean maid and impregnated her with a child who became the son of God.[2] The British

[1] A most imaginative, delightful and unjustifiably neglected novel by C. G. Finney, *The Circus of Dr Lao*, appeared some thirty years ago, in which Appolonius figures prominently.

[2] *de natura animalium*, vi. 71.

Merlin, too, was fathered by a demon who crept into his mother's bed at night.

Practically every part of the world has told stories of gods going up and down as men, and of deaths and resurrections so strikingly alike as to put them beyond the bounds of coincidence. But the parallels between Christian and pagan mythologies do not end there. The cult of Isis had a professional priesthood and performed mystery plays to celebrate the death and resurrection of Osiris. According to Ezekiel women in Babylon wept for the death of Tammuz. In Phrygia they wept for Attis, who, born of a virgin, became the lover of the mother goddess Cybele, but castrated himself and died to ensure fertility to the corn. Out of his blood for the first time violets sprang, and of course this calls to mind:

> *I would give you some violets, but they*
> *withered all when my father died.*

or later,

> *And from her fair and unpolluted flesh*
> *May violets spring.*[1]

After his death Attis was changed into a pine tree, and his cult spread rapidly under the Empire. Like the god, his priests became castrati and thus carried later Christian celibacy past what we might call the point of no return. But there was much else they taught that was also part of Christian doctrine; the necessity for baptism, for example, a doctrine of life after death, the delights of the eucharist.

In *The Golden Ass* Apuleius paints a sad and ludicrous picture of similar castrated priests, dedicated this time to a Syrian goddess. They dress in saffron yellow robes, rouge their cheeks and paint their eyes. Like Chaucer's Pardoner they cheat the gullible and offer false relics for veneration. They travel from town to town, play the melancholy Phrygian horn to attract audiences (for they are mendicants), and to satisfy themselves in their beds buy a muscular but much overworked young slave.

[1] *Hamlet*, IV. v and V. i.

As early as 40 or 30 BC the priests of Attis were a familiar sight in Rome. Carrying images of Cybele, wearing medallions on their breasts, they walked the streets, playing flutes and tambourines and gathered alms from passers by. On the 22nd of March each year they had a pine tree cut down and brought into the sanctuary. There they wreathed it in violets and tied a figure that represented Attis to its trunk.

Then for three days they kept vigil. On the third day the priests danced before it. Toward evening the music grew louder. They began to whirl like dervishes, cried out, slashed their arms to emulate the god. Occasionally in a frenzy of possession a young worshipper whipped out a knife and castrated himself before them all.

At last the body of the god was lowered into its sepulchre. A bull was sacrificed. Worshippers crowded forward to wash away their sins in the arterial blood that spurted over them, and then suddenly above the flaring torches a light shone out like an abruptly risen star. The cry went up that Attis had been resurrected, and there followed what was called the *hilaria,* the Festival of Joy. It is possibly no coincidence that the sanctuary of the Phrygian Cybele lay on what is now Vatican Hill.

But to be miraculously born was not even a purely eastern concept. After all, was not Charlemagne descended from a swan maiden? Even the pre-Christian Welsh and Irish had similar stories. Robert Graves goes further. In *The White Goddess* he says that such a child was always born on an intercalary day just after the winter solstice, thus at Christmas. As he explains it, the ancient 365-day year was divided into thirteen moons or months of twenty-eight days each, with one day added at the end to make up the proper number. This, if it were true, would explain innumerable references in popular storytelling to a year and a day. The fact that the moon lasts, not twenty-eight days, but twenty-nine and a half does, he admits, present difficulties, particularly as the ancients knew this quite as well and perhaps better than we. But Mr Graves has never been one to let facts spoil an otherwise happy theory.

In Syria the equivalent to Attis was the incestuously-conceived Adonis. Like Attis he was a god of vegetation. Like Attis he suffered a violent death (as indeed did most gods, for sacrificial reasons), and like Attis he was the lover of a goddess, this time of course Aphrodite, the sea-born, risen from the foam at Paphos. And so conscious were second-century Gnostics of the parallelism with Christianity that they are said to have equated the name of the Virgin Mary with *mare,* the sea, though her name is more probably a corruption of the Hebrew Miriam.

Like the others Adonis was resurrected at the time of sowing, a time sacred to the dawn goddess Easter. And Adonis too gave birth to a flower, not a violet this time, but a rose.

> *Spring, says your Alexandrian poet,*
> *Means time of the remission of the rose.*[1]

It is perhaps worthy of note that in the year 389 St Jerome founded a religious house in Bethlehem, which in Hebrew means House of Bread. Near that house of bread there lay, not surprisingly, a grove sacred to the corn-god, Adonis, and according to Jerome, the pagan worshippers had simply stolen and ascribed to their god happenings in the life of Jesus. Needless to say, the evidence points in the other direction.

Not that it makes any difference. Christ, presented by his disciples as the only begotten son of a father-god and ultimately a sacrifice for our redemption, was in fact obeying laws older than the words of the prophets which all his life he had been bent on seeing fulfilled. Not only was Judas Iscariot merely doing his duty in the service of the state. He was doing that duty to Christ as well, for without him or someone like him the Christian religion would never have spread as rapidly as it did. It would probably not even have survived.

St John goes so far as to suggest that what was really the earliest of all things, the serpent in the garden, the serpent lifted on Moses' banners in the wilderness, became in the fullness of time Christ lifted on the cross.[2] So beginning and end were the

---

[1] These are the opening lines of a poem of Lawrence Durrell's in *The Tree of Idleness*, London, 1955. Durrell has of course read widely in these mysteries.

[2] John, iii. 14.

same. One might add that the cherubim or storm clouds or horned bulls guarding the way eastward out of Eden found a not inexact parallel in the darkness that came over the earth at the crucifixion.

But the chief point is that all these religions grew out of sacrificial magic, formulated similar moral laws, accumulated similar rituals, created priestly classes and involved the worshipper emotionally because the worshipper's very life depended on the growth of the corn. Now in the main the long later adherents to the old sorcery, to *la vecchia*, were inhabitants not of Rome or Jerusalem or any other city. They were peasants of the most primitive sort for whom the growth of corn and the stability of the natural world by which they lived were matters of tangible concern, and who knew with a dumb stubbornness that the church, by dealing almost solely with matters of the spirit, had gone astray of the point. For magic, like modern science, is based on the principle of causality, and this they could understand. The cults of Attis or of Mithras had been halfway houses. Christianity, when it grew away from its origins, was not.

Equally important, "Magic and magical rites are traditional facts. Actions which are never repeated cannot be called magical."[1] In Christian ritual, repetition was never employed except to plead or to involve the worshipper more deeply in the service. But it did not move the magic forward. The peasant is at heart conservative and not easily weaned from his traditions. Christian ritual, appearances to the contrary, is not in the same sense traditional, for it lacks the element of causality or progression. It does not act as magic acts; instead it persuades, and we must not confuse ritual with technique.

So much for the later followers of a *vecchia religione*. But we are concerned with the heretic too, and in almost every example of heresy that has come down to us that devil-driven heretic was a man who, devout as he may have been (and most heretics had started by being praeternaturally devout), yearned for a simplicity, for that kernel of primitive need out of which his church had originally grown.

[1] Mauss, *A General Theory of Magic.*

A prehistoric painting, the man-animal dancer, in the cave *Les Trois Frères* (in Ariège, France). (*Mansell Collection*)

The ecstasy of the Bacchanalia painted on a Greek amphora; despite fantastic elements, this would seem to be a depiction of a real event. (*Mansell Collection*)

A more controlled and 'civilised' view of the horned god Pan, in a Roman sculpture; he is depicted teaching Daphnis to play the syrinx. (*Mansell Collection*)

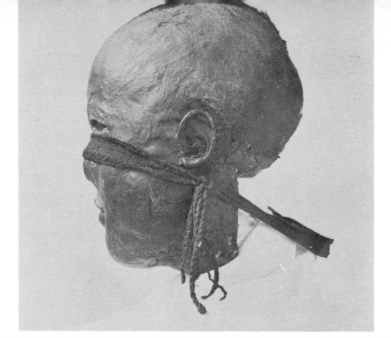

Above, the head of a young girl, victim of a ritual sacrifice in the Danish Windeby bog. (see chapter 4) *P. V. Glob, The Bog People (Faber & Faber)*

Below, a detail from the Gundestrup Cauldron, showing the method of sacrifice. *P. V. Glob, The Bog People (Faber & Faber)*

HILDEGARDIS a Virgin *Prophetess*, Abbess of St Ruperts *Nunnerye*. She died at *Bingen* A° Do: 1180. *Aged* 82 *yeares*.

W. Marshall sculps

St Hildegarde of Bingen (1098–1180). (*Radio Times Hulton Picture Library*)

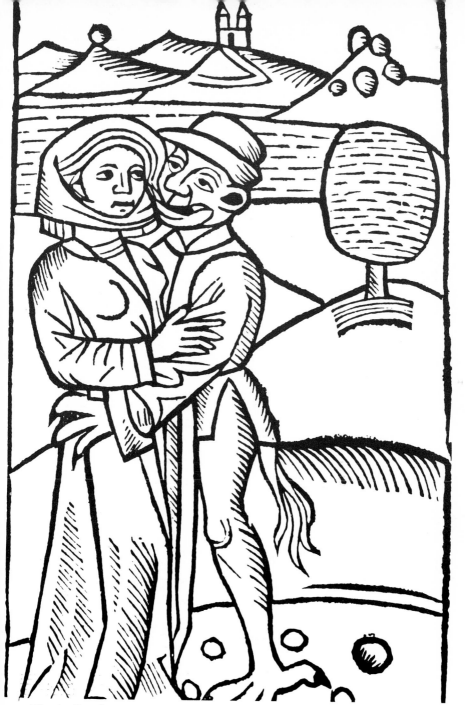

The devil embracing a young woman, in a woodcut dated 1489. For three centuries the devil appeared to many a young country girl.

The anti-establishment impression of the devil, as depicted in the confessions of many witches—and clearly it was important to the establishment that he look as reprehensible as possible. (Both *Mansell Collection*)

Above, a most comprehensive depiction of the activities of witches, from a sixteenth-century engraving. (*Mansell Collection*)

Urbain Grandier, the priest of St Peter's Church in Loudun, burned at the stake for his part in the now-famous events that took place there. (*Radio Times Hulton Picture Library*)

Of course the early church was aware of this, and tried to embrace in its own practices as much of pagan custom as it could. So it fixed feast days to coincide with the farmer's calendar and built places of worship in spots long made holy by primitive usage. For centuries there were sanctuaries, wells, even burial grounds used by pagan and Christian alike, and St Paul's in London was remembered well into the Middle Ages as a shrine sacred to Diana. Indeed one can go further. Saints' haloes are found in Pompeii girdling the heads of pagan gods and heroes, and in the catacombs Christ very often appears as Asclepios.

In a word the Christian year was evolved out of the pagan and Christian mythology out of a mixture of mythologies older than history. Canaanites had sacrificed their kings. Asclepios had raised the dead as Jesus was said to have raised Lazarus and Jairus' daughter, and the beasts in the stable at Bethlehem echoed memories older than any of this. Christ's miraculous draught of fishes, his stilling the tempest, his feeding the multitude, his miracle of the wedding wine, all these were parts of an age-old story. Mithras, Herakles and many kings had given their blood and bodies in sacrament. Mithraism had even promised a second coming.

But several factors caused the fresh evocation of ancient beliefs to take a hold on people's imaginations, for of course Christianity spread—not as rapidly as has been supposed, but with measurable speed—all over the Mediterranean world. Gibbon in his famous fifteenth chapter lists five reasons: the inflexible and indeed intolerant zeal of the early Christians; their doctrine, nowhere else so explicitly affirmed, of a future life; the power ascribed to the church of performing miracles; the pure and austere lives of the first converts; and, perhaps most important of all, the union and discipline they maintained in their little republics.

In addition he has much to say about the advantages enjoyed by a body composed of zealots vis-à-vis a society radically tolerant of differing opinions. He points out that Augustus asked that sacrifices to his well-being be offered up in the temple at

Jerusalem, but that a Jew who had paid the same homage to Jupiter would have been abhorrent both to himself and to his fellows, and that the utter intolerance of early Christians, their positive detestation of pagan beliefs are traceable without question to the inflexibility of the Jews who were their predecessors.

"The Jewish religion," Gibbon says, "was admirably fitted for defence, but it was never designed for conquest". It had had its origins not in a nation or even in a tribe, but in the divine promise made to a single nomadic family. The Jews had permitted no marriage of one of their number to an alien, no political alliances, no reception of foreigners into the congregation, no teaching of Judaism to the gentile, no diminishing of the inheritance, in other words, by subdivision. Instead of courting strangers they had shunned them, and it is possibly for all these reasons that a vigorous Jewish state still exists today. Modern psychiatry holds that monotheism is most easily accepted by those who in childhood were accustomed to revere their fathers. This the Jews did, perhaps because of their very cohesiveness.

And it is interesting to read Freud in this context, for in his *Moses and Monotheism*, written late in life, he postulates that Moses was not in fact a Jew, but an Egyptian. Hebrew monotheism, he says, originated in the writings of the heretic and anti-paternal Akhnaton, and if this be true, he suggests that the Jews murdered Moses as tribal fathers and other godlike leaders had been murdered, and that later they not only hated and adored him, but adopted his monotheism in penance for the crime.

"No other portion of the history of religion," he writes, "has become so clear to us as the introduction of monotheism into Judaism and its continuation in Christianity—if we leave on one side the development which we can trace no less uninterruptedly from the animal totem to the human god with his regular companions (each of the four Christian evangelists still has his own favourite animal)."

I said the Jews had found strength through isolation. Christianity, however, armed with all the strength of Mosaic law but released from Mosaic inhibitions, had offered itself to the world. Gibbon points out that the first fifteen Christian Bishops of Jerusalem had been born and brought up as circumcised Jews. And therein lay one aspect of its greatness. But therein lay also the seed of dissension. Jews had never allowed the heretic into the temple. Christians, in their proselytizing zeal, opened the door wide and were horrified to see how easily the devil made himself at home.

So far, Gibbon.[1] But it seems to me that in the light of later knowledge there are several other factors that have to be taken into consideration, for today we know more than he about both anthropological history and primitive superstition. First, Jesus was no mythical Tammuz or Adonis, but a contemporary as real as (say) Marcus Gnipho, a man whom we will presume people had met, with whom they had talked, travelled and broken bread. It was not the rumours, indeed (if you like) the evidence of reincarnation that moved them. After all, Attis had been reincarnated every Easter for as long as anyone could remember. But in Christ's life the myth had been turned into what seemed a practical reality, and the vague promise of a future life into irreversible doctrine.

Second, heretic though he may have been to a man like Caiaphas, Christ was a Jew, and unlike Attis and other similar figures, heir to a vast rabbinical tradition, but also, as the genealogists affirmed (and all men were familiar with epic genealogy), the lineal descendent of the divine Hebrew kings of the years before the diaspora. This linked him with the beginning of the world. It made him every man's cousin, a part of every man's family and thus a part of every man's private and secret magic.

Third, he had taught that, far from being at the mercy of faceless and unpredictable spirits, the individual was master of his fate and could, by choosing the path of asceticism ensure an

[1] That famous fifteenth chapter of *The Decline and Fall of the Roman Empire* has been much criticized for what is called its anti-Christian bias. But then everyone except the churchmen who has written about the church's first thousand years has been accused of the same thing. It is a matter, however, not of opinions, but of facts, and even some of the churchmen, scholars like Fisher, Gwatkin, Glover, have been content to let the facts speak for themselves.

immortality of his own. We were all the children of God and as important in the eyes of heaven as Augustus.

Thus Christ appealed not so much to the rulers as to the ruled. And to understand just how pertinent this was to the spread of Christianity we have to be able to bring vividly to mind just what their daily lives were like, the lives of the slaves, the outcasts, the failures, the sick, the women (to whom he particularly appealed; and of course women made up half the population).

In the second and third centuries Rome was a crowded, noisy city where nearly a million people lay jumbled into an area of five or six square miles bordered by a swamp and, on its western side by an unruly river that frequently flooded the low-lying fields. For the sake of cheapness, and because foundations could not easily be sunk in the marshy ground, builders had early learned to build upward instead of out, so that behind the great squares and palaces, the Campus Martius, the temples on the Quirinal, the Forum Romanum, lay almost innumerable narrow streets like modern Neapolitan slums, with working-class flats piled cheek on cheek and blotting out the light, or with *insulae*, shops of timber and sun-dried brick where the living quarters were built up overhead.

Here, sometimes three and four to a room, lived the hundreds of thousands to whom the glorious Roman Empire might as well not have existed, the carpenters, roadmenders, smiths, the weavers and bricklayers, the servants and waiters, the boat builders, the oarsmen and carters and God knows who else, the sick, the unemployable and the unemployed. What to them were Jupiter and Diana of the glades? What to them were nymphs and river gods? At dawn they ate their *ientaculum*, their bread and salt and bit of cheese. Then parents and older boys slipped into sandals and sallied out to work, and the daughters, barefooted and wearing nothing but tunics that reached to their knees, started the chores, looking after the younger children, fetching water from the well, washing, cleaning the flat, filling the oil lamps, kneading dough and laying it under the ashes to bake, shopping in the street market to find the porridge, the olive oil, the onions, pulse and garlic that would make the *cena,* the scanty second meal of the day, and even when money was scarce, fetching a pitcher of black or yellow wine from the amphora to mix with water and set near the fire to breathe.

What did they know about Cicero, or Virgil's *Eclogues,* about Sabine farms and the magic of Sirmio? History was a few half-remembered scraps about geese that had saved the city, or Curtius leaping into a chasm to close it, or that Augustus had been so rich he could wear four tunics all at once. History was grandfather mumbling endless reminiscences of his ineffectual part in the campaigns of a Septimus Severus he had never seen against enemies of whom he had not even known the names. What was Rome to them except lying soaked in sweat on summer nights while the baby cried and one rocked it with one's foot, or shivering half the winter in a threadbare cloak, a city of hagglers in markets where the clipped coin contained less and less silver and work was perpetually worse paid and harder to find, where taxes went up with every change of political direction and there was no prospect whatever, not even a hope or a thought, of economic change or development, where the only news was of broils, commotions, sickness and civil war? What had auguries, household gods, Sybilline books ever done for them, or the fashionable society of a Pliny, or the Pantheon filled like a zoo with relics of discarded superstition?

To many such people the intense, the fervent and the seemingly irrefutable doctrine of their own immortality and importance in the scheme of things must have tasted like a drink of fresh water. They began meeting in little secret groups to pray, first a few members of a family, then a neighbour woman or two. It must have given a sense of much excitement to be for the first time admitted into a hitherto mysterious, but already powerful society. There was no disputation about doctrine, no mine or thine, no question but that so long as the few held together the kingdom of God was within them. Sitting at the *agape,* or love feast—of fish, perhaps, bread and wine—singing a small song with voices unaccustomed to the measure, reading a letter from unknown brothers somewhere out in the dark, or composing one, reciting copied and recopied verses or scraps of Jesus' sayings, but above all when saying the "Our Father", whose words embodied a concept so new as almost to be frightening, it is likely that for almost the first time in the history of urban man they recaptured an old neolithic sense of mystical and hypnotic union.

Always there were risks of informers and blackmailers, soldiers and Jews. One could be trapped whenever one met. "Every day we are besieged," Tertullian writes in his *Apology*. "Every day we are betrayed, most of all at our gatherings and congregations." So he advises that they meet only by night, or else "let three be your church".

But no matter. For this secret one would gladly be imprisoned. One would go to the northern mines. One would suffer torture and if one happened to live at a time of particularly vicious persecution one would die with Christ's name on one's lips.

So the aged Polycarp, Bishop of Smyrna, who had sat at the feet of St John, when he was arrested and required to curse Christ he answered, "Six and eighty years have I served him and he has done me nothing but good, and how should I curse him, my Lord, my Saviour?" So he was burned to death. Or there was the ninety-year-old Pothinus up in Gaul who was so beaten and kicked by an anti-Christian mob that he survived only two days.

But one of the most moving stories (and there are many hundreds) is that of the little slave, Blandina, in Lyons, "an insignificant creature," Gwatkin calls her,[1] who lay in prison with several companions accused of being ringleaders in a Christian conspiracy. According to letters sent to Christian groups in Asia Minor she "tired out relays of torturers until her body was so broken and torn open that they only wondered she was not dead". But they got nothing out of her except, "I am a Christian and we do no evil".

After the torture she and her by now ragged companions were thrown into a cellar dungeon where they lay for several

[1] Gwatkin, Henry Melvill, *Early Church History to AD 313.* 2 vols., London, 1912.

days waiting for the appointed time of the games with their legs forced open in the stocks. Since Roman law did not allow the execution of a virgin, if she was unmarried (and there is no record of a husband) she had then to be deflowered.

When at last they were taken to the arena Blandina was crucified and left hanging all day in the expectation that the beasts would tear her down. But they ignored her, so she survived and watched one by one the deaths of her companions. *"Salvum lutum! Salvum lutum!"* the crowd had roared on another occasion (Good luck in your bath!) when they saw women drenched in blood. Nothing of the sort happened here, or else it went unreported. But at last she was cut down and tied, still unrepentant, to a pillar to be scourged, then played with and dragged about by the beasts, then put into a net and tossed by a bull "to the crowd's great satisfaction". Still she did not give way to panic, so at last when everyone had grown tired of the sport she was taken into the centre of the ring and butchered by the beast-finisher. "Whoever sees such a thing," Tertullian writes of a similar martyrdom (that of Perpetua) "is beset by doubts, burns to look into it, and when he has learned the causes longs to act likewise".[1]

Such little histories, recounted in a thousand gatherings, gave the survivors a sense of spiritual unity which no material triumph could have done. Pain and death were not to be feared, but actually to be hoped for, and martyrdom washed away more sins than a lifetime of prayer.

Indeed the new faith offered answers to every imaginable problem. If one felt so much as a spark of resentment at having been wantonly neglected both by the state and by its old gods Christianity could explain it, for to Christians, pagan gods were particularly odious creatures. They were nothing less than rebel angels, demons who had been cast into outer darkness. Thus they had been the first and greatest heretics of all. For what had they done but usurp God's place in man's affections and, calling themselves by various names, Jupiter, Venus, Apollo, succeeded for centuries in hoodwinking the entire human race? So in the

[1] *ad scapulam*, 5.

early days of Christianity any homage to one of the old Pantheon was, as Gibbon has it, "direct homage to the demons, an act of rebellion against the majesty of God."

In the third century Minucius Felix says more or less the same thing. "They are demons. You may believe their own testimony, for they have confessed the truth. When adjured by the only true God, poor devils, they have quaked with fear in men's bodies (i.e., in the bodies of the possessed) and either come forth at once, or gradually disappeared."

A hundred and fifty years later Theophilus of Alexandria goes even further. "Homer and Hesiod," he says, "were inspired by a deceitful spirit, for many a demon who has been exorcised has confessed that he was once active in those poets."

That only by the way, except that here we have one of the first indications that the new church intended to throw out the baby with the bath water. But so much was Christianity at its beginnings a religion of gentleness that in the early days a soldier was usually denied the sacraments because he was a professional shedder of blood. And the simplest of Christians knew that, if not he, then at least his presbyter, his priest, his bishop had become capable of miraculous deeds. On every side one heard tales of men who possessed the gift of tongues, of vision, of prophecy. They expelled demons, and these demons issuing out of the mouths of the damned—often in public exorcism—generally confessed themselves to be one of the fallen gods.[1]

Of course these same poor were to be the first whom the hierarchy of the church later abandoned. And I ought to point out here that because we are concerned not so much with the church as with the devil who opposed it, because we are in a sense devil's advocates, it is the poor, the devil-driven whose point of view will be most strongly be put forward. That there were holy

---

[1] It is interesting and indeed informative to note that in the whole of church history no saint has ever claimed the gift of miracles for himself. The stories are always at second hand. Thus Bernard of Clairvaux is loud in praise of St Malachi's miracles, but he never mentions any of his own, though in later generations he is credited with many. Nor could such reticence be ascribed to a natural humility. An abbot, and Bernard was Abbot of Clairvaux, would be the first to see in a miracle vouchsafed to him incontrovertible evidence of the community of his Order with God.

men among the clergy no one disputes. Their intensity, their purity and their devotion kept many a light burning in the darkness that was to come. Indeed even that purity was sometimes called the devil's work when it opposed current doctrine, and as we shall see, priests as well as laymen died in the public bonfires.

But partly because of such men it took almost fifteen hundred years for the great mass of people to understand that whatever they suffered, it was for them alone to bear, that whatever inward power they had found was untranslatable into doctrine, that their new religious leaders were to prove as avaricious and solicitous for temporal power as the discarded emperors. For almost fifteen hundred years they were to wait for miracles and for a second coming that were daily promised, but that never came. And when at last they cried out to be given back the simplicity, the charity on which the church had been founded, when they were seized by their own inward, mystical revelations of goodness or love, when they dared act as they thought Christ would have had them act, they were to be called heretics becaues their revelations differed from those that had been authorized, put to the torture and at last slaughtered as cruelly as their ancestors had been slaughtered for avowing Christ in the first place.

As someone said, Christianity perpetually favoured the sheep at the expense of the goats, and in one's anger and indignation at its irrational, its anti-human doctrines enforced with so much pain and blood on the defenceless, one has to say straightforwardly that it was the greatest cultural disaster that has ever befallen us. What a drouth, what a waste of lives spent haggling empty complexities, what a perversion and exploitation of Christ, what a twisting to organizational advantage of our primordial and deeply rooted concepts of the divine!

One single mitigating argument comes to mind. The classical age was burnt out. Law and the old, lovely equilibrium were tipped out of balance. The investigative mind had grown tired and people's sweet lust for earthly perfectibility had lost any sense of direction. Rome was dying as Egypt and Greece had died, and there was nowhere left for the acquisitive mind to drop anchor. They thought they had destroyed the classic world, those ponderous ecclesiastics. All they had done was walk into a vacuum and leave the devil, half Satan, half Apollo, the only familiar face out of the old school, standing on the brink.

And when they found out, the poor, what had been done to them, then they were to turn with the rage of love rejected and with almost stupefying force to whatever opposed ecclesiastical authority, to murdering priests, to open rebellion in the sacristy, to Protestantism, to the very human devil, to the eternal damnation promised in the Athanasian creed to every man who failed to accept the Catholic faith. And at last, only yesterday in human history, when it became clear that even the devil's hands were empty, then they took matters into their own. Where they will turn next when these hands prove fallible too is a matter for speculation. The world is still younger than we imagine.

To revert: for the reasons I have given or in some similar manner the new teaching appealed to the poor. They were the first converts who appeared in any numbers. But far from the spread of Christianity having been rapid, by the year 250 in Rome, according to what seem the most reliable estimates, Christians numbered only about five per cent of the population or about fifty thousand souls. According to Optatus, there were some forty churches in Rome at the time of Diocletian.

There is an interesting description in Gibbon of the difficulties any would-be Christian faced in his daily life, and these for anyone engaged in trade or fond of social intercourse, would have been almost insuperable.

"The innumerable deities and rites of polytheism," he writes, "were closely interwoven with every circumstance of business or pleasure. . . . Peace and war were prepared or concluded by solemn sacrifices. Public spectacles were an essential part of the cheerful devotion of the pagan . . . and the Christian who with pious horror avoided the abomination of the circus or the theatre, found himself encompassed with infernal snares in every convivial entertainment, as often as his friends, invoking the hospitable deities, poured out libations to each other's happiness. When the bride, struggling with well-affected reluctance, was forced in hymeneal pomp over the threshold of her new habitation, or when the sad procession of the dead slowly moved toward the funeral pile; the Christian, on these interesting occasions, was compelled to desert the persons who were the dearest to him, rather than contract the guilt inherent in these impious ceremonies. Every art and every trade that was in the least concerned in the framing or adorning of idols, was polluted by the stain of idolatry."

Thus music, painting, drama, ornamentation, eloquence, poetry, all flowed from the same impure sources.

Three reasons I have listed for the spread of Christianity. A fourth lay in this: that not only had the church the unifying genius of Paul behind it, and his positively Roman sense for organization, it had within it a host not just of leaders, but of simple men and women whose goodness and austerity astounded even their enemies.

To them, the story of Jesus, his wonderful birth, the sweet acts of justice and love that his apostles wrote about, the necessary horror of his death, were all simple and straightforward reality. For this they lived, and for this many of them died.

And if we try two thousand years afterward to strike a balance between the old and the new, paganism suffers from one nearly fatal handicap. The emotions it roused, the beauty and majesty of its finest concepts, the noise, the colour and frenzy with which its mysteries were expressed have come down to us only as echoes, in fragments and at second hand in Greek and Latin texts translated for the most part by unimaginative nineteenth-century schoolmasters. The gospels, on the other hand, lie before us in the finest English prose we have ever read. As Samuel Butler put it to those who would make any sort of judgment, unfortunately God wrote all the books.

7

Sir Walter Scott commented somewhat wryly in his *Letters on Demonology* that Satan's power was much enlarged by the coming of Christ. One could go a good deal further and say that Satan as we know him was invented lock, stock and barrel by the early church fathers as an efficient cat o' nine tails with which to whip the recalcitrant. For from a world full of sunlight it had been turned into a world crowded with evil and with evil spirits.

Yet even this, true as it may be, is not inexcusably true. We tend to forget how limited people were by what seems now an absurd ignorance, not only of the workings of the world, but even of what went on in their bodies. God alone knew what monsters lurked in the great, loutish seas beyond Ireland, and why not monsters too to account for the visible sicknesses and aberrations in human action? If a thousand years later so vigorous and intelligent a man as St Bernard could be certain the world was flat, how can we condemn him for believing with all his indomitable soul that there were demons working to contravene God's ordinances?

This being said, it is still true that when they themselves had been persecuted they had cried out for tolerance. Let church and state be separated so that Christians need not blasphemously worship the emperor. Let there be freedom for all religions so that Christianity could win converts by persuasion, by sweet reason, compete on equal terms as it were and allow the truth to prevail.

But as soon as Constantine had had that opportune vision of his of a cross in the sky (he had earlier claimed the inestimable privilege of a conversation face to face with Apollo), as soon as the truth had struck him like a thunderclap on the road to Rome and Christianity was made the official religion of the empire, Christians turned into the most intolerant sectarians in human history. Thus the devout Emperor Theodosius in 380: "We . . . will that all our subjects steadfastly adhere to the religion which was taught by St Peter to the Romans. We brand all senseless followers of other religions with the infamous name of heretics and forbid their conventicles assuming the name of churches. Aside from the condemnation of divine justice, they must expect the heavy penalties which our authority, guided by heavenly wisdom, shall think proper to inflict."

Only the Jews had ever spoken in this tone, and then only within the tribe. No other people had ever felt such arrogant assurance. So in an access of zeal Christians began burning pagan temples, and if we feel contempt and loathing for the barbarians who destroyed the almost incomparable temple of Diana at Ephesus, what shall we feel about Christians who deliberately fired the temple of Daphne at Antioch?

As Oesterreich says in his study of demoniacal possession, "The invasions of the barbarians who conquered the Roman Empire destroyed infinitely less than did the Christian hatred and persecution of the heathen. Never in the world's history has so vast a literature been so radically given over to destruction".

The temple at Delphi was officially closed in 390, and it seems that at some later date the Adyton, the sanctuary itself, was painstakingly destroyed by Christian zealots. Archaeologists have spent several hundred years searching for that famous chasm in the rock over which the Pythoness sat. That it existed there is evidence aplenty. Xenophon and Plutarch saw it. Nero even had prisoners thrown into it. But no modern student has ever found it, and how it was filled or destroyed nobody knows.

Within three years of Theodosius' pronouncement the first seven heretics were consigned to what must have begun to look like an everlasting bonfire at Trier. From then on the divine truth was almost annually reinterpreted, each interpretation becoming in turn inviolable and superseding all others. For over a thousand years the truth was a will o' the wisp, now visible here, now there, and with only that for a flickering daylight the church inaugurated an age of sanctimonious barbarism that for extent and duration has no parallel in human affairs. Or perhaps one should not say "the church," but rather those politicians in or out of the church (and they were legion) who made use of a new and infallible authority for ulterior purposes.

I said earlier that almost three hundred years after the death of Christ, Christians made up only five per cent of the population of Rome. But it took only another few generations before paganism had to all intents and purposes disappeared. Never except under grossly authoritarian governments has any idea found such universal acceptance. Against that authoritarianism neither reason nor humility nor faith nor even individual revelation, none of the phenomena on which the authority itself was based carried any weight. It is quite impossible, of course, to believe that those clerico-politicians cared two pins about religion, but with an utterly consistent ruthlessness they simply branded whoever opposed them as a bed-fellow of the devil. And they attacked not only differing opinions. It is a commonplace of church history that they attacked not only the heretic himself, but his family, his friends, his associates, his sexual habits and his domestic economy. The Catharists, for example, the Bogomils (or beloved of God), a splendid sect given to purity and simplicity of life, they called *bougres* from the start, and thus originated the word "buggers" as we know it today.

But I began by talking about Constantine, who dealt Mediterranean paganism its deathblow. By the end of the third century, threatened by barbarians on many fronts and by an almost interminable struggle for political power at home, Roman valour and Roman discipline were simply no longer enough. By the year 272 Aurelian had built twenty-one miles of walls round the city. Rome no longer attacked; she had turned in upon herself, for by then the great legions were nothing but an army of mercenaries. In 312 Constantine, a tall, tough, affable, soldierly man, the bastard son of a Serbian innkeeper's daughter, found himself at the head of an army marching from Gaul to Rome—and with armies four times the size of his own barring the way. Prudent, ambitious, cruel almost on sporting impulse, an opportunist both in marriage and murder, but unquestionably a man of great courage and political adroitness, he started that southward march under the immediate necessity of making new allies, and making them quickly. What better than by a single stroke to acquire the allegiance of fifty thousand or so Christians who had thus far kept aloof from politics?

In hoc signo vinces he saw blazoned across the sky, by this sign you shall conquer, and it was a revelation every bit as momentous as that of St Paul on the road to Damascus, for it was to inaugurate twelve hundred miserable years. Gibbon compares him to Henry VIII. "The policy of self advantage," he writes, "was equally the pride of both; neither the one nor the other had the faintest idea of principle. They both plundered the rich establishments which they overthrew; they both resisted error and assisted truth, only as far as the one prejudiced and the other served their own interests."

Barthold Niebuhr in his acutely reasoned *Römische Geschichte*, written well over a hundred years ago, says of him that "His motives in establishing the Christian religion appear to have been odd in the extreme, for whatever religion he had in his head must have been a jumble indeed. He stamps the *sol invictus* on his coins. He worships pagan deities, consults the haruspices, adheres to heathen superstitions, and yet at the same time he shuts up the temples and builds churches. In his role as president of the Nicene Council we can only look at him with disgust; he was himself no Christian; he never so much as allowed himself to be baptized until he was at the point of death. He had simply taken up the Christian faith as a superstition, and then mingled it with his other superstitions."

Rome had loved action, enterprise, pleasure and knowledge. The Christians loved none of these, and during the black, dead centuries before the Renaissance they were to cut themselves off from any earthly delight, for their governments were, in the vast majority, administrations of businessmen, and their business was the manipulation of people's fears and hopes for the acquisition of money and the exercise of political power. Sexual desire was a crime, marriage a weakness, celibacy the only pure state. They had no concern for public welfare, no interest in abstract but irreligious speculation. Music did not move, nor casual joys amuse them. The loveliness of landscapes had no meaning, or the majesty of trees. The blueness of skies was nothing but the colour of the Virgin's robe. Greek science, the work of Hippocrates and Galen, these they abandoned, for the health of the body did not concern them, or the measurement of the world. Aristotle had proved the earth to be a sphere. Eratosthenes had with remarkable accuracy measured its circumference. Heraclides Ponticus had demonstrated that it turned on its axis and Aristarchus that it probably revolved around the sun. But all this they swept under the carpet or ignored, so almost until the time of Copernicus, geography, astronomy, medicine and mathematics remained matters for study and experiment only in the Arab world.

Drama, sculpture, poetry, history, painting, architecture and what Tertullian called the bloody, wanton theatre died; so did literary scholarship, and even the old waves of fashion or opinion, like pulsebeats in the body politic, became either matters of doctrinal argument or else private and thus of little account. They had no style, these people, no sense for the earthly, the natural, no love of variety or wit or foolishness or unorganized amusement, or even of life itself, nothing but a profound earnestness, an all-embracing gloom. And early in their history, even that initial purity of theirs, that incorruptibility, was corrupted by the need to evolve doctrine, to govern a growing organization, to detect and punish differences of opinion.

It is a commonplace that women had never acquired equal status in Greece, and rarely in Rome. Only barbaric Gauls and Germans had treated them with any respect, consulted them on important occasions, and acted indeed as though they were wise and almost sacred beings. But under Christianity they were degraded almost from the start. For Christianity not only deprived them of what status they had had in the classical world as actors through persuasion or emotional power, like Medea, Antigone, Cassandra, as equal partners of their husbands, like Andromache, or heroines, like Alcestis, or veritable saints, like Iphigenia, or simply as delightful and idyllic girls, like Nausicaa; it not only deprived them of the privilege of enchanting, like Psyche, Daphne, Helen and their many sisters; it even deprived them of their roles as magic-bearing bodies; it turned the old carnal mystery of virginity (which to be potent had to be intrinsic—in the soul) into an abnegation of nature, and magic-inducing menstrual blood into an object of horror. Like virgin Roman vestals, nuns were of course virgins too, but for a different reason. They were brides of Christ, and might not breed lest they produce an heir to the kingdom.

As all men knew, women were nothing but temptresses, and in their very natures, being descended from Eve, given to deception and carnal appetites. "If the world could be rid of women," says Cato of Utica, "we should not be without God in our intercourse." "Better a churlish man, than a courteous woman", we read in Ecclesiasticus. According to St Bernard, "their face is as a burning wind, and their voice the hissing of serpents".

Faithless, credulous, weak of memory, undisciplined, liars out of habit, vain, slippery-tongued, "bitterer than death", Sprenger calls them in the *Malleus Maleficarum*, and so far as concerned intellect or understanding of spiritual things, they were simply an inferior race. Of course by God's mercy even a woman could in the end redeem herself, but only if she held both to her virginity and to an iron obedience. The high-born adulteress and the patient Griselda are both prototypes of medieval romance.

And indeed in the *Alphabet of Tales* we read of a man who

killed his own daughter in the market place, for he would rather be known, he said, as the slayer of a virgin than as the father of a strumpet. One Alexandria (again in the *Alphabet*), because a young man had seen and desired her, caused herself to be immured in a room like a grave with only a hole through which food could be passed to her. She would not, she said, be a cause of sin to any man made in the image of God. "From the beginning of the day," she told a questioner, "I fall to my prayers. Then I do linen work. Then I think of holy martyrs, confessors and virgins. Then I take meat and drink, and then toward evening I go to rest and worship Almighty God. And thus I abide the end of my life with a good hope and a belief that on the day of doom I shall be saved."

Democritus put out his eyes because he could not look at women without desiring them, and according to Tertullian such idolatry was the midwife that brought all of us into the world, and lust the shameful part of nature that gave us birth.

Always, in every action or enterprise or exhortation, that spiritual and intellectual arrogance, that sanctimonious inflexibility; even a hypocrite found it useful for the successful exercise of power. Every creature who had lived since the time of Christ and still worshipped other gods was damned to everlasting fire and could expect no pardon. The love of one's enemies that Christ had preached was turned to bitterness and contempt.

"How I shall laugh!" that same lawyer and martyrologist, Tertullian writes (and he was certainly no hypocrite, simply verbose, impatient and bad-tempered, like Carlyle), "How I shall laugh, how rejoice, how exult when I behold proud monarchs and gods groaning in the lowest abyss of darkness, magistrates . . . liquefying in fiercer fires than they ever kindled against Christians, philosophers blushing in red-hot flames along with their deluded followers, poets trembling before the tribunal, not of Minos, but of Christ, tragedians more tuneful in the expression of their sufferings, dancers. . . ."[1] It was this same Tertul-

---

[1] Tertullianus, Quintus, *de spectaculis*. This diatribe was written about the year 198 in derision of the pagan love of games and circuses. And yet, years afterward he told Scapula that it was a fundamental right of human beings to worship what they thought proper.

lian who decided that Pilate was a Christian at heart, *"pro sua conscientia Christianus"*. And indeed he was not even alone in this. Both Pilate and his wife were eventually canonized by the Coptic church. One cannot help wondering what wry talk passed between him and Jesus when they met in the colonnades of heaven.

Peter crucified, Paul beheaded, and within a few generations of Christ's death a violent argument already raging about just how his teaching ought to be interpreted. Of course in the first two centuries there were no scriptures generally available and thus there was no standard of orthodoxy, simply a tradition which each priest or bishop had to interpret as best he could. Only St John, as far as one can judge, kept hold of the essentials, for he is said to have lived almost to the turn of the century, and when he could no longer stand, to have preached sitting in a chair. "Little children, love one another", was always his text. The time was to come only a few hundred years in the future when the church would say to children, "Act like old men", for no invention could ever be allowed, no freshness, no play, no individuality. "Copy, imitate, copy and be silent", were to be the watchwords.

In the course of a millennium and a half, heresy went through three stages. The first was simply schism in the parent church, when the heretical was whatever opposed the doctrine of the prevailing party, and when, as Gibbon points out, that party exercised its spiritual authority with ever-increasing severity. The second was of sects that grew up, principally in France and Italy, and almost all of which were made up of rebels harking back to the faith's earlier simplicity. Their members were hunted down with all the violence of later pogroms against the Jews. And the third was the rebellion of individuals, when the corruption, the luxury and the naked authoritarianism of the clergy had become too much to bear.

In a history of the devil, early heresies deserve little more than to be mentioned, for although St Augustine tells us there were over two hundred of them, the terrible heat they generated has of course long died away. There were the Ebionites, a sect of paupers who had the effrontery to deny Christ his miraculous birth. The Gnostics, learned and wealthy, dared to enquire into the nature of evil. There were the Montanists, the Novatians, the Sabellians, the Patripassionists, the Monarchians, and most of them, according to the encyclopaedic but unimaginative Origen, were no better than executioners of God. That even they might finally be saved ought not, he thought, be preached to the common people, lest they be freed from the terror of hell-fire. When did the cleansing fire come, he wondered, when a man died, or at the time of the Last Trump?

The Monothelites argued about whether or not the incarnate Christ was possessed of two wills, his and his father's. The Pelagians admitted free will, but Augustine opposed them, pointing out that freedom of the will actually meant union of the will with God's law. Homoeusians disputed with Homo-ousians about whether the Son was the same as the Father, or simply a like essence. In other words, what had used to be philosophy degenerated into speculative fancy, and for these and similar cogitations men pored over manuscripts, scratched away at critical editions by the thousand, spent their whole lives and died.

Gradually, very gradually indeed, doctrine evolved out of controversy and political manoeuvring, both doctrine and the power to enforce it, and when the central power of the papacy felt strong enough to anathematize its opponents, then it thundered out that not only had the whole of pagan religion derived from Satan, but so had all the heresies. The great St Cyprian himself, before he was beheaded, taught that there was no salvation to be found anywhere in the wide world except in the visible church. The trouble was that by then the church had acquired almost as many tongues as it had iron-eyed and argumentative leaders. Before Nicaea the church could reprove, depose or excommunicate. But as soon as church and state became one it could kill. And of course this is true not only of the early Catholic church, but of any organization in history that has had both power and a monopoly of the truth. One can take it as an axiom that nothing so hardens the heart or deadens the judgment as a conviction that one is irrefutably right.

And those early church fathers were concerned not only with establishing doctrine, not only with absorbing such aspects of paganism as seemed advantageous, but also with manipulating the very climate of opinion. I mentioned earlier that the Christian year was evolved out of the pagan, and this had been largely a matter of necessity. But it became more than giving old gods or goddesses Christian names. Thus in 273 Christ's birthday was formally fixed at midwinter to coincide with the Saturnalia and with the birthdays of Dionysus, Mithras and Apollo, and in the third century, according to the Julian calendar, midwinter fell on the 25th of December.

The 2nd of February, the day of purification in Rome, became the feast of the Purification of the Virgin. Mosaic law had laid down that for forty-one days after the birth of a son a woman was unclean, and forty-one days after Christmas would have ended on the 4th. But it was important that the pagan holiday be superseded. By the same token August 15th, the Assumption of the Virgin, had formerly been the feast day of the Mother goddess Artemis or Diana. Midsummer Day, which had always been a pagan festival, was given to John the Baptist, and became his birthday, and this holiday too came late because the calendar was faulty.

Nowhere in the gospels is there any mention of infant baptism, but by the time of Irenaeus, about 180, it had become obligatory (as it had been obligatory for the priests of Attis) and a prerequisite to salvation. In 325 the creed was argued and established, and for four hundred years the body of dogma grew until Christ himself would have been hard put to it to recognize his teachings. About 370 the Emperor Valens decided that practitioners of divination and sorcery, being by their very trade opponents to Christianity, had become politically dangerous and were to be persecuted. By 425 a law was passed, forbidding games on Sundays. A few decades afterwards Augustine invented purgatory and the doctrine of the body's resurrection.

Even that late, however, the old gods occasionally fought back. Augustine quotes in *de civitate Dei* the reply of an oracle to a man who had asked how he might reclaim his wife from

Christianity. "You will find it easier to write on water or to fly like a bird," the priestess had said, "than to bring your wife back to sanity once she has polluted herself. Let her keep to her foolishness if she likes. Let her sing dirges for her dead god whom rightminded judges condemned and who suffered his violent and ignominious punishment."

In 609, when the ineffectual Emperor Phocas at last handed over the Roman Pantheon to the church, Pope Boniface IV dedicated it to the Virgin and All Souls, and there All Souls' Day, the feast of the dead, was celebrated on the 1st of May. For well over a thousand years the dead had been covered in flowers on their day of commemoration. The dead man and the seed had had the same prospect of rebirth. But the early church wanted men to live in terror of hellfire, so eventually All Souls' was moved to November, when no flowers bloom.

In time every day of the year, sacred to one god or another, was given to some obscure saint or martyr, Thelasius and Apian (who was perhaps a beekeeper), St Marguil and St Onuphrius, men and women of whom nothing is remembered and who may for that matter never have existed. Artemis, the lovely huntress, became St Artemidorus, Venus, St Venere, Dionysus, St Dionysius, and Celtic St Brigit was even called for a while the mother of Christ. Like Marxism, Catholicism dominated and diminished the individual by dictating his every thought and finding a doctrinal explanation for every one of his activities. Power fed on power, certainty on certainty, casuistry on casuistry.

But Rome had never conquered the north, and for a good many centuries Christianity remained to northerners the badge of a foreign power. Augustine might convert his Ethelbert and, more to the point, he might, when the British refused full submission to the Roman ritual, threaten Saxon invasion, thus displaying a penchant for naked power politics in the name of Christ, but meanwhile the Teuton, or the Welsh or Scottish peasant pursued his immemorial customs and sacrificed to his immemorially ancient gods. Bishop Boniface might in 740 hew down an oak consecrated to the god of thunder and turn the timber into a church. But the Friesians could with equal determination eventually murder him and tear down the church he had built.

Gradually, however, church and state almost everywhere became interdependent powers, and more and more men, anxious to gain a foothold where power was to be found, sought or bought ordination. Fines originally exacted as punishment for crime gradually became the basis of a whole system of indulgences, a dispensation of pardon to build a capital base for expansion. The old pagan ordeals to test guilt or innocence—thrusting a hand into boiling water, walking over red hot ploughshares—became useful in drawing confessions out of confused and ignorant mouths, and it was not until the fourth Lateran Council in 1215 that priests were forbidden to bless or consecrate such ordeals. Meanwhile in the east the church authorities had had a hundred thousand Paulicians put to death for maintaining, among other things, that Satan was lord of the visible world, but that Christ had been sent to deliver men from the body. It was a heresy remarkably similar of course to that of the Manicheans and of the Catharists hundreds of years afterwards.

As the church leadership acquired political power it attracted to itself the moneyed classes, and as they acquired money churches began to look merely contemptible if they remained simple. New and imposing buildings were erected and furnished at inflationary cost. One had to keep up with the times. More and more often the altar cross was crusted with precious stones. More and more saints' pictures were painted to replace what was now considered the primitive art that had decorated innumerable temples. The poor prostrated themselves, but the ignorant who had never beheld such splendour actually worshipped the pictures, and thus earned the contempt of a clergy that was only half educated itself. Tales began circulating from village to village of statues that had miraculous powers.

A good many, of course, were down-to-earth folk and not so easily fooled. One story current was about an adulterous wife whose lover had murdered her husband. When she was told that the corpse had worked certain miracles, "that's as true", she cried, "as that my arse can sing". At once, *mirabile dictu,* her arse began to sing, and the plain fact attested by many witnesses was that for all her efforts to stop it, it burst into song every Friday thereafter for as long as she lived.

The moral was obvious, and miracles bred money. So priests began vying with each other to acquire saints' relics, their hair, their bones, a scrap of their clothing. More and more frequently these relics were seen to work miraculous cures. And so in the course of a generation or two many a church turned rich corporation, for its priests were able to lay hands on quite large numbers of money-making relics. To take one example, the Chapelle du Marché at St Omer acquired fragments of the manna that had rained from heaven, a bit of Christ's cradle and of his winding sheet, some strands of the Virgin's hair, a piece of her robe and even a section of the window through which the angel Gabriel had entered at the Annunciation.

To be sure, many a humble parson, full of the joy of unquestioning acceptance as he may have been, began to be both embarrassed and worried by such pandering to credulity, and even in high places there were individuals seized with a growing discomfort at the direction the great body of authority was taking.

All over Europe at a simpler level there were thousands upon thousands—men and women—who were simply unconcerned, the souls at rest who lived immured in cloisters and were content for days to drift like shadows, hundreds falling each day between Matins bell and Compline, until an immortal patina had covered up the transitory. *Shave the head and tie the beard, and say it was the desire of the penitent to be so bared before his death; you know the course is common.* This of a common malefactor, and shaving for both priest and sinner was token of purification. For another it must often have looked more a matter of imprisonment than joy. He would be

a stubborn soul
That apprehends no further than this world.[1]

[1] *Measure for Measure,* IV. ii and V. i.

Hundreds of years earlier Benedict had been so disturbed by the frivolity and licentiousness of unsuitable prelates that he had fled to his cave in the Abruzzi. In the tenth century Ratherius of Verona had preached about God as a spirit, only to be met with a positive outcry of priestly indignation. A spirit had no head. God was nothing if he had no head. So perhaps ignorance had to be cured before one could cure licentiousness, simony and corruption. This same Ratherius cried out over and over again at the sight of stupid and prurient priests and at the negligence of bishops.

In the twelfth century Arnold of Brescia, a republican, a priest and a pupil of the great Abelard, sent out a ringing call to the church to return people their property and reacquire the simplicity expounded in the gospels. The popular response was so immediate that both noblemen and clerics became alarmed and looked about for charges of heresy that might be brought against him. But he was orthodox in doctrine, and in his private life an irreproachable ascetic, so that even the redoubtable St Bernard (who had already once been worsted by Abelard) was forced to acknowledge that Arnold neither ate nor drank, but like the devil himself "thirsted after the blood of souls".

In early days Satan had invariably been a spirit, but by the time of St Martin in the fifth century he had become palpable, weighty and of course visible. Being the antithesis of God, he was often quite unbearably ugly, and during the next several hundred years there are literally thousands of records of how and in what shape he was seen—as an imp, as a black man, a gargoyle of quite hideous proportions, a nightmarish figure that could insinuate itself like a sickness or some intolerable stench through a keyhole, and yet had fingers so powerful that when he got in he could strangle a grown man. He was never the jocular gentleman of the nineteenth century, the elegantly dressed lawyer, the Shavian, the nimble bargainer for souls, but in fact the most grotesque and bloodchilling apparition a man could imagine, a great bat spreading his leather wings between heaven and earth. Not since Bronze Age Europe had he been so nearly ubiquitous as now, peering unexpectedly over one's shoulder, crawling out of one's pocket, as a toad, a buzzing fly in one's food, one's hair, wherever one least expected. Peter the Venerable saw him leering in lavatories. He was an incubus who made corrosive love to a woman, sometimes taking her husband's place and implanting semen stolen (according to Sprenger) by a succubus in the shape of a girl who had made love to another man in his sleep. For devils, being cold and inhuman, could not manufacture semen of their own. He was a rat who gnawed through the timbers of a ship, or a barely visible exhalation that seeped like smoke out of the mouth of someone bewitched. He was the black goat that carried the body of William Rufus out of the New Forest. To King Arthur he was an enormous cat caught in the lake at Lausanne. To Etienne de Bourbon's priest he might appear as the Virgin Mary, to an anonymous chronicler as a Benedictine monk, and in 1138 to the Abbot of Prüm he became a little black boy who emptied the wine barrels.[1] In what form he appeared to square-shouldered Martin Luther is I think not recorded, but Luther threw an inkpot at him. He was a grey effluvium that grew like a monstrous mole out through the shoulder of a disturbed and adulterous wife, and to a lay brother of Vaux-Cerney (according to the *Grandes Chroniques de St Denis*) he appeared consecutively as a tree from which issued a hideous stench of corruption, a giant, a black monk and a beast with ears like those of an ass, all on one Saturday morning.

It was this devil of an infinity of shapes, we are to believe, who induced simple people to hate and slander the church. Priests complained on many occasions about deluded peasants who, meeting them in the road, started crossing themselves in superstitious dread. Cardinal Vitry (he studied at Paris and ended by being elected Patriarch of Jerusalem) was a man of unimpeachable honesty, and he reported that in one country district where many had died of the plague, villagers seized the local

[1] It was the predecessor of this Abbot, incidentally, who in 906 first recorded the famous *Canon Episcopi*, wherein we read of certain women "who believe and declare that they ride upon beasts with Diana, goddess of the pagans . . . in the dead of night". As Kittredge makes plain in his *Witchcraft in Old and New England*, Harvard, 1929, these women had nothing to do with witchcraft. They had simply reverted to paganism. But more of this later.

priest while he was officiating at a funeral, pitched him helter-skelter into a grave and buried him too. "So horrid are the inventions of the devil", the Cardinal writes.

In time a good many parish churches came to be frequented only by the poor, for only the poor and the mystically inclined still found spiritual succour there. The chaplains of princes and noblemen became so grand that they were independent even of bishops. And writers of many sorts, clerical as well as lay, bear witness to the avarice, the lechery and the sheer corruption on every hand. In 1100 a pink and white stripling with whom an Archbishop had fallen in love was made Bishop of Orleans. All over his diocese he was nicknamed Flora in honour of a local whore, and this so amused the working classes that they made up bawdy songs to sing about him in the taverns. In 1198 the Archbishop of Besançon was accused by his own chapter of simony, perjury and incest. A Dutch Archdeacon is said actually to have murdered his bishop by causing a stone to fall on his head so that he might himself be elevated to the See. A certain Bishop of Toul had for mistress his own daughter, the child of a nun in Epinal.[1]

It must be remembered that priests had the disposal not only of people's souls, but of their bodies too, and that they used their influence in practically every corner of mediaeval life. They not only hired architects and builders, victuallers and inn-keepers, tanners, cloth merchants, carters, gardeners and a host of menials; through their powers of bribery and their supposed spiritual ascendancy they influenced the law. They taught the physician how to go through a mumbo-jumbo that had learned nothing since Hippocrates. They sat with the king in his closet,

[1] Hughes, Pennethorne, *Witchcraft*, London, 1952. Unfortunately Mr Hughes fails to tell us in his urbane and highly readable little book where the story comes from. I quote it without having verified it because like certain others of his tales it is both vivid and apposite, but with the caveat that Mr Hughes is not always entirely accurate. Thus, to take one example, he writes elsewhere in the same volume that cats were not domesticated in England until the sixteenth century. Perhaps he was thinking of witches' familiars. But if he had glanced at Langland's "C" text or at the Wyf of Bathe's *Prologue*, both written in the fourteenth century, he would have found cats indoors and living there very comfortably indeed.

the lord at his table and rode with the leader of troops in the field. For a fee they said the Ave and Paternoster, buried the dead and even chose those among the utterly impoverished who might earn a few pennies by singing for their souls.

Etienne de Bourbon tells of a poor man in Lorraine whose mother had died. But the priest refused to bury her without a fee, so the peasant stuffed his mother into a sack, carried it to the priest's house and offered this weight of what might be cabbages as a pledge for the money. So taking up his cross, the priest went to the peasant's cottage, only to be told when he got there that the corpse lay in his own bed, and that he "might lay her in the earth or in salt, whichever pleased him best".

Langland describes for us in his *faire felde ful of folke* the palmers and pilgrims who lied about journeys to Rome, the friars of all four orders who preached the word of Jesus only for profit, the hermits with hooked staves journeying to Walsingham with their wenches lolling along behind, the parish priests who complained that their parishes were too poor to keep them and asked leave to preach in London, *for silver is swete*.

Chaucer's prioress who fed her little dogs with milk and white bread, or his monk who loved hunting are little better, and only the poor parson does his duty simple-heartedly, for he says *if gold ruste, what shal iren do?*

"I remember," says the good Abbot Moses in the *Alphabet*, "I remember to have so despised meat and drink that for two and three days at a time, meat and drink were never in my mind. And I have so abstained from sleep, notwithstanding great temptation from the devil, that many nights and days I slept never a jot, but said my prayers unto Almighty God. . . . But monks are not so nowadays."

Yet the age was bigger than the sum of its parts, for it was an age given to a widespread popular enthusiasm for any ecclesiastic who seemed actually to practice what he preached, an age not only of ecstatic visions, but of spiritual strait-jackets that forced the normally unimpressionable into outbursts of emotionalism.

And so terrible was the need to believe and the longing

among simple folk for purity that a St Asella could grow carti-
laginous lumps on her knees from kneeling on hard stones to
pray, and nuns never dared (for fear of impurity) take off their
clothes to wash until St Brigit was told in a vision that she might
without offence bathe once a fortnight. It was an age that could
breed a St Francis who developed stigmata vouched for by
several witnesses and who seems genuinely to have possessed
the power to effect cures, or a Christina von Stommeln who,
having solemnly married Jesus, spent a long life being almost
daily tempted to infidelity and suicide. "Good Brother Peter,"
she says, "talk to me of God,"[1] while huge iron nails are driven
by the devil's agency into her knees and thighs. Oddly enough,
or perhaps simply to illustrate the moral obliquity of women,
these tortures ceased abruptly after the death of Peter, who had
been her confidant for many years.

It was an age when simple men and women of all classes
could sometimes feel a love of God, an apprehension of Grace
so piercing and beautiful that all the delights of the physical
world became by contrast mere vexation of spirit. The Eucharist,
the eating the body and blood of Christ, was to them not a
symbol, but a stark and powerful reality. God was more than
God. For five thousand years he had been food. The king was
more than king; he was life. The devout felt this in every fibre
of their bodies. Bread was indeed flesh, and wine blood. And
the gentle old priests whom Guazzo saw carrying stones in their
barrows and mixing mortar to build a chapel in the dappled sunlight; they also were characteristic of the time.

It was an age too when the Blessed Jacobus di Marchia could
report that at the time of the visit to Fabriano of that enormously learned pope, Nicholas V, Nicholas who had engaged
Phillepho to copy the *Iliad* and the *Odyssey* and given him for his
work a palace, a farm in the Campagna and ten thousand pieces
of gold, at the time this pope visited Fabriano such a great
number of heretics was burned that the city stank for three days
of roasting flesh.

[1] This was a young Dominican friar, Peter of Sweden, then studying
at the friary at Cologne. He later wrote a biography of Christina.

8

One of the greatest of all heresies was that of the Albigenses, who in their purest and most fanatical form were called Cathari. They were spiritual descendents of the Manicheans, a sect of dualists who in their western incarnation first appeared in the neighbourhood of Toulouse early in the eleventh century.[1] They held that this world is governed by two separate forces, one for good and one, which was called the Demiurge, for evil. God the Father was God of all things temporal and visible, of death and of the flesh, and this world was the only true purgatory and hell.

Christ's kingdom, on the other hand, was not of this world (he had never really existed except in spirit) and therefore we who are burdened with flesh and with sin long perpetually for the golden age of a half-remembered heaven. What was therefore to be done? Man had to become a new Adam, to rediscover his primal purity, for, contrary to church teaching, there was no

[1] To describe Manichaeanism would require a chapter to itself. Aside from recognizing only two forces that acted upon man, one of light and one of darkness, they practised an asceticism so rigorous that they abjured not only idolatry, sorcery, avarice and falsehood, but even fornication, and thus were quite patently opposed to the continuation of the species. To investigate the history of such concepts of purity, however (and it is a very deep and widespread obsession), would require not a chapter, but a volume.

fleshly resurrection, and God's absent simplicity and goodness could be exemplified nowhere except in one's daily actions. They might have said with Meister Eckhardt, "If God could back-slide from truth I would stick to truth and let God go".

Arising out of this belief came a contempt for the avarice of the church, so they preached against a host of ecclesiastical abuses, the pomp of bishops, the luxuries of monastic life, the political power demanded by what ought to be simple prelates. And they renounced, not Satan, therefore, but what they called the harlot church of their persecutors, whose priests were venal, whose veneration of relics was hypocritical and whose prayers were more inimical to the truth than useful for salvation. Had they not been devout in the first place they could not have turned heretic.

These Cathari called themselves *boni homines*, the good men, and in their small societies practised a strict austerity. Three days of the week they fasted, and of course chastity among them was the rule rather than the exception. They ate no salt, for that preserved the body, no meat, no cheese, no eggs or milk, for it was evil to kill or devour any living thing. At communion they simply broke bread together as had been done at the Last Supper, and their piety, their gentleness and their obvious sim-plicity induced so many poor peasants to follow them that the church was forced to take immediate and drastic steps for their suppression. But as we might have expected, during their exam-inations before the ecclesiastical courts, some of the weaker did indeed confess to having seen and been traduced by the devil. He was a black man and occasionally seemed to have two faces.

The earliest of these Cathari had been put to death at Toulouse in 1022. But in spite of repression the movement grew. It spread like a fever all over southern France. St Bernard preached against it with an eloquence that had never failed him but once in his long and thunderous career. How odd, one thinks, that they should have broken so many arms and legs in trying to mend men's souls!

But in spite of Bernard's power in disputation, in spite of the severity of St Dominic, in spite of discouragement and persecution, the movement grew for two hundred years, and did so with a greater rapidity than Christianity had done after the death of Christ. For common people venerated the Cathari and noblemen actually protected them. In Languedoc, in Toulouse, in Savoy they formed what was almost an enclave in the heart of Catholic Europe.

So Innocent III decided upon drastic measures. As John Arden said recently, everything done in the name of God and good order becomes done against *us*. And so it was then. In 1207 Innocent excommunicated Raymond VI, Count of Toulouse, as an abetter of heretics, and soon afterward ordered the Cistercians under St Bernard to preach a crusade against the heretics themselves. One wonders over and over again why these men, spiritual fanatics as they were, exercised their fanaticism so largely on the temporal plane. Even now we are only gradually escaping from the prisons they built, and there is no certainty that we shall ever really be free.

A military campaign was mounted, and Arnold, Abbot of Citeaux, along with Simon de Montfort, fulfilled his commission with an almost insatiable cruelty. Hundreds of thousands were burned, hanged, put to the sword or else driven off into the forests.

When, for example, Béziers was besieged by the crusaders and a hundred thousand men were said to be in the city, a good number of them heretics, the besiegers scaled the walls and clambered in to open the gates. "Learning from their own confessions that there were devout Catholics mingled with the dissenters in the city, they sent word out to the Abbot, saying, 'What shall we do? We cannot distinguish between the good and the evil.' The Abbot (Arnold, afterward Archbishop of Narbonne) fearing as did many others that heretics would feign themselves to be Catholics out of a dread of death, but return to their apostasy again after he was gone, is said (no doubt with a certain nonchalant ferocity) to have answered, 'Kill them. God will recognize his own.' So innumerable multitudes were killed in the city."[1]

[1] Caesarius of Heisterbach, *Dialogus miraculorum*, ed. Strange, vol. I. Cologne, 1851.

Arnold himself reported to the pope that they had spared neither rank, age nor sex, but had slaughtered some 20,000 of the inhabitants. And what was their heresy again? "A zeal for purity of life and an opposition to the claims of the priesthood, as well as to ecclesiastical abuses in general."[1] But of course, according to the mediaeval church, they were so much under the thumb of the devil that when one fought them all the normal rules of morality might go by the board.

And yet, parenthetically, I ought not to pass on without telling a story about Bernard that explains something of the inward man. Riding on a journey, as we read in the *Alphabet*, he stopped one night at a farm and asked for food and shelter. After supper he and his host fell to talking about the monastic life, and he was asked point blank why he had abjured the world and so restricted himself. "You can pray just as easily here as there," the man remarked.

Bernard is said to have sat lost in thought for a moment and then to have replied, "I will make a bargain with you. Go into the corner and say your Paternoster. If you can come back to me and swear that you have thought of nothing else while you were praying, I will give you my horse."

The peasant laughed and went to do as he had been told. A moment later, however, he returned, crestfallen, but honest. He had said only a dozen words, he confessed, before the thought struck him—would he be given saddle and bridle too?

But we were talking about heresy, and to go from the general to the particular we can read in the Chronicle of Ralph, Abbot of Coggeshall, how one particular heretic (or suspected heretic) was handled. It seems that William, Archbishop of Rheims, was riding one day outside the city accompanied by one of his clerks, a certain Gervase of Tilbury. This Gervase later became rather an eminent historian. He had been brought up in Rome, taught law for a while in Bologna, and was eventually made Marshal of the Kingdom of Arles. He died, probably back home in England, in the year 1211. In any case, the chronicler informs us that:

"Gervase, seeing a maiden walking alone in a vineyard, and

[1] Fisher, George Park, *History of the Christian Church*. London, 1890.

impelled by the wanton curiosity of youth, went aside to her, as we have heard from his own mouth in later years when he was a canon. Having saluted her and asked whence she came and who were her parents, and what she did there alone, having also observed her comeliness for a while, he began at last to address her in courtly fashion and prayed her of love *per amours*. 'Nay,' replied she with a simple gesture and a certain gravity in her words, scarce deigning to look at the youth. 'Nay, good youth, God forbid that I should ever be your leman or any man's; if I were once thus defiled and lost my virginity, I should doubtless suffer eternal damnation without any help."

The Archbishop, coming up and hearing the heresy, ordered that the girl should be arrested for a suspected Manichee. So she was taken into the city. There they disputed with her, but she told them she was not sufficiently well instructed to refute their arguments. She had a mistress, however, who was. Thereupon the mistress was fetched, and argued so well that the clerics understood at once "how the spirit of all error spoke through her mouth".

So the two women were clapped into prison for the night. Next day they were again summoned before the Archbishop who sat with his clergy in the hall. And still they would not renounce their errors, so they were sentenced to be burned at the stake.

The fires were already laid. But one suspects that even the Archbishop felt uneasy at burning a woman alive simply because she was chaste. He needed some additional bit of evidence, something that would clinch his case once and for all. And lo, out of his mouth, or out of Gervase's telling the story, that evidence came.

"Madman," the old woman shouted, "I fear not your flames." And pulling a spool of thread out from her bosom, she held the end of the linen and tossed the spool itself clear out of the window. "Catch," she cried, and at once by the agency of the devil she was whisked up out of the window and flew away no one ever discovered whither. So of course the case was proved beyond any question, and as for the girl:

"when no persuasion of reason, no promise of riches, could recall her from her foolish obstinacy; wherefore she was burned to death to the admiration of many who marked how she uttered no sighs, no tears, no laments, but bore with constancy and firmness all the torments of the consuming flames, even as the martyrs of Christ (yet for how different a cause) who were slain in former times by the heathen in defence of the Christian religion."[1]

One touch here ought to be pointed out, that the witch was pulled out through the window by a thread, for thread, string, garters always had a great significance among sorcerers. I have already mentioned the cave-drawn figure in Cogul who wears garters. In Brittany it was the custom to wear a red garter as a sign that one had made a pact with the devil, and later witches when they describe their devils never fail to mention when they can the silk laces or points or the garters he wore. Margaret Murray observes that friends of the bride always fought for her garter. One sixteenth-century witch in Durham was accused of measuring waists so that she could make belts to preserve folk from fairies. At the siege of Acre Richard I issued garters to his soldiers to put them in good heart. Many a prisoner accused of witchcraft strangled himself with a bit of string which no one had seen on him before, and the devil, if he appeared in a modern film, would very likely (without anyone knowing the reason) be wearing a string tie.

Most early Franciscans held as an article of faith that Christ and his apostles had owned little or no property, and Coulton tells us that the popes had for some years favoured this doctrine.[2] But John XXII (1316–1334) was only too strongly aware that the doctrine of Christ's poverty lent itself to propaganda against a possessionate clergy, so in 1323 he condemned it as heretical, thereby contradicting the decision of his predecessor, Nicholas III.

[1] Translated by G. G. Coulton, *Life in the Middle Ages*. 4 vols. Cambridge, 1928–30.
[2] Coulton, op. cit.

This convinced a large number of simple Franciscans that John himself was heretical, and these rebels, the Fraticelli, came out in open rebellion against papal doctrine. In Italy, in France and even in England they were arrested and burned wherever they could be found, and Coulton abstracted a most moving story about one of the Fraticelli from a manuscript in the National Library at Florence, a circumstantial account of the trial and execution of one Brother Michael of the Poor Brethren of St Francis, a devout and simple man who had come to Florence to preach the gospel according to his lights.

Having been betrayed by certain women for saying that God's word carried more weight than that of the contemporary church and that they should abide only by what was written in the gospels, he and certain companions were arrested by soldiers and taken to the Bishop's palace.

There over a period that lasted several days the Bishop tried to force him to sign statements of various sorts, notably one that John XXII was "a Catholic and holy man".

"Nay, but he is a heretic," said the friar. So he was sent back to prison, bound and with his feet in the stocks. As a matter of fact even orthodox contemporaries considered John XXII a particularly worldly person, for he had amassed enormous possessions by systematizing the collection of first-fruits from bishoprics and other rich benefices. But his orthodoxy, at least, was beyond question. He had even had one of his bishops flayed alive on suspicion of heresy.

As far as Brother Michael was concerned, there followed numerous further interrogations, and at last when he still refused to abjure his heresy his hair was cut to obliterate the tonsure, his fingertips shaved where they had been dipped in holy oil, and he was condemned to be burned at the stake.

The writer seems to have been a disciple and friend, for with an enormous crowd he followed the procession halfway across the city, and is able to quote over and over again what people shouted and what the friar replied.

"Alas, why wilt thou die?"

"I die for Christ."

"Nay, thou diest not for Christ."

"I die for the truth."

"Wretch, thou hast a devil."

"Nay," the quiet answer. "Nay, God forbid."

At the Canto del Proconsolo: "Brother Michael, pray God for us."

At this the condemned man looked up. "Go with God's blessing," he said in a clear voice. At the Baptistry someone cried out, "Repent and choose not to die," to which came the answer, "I repent me of my sins," At the Cornmarket: "Fool, why wilt thou die?" and the answer, "I die for Jesus Christ." Another: "The people's voice is the voice of God," and Brother Michael replied, "It was the people's voice that crucified Christ."

For many hundred steps the shouts, the jostling, the prayers, the imprecations and the quiet replies. As he went toward the Porto alla Giustizia the throng crowded uncomfortably close, saying, "Recant. Recant. Wherefore wilt thou die?" But he: "Christ died for us."

"When he came to the stake (so far as I could see and as I heard from others) he went boldly into the hut, and while he was being bound to the stake, many thrust their heads in to pray him to recant; but he stood firm and firmer. And as one told me for certain, he asked him, 'What is this for which thou wilt die?' and Brother Michael made answer, 'This is a truth which is lodged in my soul, so that I cannot testify to it except in death.' Then to affright him they made smoke twice or thrice round the hut, and many other frightful things; and the people round besought him all the while to change his mind, save only one of the faithful who comforted him. . . .

"And one of the captains, seeing his constancy, said, 'What perversities hath the devil put into this fellow's head?' And the youth made answer, 'Perchance this is of Christ.' At last, having besieged him with many arguments, they set fire to the hut from above; and then Brother Michael, having finished his *Credo* (which he had begun as he entered into the hut) began to sing the *te Deum*; and, as one told me, he sang perhaps eight verses, and then made a sign as though he sneezed, saying these last words, 'Lord, into thy hands I commend my spirit.' When the bonds were burned he fell dead to the earth upon his knees, with his face to heaven and his mouth wide open. . . .

"Then some besought of the captain of the horse as a favour, that they might bury the body. And the captain . . . gave them leave and departed with his sergeants. And those young men took away the body and wrapped it in a linen cloth, and carried it and buried it in a grave at some distance from the stake, and folk returned to their homes; and it was the twelfth hour when he left the palace, and he died a little before the thirteenth hour. And while folk went homeward, the greater part thought it an ill deed, and they could not say enough evil of the clergy. One said, 'He is a martyr,' and another, 'He is a saint,' and another the contrary. And thus there was greater noise of the deed in Florence than there had ever been.

"And on Friday night the faithful went, the one not knowing what the other did, and found themselves together at his grave and carried him away secretly.

"Wherefore on Saturday morning many who went to see him found him not. . . ."[1]

And surely, as the poet has it, when these things happened, Christ and his angels slept. But gradually all over the continent such cruelties reawakened a longing in many devout believers for the past, not only for the innocent relationship with nature which had been the earliest religion, but also for the simplicity of the earliest Christian teaching which had given the individual believer a sense of his own importance. And not only this. Men similar to the *boni homines* and the Fraticelli, finding that the church would not take purity for an answer, turned away from the church altogether, back to older gods, to the foundations of a witchcraft that was to flourish all during the next three hundred years. Not the witchcraft of Sabbaths and broomsticks, but the magic of Bronze Age men who still lived in normally unfrequented places all over Europe in round, turf-covered dwellings half buried in the ground.

The strange fact that has to be faced about heretics is that

[1] Translated by G. G. Coulton, op. cit.

many of them erred simply in trying to emulate Jesus. Thus St Gregory, Bishop of Tours, tells of a man of Bourges who in 591 went to Gévaudon and set himself up as Christ, curing the sick and preaching, accompanied by a female companion he called Mary. He took from the rich and gave to the poor and, as Gregory remarked, unquestionably did so with the devil's help, for he amassed a following that must have numbered almost three thousand souls. In the end, Bishop Aurelius of Le Puy had him seized and decapitated as Antichrist. As for Mary, she was tortured until at last she confessed that she too had been the devil's servant.

Antichrist was not simply the devil magnified. He was as old as the book of Daniel wherein the horned goat cast the very stars to the ground and then stamped on them.[1] In Revelation he was a great red dragon with seven heads and ten horns. "And the great dragon was cast out, the old serpent called the Devil and Satan, which deceiveth the whole world: he was cast out into the earth and his angels were cast out with him."[2] Norman Cohn reminds us that in the twelfth century St Hildegard of Bingen saw him in a vision, "a beast with monstrous, coal-black head, flaming eyes, ass's ears and a gaping, iron-fanged maw".[3] This was the ultimate monster; this was heresy incarnate, and one felt for it nothing but loathing and a terror like the vast, dead middle of the night. As early as the third century theologians had maintained that Antichrist, when he appeared, would turn out to be a Jew of the tribe of Dan. St Thomas Aquinas accepted this as a fact, and in pictures Jews were generally portrayed wearing horns. It was fairly generally believed that they worshipped Satan in their synagogues in the shape of a toad or a cat, and invoked his aid in making black magic. In the *Prioress's Tale* Chaucer was simply setting down the casually accepted superstition when he had the Jews murdering a little Christian boy for singing his *alma mater redemptoris* to the Virgin as he passed their houses. On the other hand, by the time of Luther

[1] Daniel, viii. 10.
[2] Revelation, xii. 9.
[3] Cohn, Norman, *The Pursuit of the Millennium*, London, 1957.

Antichrist had become either the pope or else the son of a bishop and a nun.

I mentioned the Christ of Gévaudon, but he was by no means unique. People simply felt an enormous longing for spiritual leadership, and the proper authorities would not supply it. St Boniface, for example, an Englishman struggling to reform the Frankish church, was vexed by the rebellion of one Aldebert, a Bishop who had abandoned his See and gone to preach to the common people near Soissons. This he did with such fervour and eloquence that peasants flocked to him by whole villages (half emptying the churches), crowding round the plain wooden crosses he set up on country roads.

Aldebert practiced the same apostolic poverty later preached by the Fraticelli. He claimed to be able to effect cures, for like Christ he had been born of a virgin who had had to have the side of her belly opened for his delivery. In 744 Boniface held a synod at which Aldebert was defrocked and excommunicated. But the man continued to preach, and indeed so huge was his following that he died eventually without even having been arrested.

In the twelfth century another Christ arose, one Eudes de l'Etoile, a Breton, and not a priest this time, but a nobleman. It was a generation of terrible dearth and famine, and de l'Etoile preached to hordes of landless peasants, some of whom had been wandering the roads for years, stubble-faced, hollow-eyed, feet wrapped in clouts so that in wintertime, as a later poet had it, when they walked on the bare ice the blood followed.

De l'Etoile formed them into bands and set them to plundering churches and monasteries where the monks sat at dinner with their double chins "as big as goose's eggs". At last troops were sent out to seize him. He was imprisoned and died eventually in a tower in Rouen. As for his followers, they were a lesser breed, so those who refused to repudiate him were convicted of being impenitent heretics and burned at the stake.

Tanchelm of Utrecht preached in the open fields too, and according to a host of authorities did so with extraordinary eloquence. The Chapter at Utrecht noted that like his master, the devil, he so shone that he resembled an angel, and so greatly was he adored that some followers even drank his bath water in place of wine at the Eucharist.[1] Like a host of others he damned clergymen unworthy of the cloth. The only priest in Antwerp, for example, was openly living with a mistress, and for such a man to administer the sacraments he thought positively blasphemous. Indeed one hears attacks like his against clerical licentiousness and luxury from every quarter and in almost every mediaeval generation. And a large part of his support may have originated in the fact that the church not only amassed enormous wealth and spent large amounts of it in good living, but condemned as usury the amassing of wealth by merchants in the towns. No Abbot ever felt the need to put something by for a rainy day because for most of the comfortable abbots it never rained. Tanchelm did not end up at the stake. He seems to have been murdered by a priest somewhere about 1115.

It is beyond the scope of this book to talk of the crusades, except to say that Urban's first crusade was not so much intended to drive the Turk out of the Holy Land as to force the church in Byzantium to acknowledge the supremacy of Rome. Knights who took up the cross were promised in payment the remission of all temporal penalties. A crusader who died was offered remission of his sins. And as for the knights themselves, many of them penniless younger sons, the crusade was an opportunity for plunder on a scale hitherto undreamed of. To the devout, the *pauperes*, the simple, the illiterate, on the other hand, those first crusades offered the shining goal of Jerusalem, a pilgrimage of ultimate sanctity, an *imitatio Christi*, as Professor Cohn calls it, "a mass sacrifice which was to be rewarded with a mass apotheosis at Jerusalem".[2]

But one unexpected joy did come out of the crusades. Guazzo, in his *Compendium Maleficarum*, talks of the golden singing birds

[1] There are many accounts of Tanchelm's career, for of course he roused violent opposition among contemporary authorities. Perhaps the best modern summing up of the story will be found in Russell, J. D., *Dissent and Reform in the Middle Ages*, Berkeley, California, 1965.

[2] Cohn, Norman, op. cit.

of the Emperor Leo, and Fortescue recounts in *The Orthodox Eastern Church* how "they told when they came back almost fabulous tales of the wonders they had seen, the costly toys, golden lions that roared, trees of jewels where enamelled birds flapped their wings and sang, thrones of ivory and sheets of porphyry".

In a word they brought back eyes opened for the first time in a thousand years to the wonders of the visible world, and it is not going too far at all to say that the sweetness and imagination of a Petrarch grew out of the first crusades as the mad and weary Quixote grew out of the last. Having opened a window on the world the papacy could never again pretend that the world no longer existed.

If in the light of a second coming promised for centuries as imminent people could find no leadership in the church, they would do holy work instead. As late as a century and a half afterwards the Pastoureaux took up staves and pitchforks and under the leadership of one Jacob, an apostate monk, marched south from Brabant, intending to cross the Mediterranean miraculously dryshod to Jerusalem. Jacob claimed to have seen the Virgin in a vision wherein she had given him a letter ordering him to free the Holy Sepulchre.

The wonder is not that such men arose but that credulity and indeed hysteria were so widespread that thousands upon thousands followed them. For several months Jacob and his Pastoureaux terrified the authorities by preaching against the sacraments and murdering priests. When they reached Paris they hunted down clerics like rabbits and pitched them into the Seine. In Orleans they burned houses wherein priests had been found hiding. In Bourges they began murdering Jews as well, and it was there that Jacob finally met his end at the hands of certain mounted citizens who hacked him to pieces. Some of the survivors tried to take ship in Marseilles and Bordeaux, but their leaders were drowned by angry sailors, and so the Shepherds' Crusade came to an end. But this, like all the other messianic risings against the church, only reflected the deep resentment of the poor and the dispossessed at having for so many centuries suffered financial and spiritual indignity at the hands of their spiritual masters.

All over the continent there were similar religious uprisings. Here, there and everywhere they started almost spontaneously, fed by awful and diverse catastrophes, by poverty and hunger, by sickness, by an almost unutterable loathing for entrenched authority that had grown fat preaching in the name of Christ. They were part of our never-ending thirst for justice which we can hardly define and for an equilibrium that invariably turns out to be a far subtler thing than we had imagined.

Then in 1260, like spirits that had turned every which way in the search for justification, the Flagellants appeared—again it seemed spontaneously—all over Europe. It simply became the fashion, like nineteenth-century spiritualism in America. There had long been flagellation in monasteries. There had been ritual flagellation and offerings of cheeses at the altar of Artemis Orthia in Sparta. But now it was no longer ritual; it was hysteria.

Thirty or forty penitents would tramp into a town, march in a body to the church, there kneel and pray in front of the building and at last begin scourging themselves with whips to which sharp spikes had been fitted. Had not the authorities thundered at them for centuries that they were black with sin? Did they not know in their bones that this life was of no account, but that they might by the most painful of sacrifices buy hope of a happier afterlife? It satisfied a man to beat himself half to death, just as it had satisfied certain primordial needs to crucify Christ or to drown one's daughter in a bog.

One friar writes of himself that he stripped naked in his cell on a winter's night and beat himself until he could hardly lift his arm and one of the spikes on his scourge had bent crooked, and that when at the end he stood there, powerless and bleeding, he wept at so much resembling the Jesus whom he adored, and then all he could do was fall to his knees on the stones, still naked and covered in blood, to pray.

Now Clement VI had himself instituted public flagellation, but as the movement spread and grew in intensity in a score or more of cities it threatened to become not only anarchic but, far more important, a sacrament that had no need of and was not profitable to the church. So in 1349 the Flagellants were declared heretical and thus servants of the devil. Some who took no notice were seized and hanged. Some were beheaded; some were burned at the stake. But a mere twelve months later men and women were doing penance by allowing clerics to beat them in front of the high altar of St Peter's in Rome. And even the church had to find justification for such a turnabout. It lay in the fact that the Flagellants had professed obedience, not to their priests, but to the masters of their cells who heard confessions and granted absolutions even though they were laymen.

The Heresy of the Free Spirit went even further. Its adherents practised deliberate eroticism as an ecstatic experience that brought them close to God. Adam and Eve had gone naked before the Fall; it was the serpent that had made them cover themselves. Adam and Eve had in their primal innocence made love and in such innocence there could be no sin. Adultery was a form of purgation; nakedness and promiscuity restored lost innocence and returned them to a golden age all men dimly remembered.

More than that, Adam and Eve had possessed no wordly goods, so one might in all innocence take from the rich and give to the poor, thus making all men equal. The naked poor, like Adam and Eve, were in a state of Grace that neither theft nor carnal pleasure could impair.

God exists everywhere, they taught, and like wine in the sea or a drop of water in a pitcher, any individual was God as truly as God was God. Primitive man, the cave draughtsman in Ariège, had seen God in everything too. Among Moslems these heretics were known as Sufis. In a mordantly Catholic Europe that not only set such store by chastity, but felt such horror, such positive disgust for the human body, their promiscuity, their deliberate advocacy of pleasure as a principle of life, their delight in the employment of the senses, their openly avowed, and shameless sexuality made them quite clearly slaves to the devil, and this of course smacks of the famous Protestant aversion to bear-baiting, not because it gives pain to the bear, but because it gives pleasure to the spectators.

But for all their idealization of the poor, their chief longing was really for an intensification of mystical experience, and of course that longing is reminiscent not only of the philosophy behind certain modern communes, but also of the release through joy of the Dionysia. At any rate, out of this heresy grew the Beghards (our word "beggar" is derived from their name), who in fact lived lives as simple and austere as had many earlier heretics. Some actually became hermits. Others formed little groups to live on whatever alms they could solicit from passersby. Still others became wanderers from town to town, and as a matter of principle ate only what they could beg, standing in the streets. They never entered a strange house, wore robes like those of the friars, and like the friars preached to little street-corner crowds. Very early they were forbidden to wear their costumes in public.

Their female counterparts were the Beguines, women dedicated to a religious life while still taking part in the affairs of the world. One has to remember that in the Middle Ages there was no career open to a woman except marriage or the cloister. And because of the interminable wars and the fact that large numbers of men were deliberately celibate, the proportion of unmarried and unmarriageable women was perhaps larger than at any other time in history. As devoutly as the great masses of the illiterate poor these women longed for some role in life, and in the Beguines many no doubt thought they had found it.

But as early as the thirteenth century the ecclesiastical hierarchy saw in Beghards, Beguines and indeed in all Brethren of the Free Spirit a threat to their own authority. These people issued unauthorized translations of the Bible into French and took it upon themselves to interpret far too many passages in ways inimical to church teaching. And of course their principle offence, like that of our modern hippies and drop-outs, was that they flouted the doctrines of those who thought themselves serious thinkers, and lived lives that were openly erotic. There was only one answer to this. About fifty were drowned or burned publicly in Cologne.

Monks were forbidden to speak to a Beguine except in church. In 1239 they were excommunicated in Mainz. But as much as a generation earlier the Amaurians, graduates of the University of Paris and followers of a certain Amaury de Bène, had elaborated the Heresy of the Free Spirit into what was virtually a theological system, a form of Neoplatonic pantheism. Fourteen of their leaders were arrested, and although three recanted and were simply imprisoned for life, the rest went to the stake. And thereafter, according to Caesarius of Heisterbach, these people who had been misled by the devil were hunted out and destroyed like vermin in greater and greater numbers. Early in the thirteenth century they had been burning Amaurians in Strasbourg. A certain Marguerite Porete, an ascetic wanderer and preacher, wrote her mystical *Mirouer des simple âmes*. For this she too was burned at the stake.

People were forbidden on pain of excommunication to give the heretics alms. Houses in which they held meetings were closed. Men have always rebelled against authority that paid no heed to their aspirations, and authority has always responded by stamping on the ants' nest that annoyed it. It reminds one of Arrabal's curé in the prison of Carrabanchel, who sent prisoners to the punishment cells for inattention at mass. Yet these people had done nothing but take delight in life, and teach that just as a drop of water is part of the sea, so each of us is part of God. And because the freedom of God must be untrammelled, theirs could not be.

Caesarius tells what happened to one heretical group in Cologne, and in Coulton's translation the story becomes vividly real, for it makes clear what a huge emotion caused so many thousands to go almost joyously to their deaths. "Many heretics were taken at Cologne," he says, "who, having been examined and convicted by learned men, were condemned by sentence of the secular courts. When, therefore, the sentence had been pronounced and they were to be led to the stake, one of them, called Arnold, whom the others confessed as their master . . .

begged that bread and a bowl of water might be given him. Some were willing to grant this, but prudent men dissuaded them, lest aught should thus be done by the devil's work which might turn to the scandal and ruin of the weaker brethren . . . for he would fain have made a sacrilegious communion with them, that it might be a viaticum to his followers to their eternal damnation. . . . They were brought out of the city and all committed to the flames together hard by the burial ground of the Jews. When, therefore, they began to burn sore, then in the hearing of many this Arnold, already half burned, laid his hand on the heads of his disciples, saying, 'Be ye constant in your faith, for this day ye shall be with Lawrence.' Yet God knoweth how far they were from the faith of St Lawrence!

"Now there was among them a comely maiden, but an heretic, who was withdrawn from the flames by the compassion of certain bystanders, promising that they would either give her in marriage or place her, if she preferred, in a convent of nuns. To this she did indeed consent in words; but when the heretics were dead she said to those that held her, 'Tell me where lies that seducer!' When therefore they had shown her master Arnold's corpse, she tore herself from their hands, covered her face in her garment, fell upon the body of the dead man, and went down with him to hell, there to burn for ever and ever."

It would not be altogether easy to differentiate the Christ that Blandina, the slave, died for so bravely and the devil that sent Arnold's anarchic little mistress tumbling so bravely into hell. So Paulus Marsus may not have been altogether mistaken. The Council that in 1415 condemned Jan Hus to the stake had just deposed Pope John XXIII for simony, sodomy and fornication. God may be on the side of the big battalions, but for a large part of human history the devil has been on the side of man.

Or perhaps it would be more proper to say that God's world was one to which these authorities had never properly been introduced and to which nearly everybody else had long ago lost the key.

So the devil who had begun by being a vague and frightening menace (as ideas about freedom have often seemed a menace) began to exemplify freedom itself. Thus far we have seen him through the eyes of the establishment. But now we must begin to look at him as his idolaters saw him, as rescuer, friend, ally against repression, provider of comforts and above all as the only remaining link with a past about which few remembered anything except that it was happier than the present.

For almost a thousand years that devil walked the villages and country lanes in the shape of a man. Very often indeed, at least according to his worshippers, he sat in their kitchens, gossiped at their doors, helped them in time of trouble, was their ally against authority—and a very fine fellow he was.

9

In one form or another the devil walked up and down some parts of Europe for at least as many years as did the pope. But we must go back a little and see what he looked like to those who did not believe in the Christian God in the first place.

I have many times mentioned a *vecchia religione*, but we must not understand by this any formal body of doctrine. And indeed *religione* is not strictly speaking accurate, for here religion meant magic; it meant divination, that whole system of setting into motion a prescientific causality as old as palaeolithic man. We practice it even today without being aware of the fact.

We saw how the primitive attached importance to his dreams because he thought himself capable in dreams of foreseeing the future. During the past hundred years or so, a good deal of evidence for such divination has been looked into, and level-headed observers have generally insisted that it does not exist independent of relevant prior experience, that we cannot foretell without having been given reason to foretell, that one thing would happen instead of the other. But then Professor Rhine proved beyond any doubt in experiments conducted over a number of years that unreasonable precognition is in some individuals a consistently measurable fact. And if this can be demonstrated in meticulously controlled conditions, then innumerable uninvestigated cases of clairvoyance and divination, though less readily verifiable, are at least suggestive enough not to be ignored.

The Marquise du Deffand, having been told that St Denis walked two leagues, carrying his head in his hands, is said to have replied, *"La distance n'y fait rien; il n'y a que le premier pas qui coûte"*. If Rhine can demonstrate, as he has beyond question, that certain individuals are consistently precognitive, that they can foretell, sometimes against odds of hundreds of thousands to one, the sequence in which certain cards will fall, and that they can do this over and over again, then the case is proved. It does not matter if only one in a thousand can do this. *C'est le premier pas qui coûte.* We may lack the power ourselves, but clairvoyance and precognition exist.

Call it intuitive perception, call it an illogical but consistently accurate leap into the dark, or acuity in the analysis of otherwise imperceptible evidence, or a higher gear in the power of logical reasoning, certain people have always claimed to possess it and most of us have at least superficial evidence that it exists. Most soldiers are afraid, but on two occasions I have heard one foretell with a calm and remarkable accuracy the day and hour of his death. John Donne does indeed seem to have had a vision in Amiens of his wife with a dead child in her arms, and Josephine Tascher, giggling at dances in the backwater of Martinique, heard when France was not even an empire that she would one day be Empress of France. As I said at the start, there seems little doubt but that clairvoyance exists in some primitive tribes. Many a reputable missionary and anthropologist has set down evidence of medicine men who identify thieves, find stolen objects and describe with uncanny accuracy what is happening to an expedition days away in the bush. We simply have to admit that these things happen and that scientific causality has so far been inadequate to explain them. We do not understand. Perhaps we have forgotten even more than we have learned.

Now for several thousand years what we call magic was based on these and similar phenomena, and in looking at them we must step carefully between gullible acceptance and a sophisticated disdain. These things contradict the scientific methodology in which we have been educated. They stand outside the borders of arithmetic, and we all know that arithmetic works.

But in many societies magic seems to have worked too, whether it did so by divination or by the power of suggestion or by means we can only guess at. People have always been practical when it came down to the hard core of their needs. And to paraphrase Lincoln, if magic had not worked, it might have fooled some of us for a very long while, but it would not have fooled all of us for as long as it did.

Of course there are many little superstitions not unrelated to magic which, half consciously and perhaps unwittingly, we still accept, sometimes even with a certain embarrassment, because we accept them without really believing they are valid. Thus adolescent girls still perform divination by plants when they play "he loves me, he loves me not" with daisy petals. Cost-conscious public bodies have been known to employ divination by hazel twigs in a search for water. Even in play we now and then avoid stepping on cracks in the pavement, for they might open and swallow us up as no doubt a crevasse might have done to our ancestors. Or we laughingly hold out a hand to a palmist; and it is not only small boys who hesitate to walk through a graveyard at night. For if "the goblin will get you" is no more than a nursery joke, a dread of ghosts or at least of some spirit influence is by no means uncommon, and if we add *Poltergeister*, messages from the dead or even a penchant for visiting seaside fortune tellers, there exists in almost all of us, so far as the supernatural is concerned, a certain suspension of disbelief.

We say "That horse has the devil in him". And the devil we cannot understand makes us uneasy, for there is something in it either magical, diabolical or divine. I have explained the lucky horseshoe and throwing salt over one's shoulder. But a host of superstitions are almost as old and just as readily explained—the evil eye, the black cat, the number thirteen, the lucky charm. In a word, two thousand years after the birth of Christianity and three hundred after the beginnings of the scientific revolution, active and perceptible spirits still exist in our preconscious minds, and influence many of the things we either do or avoid. Fairy tales are clues to the thinking of their originators, and in fairy tales there is often no gap between the wish and its fulfilment. This is the essence of magic. But like medicine, which sometimes acts more on the mind than on the body, magic is workable only by certain laws. Like medicine, it cannot live in the abstract, so like medicine it uses certain formulae or rituals to turn that abstract into reality. And these rituals, forms of incantation, prayers rather like our modern hymns, are generally spoken in an antique language, one as mysterious as abracadabra to its audience. In the India of the Prakrits it was the ununderstandable Sanskrit. Among the Greeks it was Hebrew and Egyptian. In Rome it was Greek, and in all of mediaeval Europe, Latin. The antique, like the doctor's hieroglyphic prescription, is comforting and smacks of a mystery potentially divine. The priest who chants his *In nomine patris et filii* employs archaic language, not because he could not have said the same things in English, but because of the magical properties of the words.

All during history magic has employed, not gods, but spirits or demons, and the interesting thing about demons is that they are never individualized. They have no characters, but like the djinn out of the bottle exist simply to menace or to serve. In Graeco-Egyptian magic the officiant actually prayed a god on many occasions to send down such a servant, and when the Catholic invoked the spirits of dead saints he was willy-nilly absorbing the pagan system. The miner prayed to St Barbara or the cripple to St Giles, and he was doing in Christian terms what the pagan had taught him, asking for the intercession of the spirit most appropriate to his needs.

Now, if these superstitions are alive today, it is perfectly obvious that a thousand years ago they were vastly more important. Jung calls them parts of our collective experience, the *a priori* beneath the personal psyche, and we shall see in a moment just how deeply they were embedded in people's minds.

In 596, the year before Augustine started on his mission to England, St Gregory, the pope, wrote to Theodoric and Theodebert, kings of the Franks. "We are informed," he says, "that by God's mercy the English nations are waiting eagerly to be converted to the Christian faith." It is hard to imagine that this was anywhere near the truth, for no suspicious and conservative peasantry has either time or patience for a vague, foreign and esoteric doctrine that bears no relationship to its practical experience. When in 603 Augustine appeared in the Welsh marches he was met with a barely concealed hostility, and although Ethelbert may have been temporarily converted down in Kent, the vast majority of the population proved either indifferent or openly averse to his message.

What was true in England was equally true in France, in Germany and in Scandinavia. Particularly was it true in the many almost inaccessible hamlets where an uneasy equilibrium between hunting and farming communities had only just been established. As late as the eleventh century Haakon and two Olavs tried to introduce Christianity by force into Norway, but, as theologians assert with becoming modesty, they seem to have enjoyed only questionable success. The great pagan temple at Uppsala was not destroyed until 1075, and for a long time Icelanders insisted not only on their ancient pagan custom of eating horseflesh, but also on exposing such of their children as were not actually needed.

In that pre-feudal society, however, the peasant was expected to take on the religious allegiance of his master, so once the lord had been converted the dissident tenant could be punished, not only on theological grounds, but for his political offence as well. Therefore the peasant generally paid lip service, but in the privacy of his hut or field behaved exactly as he had always behaved. His magic, his demons, the deities of field or stream, the divinity of trees, the dread of inauspicious times and places, and above all, his awe of the dead and his awareness of a life and spirit in all things, these survived. And whether, as Margaret Murray believed, these things were the forerunners of later devil worship, or whether this animism and the later Sabbaths were separate manifestations of peasant opposition to Christianity cannot in all probability ever be decided. But in modern Sicily, in a few remote corners of the continent, in the American Ozarks and in parts of Tennessee and North Carolina it survives even today. We hardly need further evidence that its vestiges are alive in us too.

To make plain just what these things were we have to begin by saying that there existed not only a tradition of great magicians, of whom we shall hear more in a moment, but that for almost a thousand years Arthurian legend was in Britain and in large parts of western Europe a code of faith, an *Iliad*, the nub of Celtic and British identity, part of the folk magic that embodied whatever people needed to believe. For our purposes, however, it is not Arthur and his knights who are most important. It is Merlin, the enchanter, the clairvoyant, the animistic nature spirit who could work miracles as great as those of the church, who flew through the air, prophesied what was to come (even his own fate) and who, they say, is still alive today, locked by enchantment either in a stone or a tree. The accounts differ. But accounts do not differ except marginally when they tell about his birth. His mother was a virgin (some say a nun), and his father the devil who seduced her in the shape of an incubus.

After God had saved the world from hell (thus, after the death of Christ) the fiends met to plot their revenge, and decided to bring about the birth of a magician who would take up arms on their behalf. One of them posted off to the wife of a rich nobleman who had three daughters and a son. He drove the woman mad so that she hanged herself. The husband he caused to die of grief. One daughter the demon seduced and afterward, for reasons never explained, had buried alive. The second he turned into a strumpet, and the youngest, after she had held out against temptation for two whole years, he at last impregnated one night in her sleep. This was the mother of Merlin, who grew into a dark, dwarfish, mercurial man, and who was, as Alfred Nutt declares, the last of the god-begotten heroes.[1]

If we except certain Welsh poems that may be as old as the sixth century, Merlin first appears in the ninth century Chronicle

[1] *The Fairy Mythology of Shakespeare.* London, 1900.

of Nennius. Three hundred years later his story was much enlarged in the *Historia Regum Britanniae* of Geoffrey of Monmouth, and in time it became so much a part of Celtic and French romance and of certain pseudo-historic Latin chronicles that its genesis and complexity have never been more than half unravelled. They probably never will be, for we are dealing here not with history, but with contemporary magic. And as so many times before, I must emphasize that the whole way of thinking of these people is unlike ours, that causality was more a spiritual progression than a material, that image and object were identical. Thus a man's spirit was also his double, his *alter ego*, an intangible essence of the man himself. Spirit and body were interchangeable, and that is how a magician (or, for that matter, a Catholic priest) could be in two places at once. As late as 1221 Joannes Teutonicus, who was obviously both priest and pagan sorcerer, claimed to have celebrated three simultaneous masses in Mainz, Halberstadt and Cologne. And indeed, what were Christian miracles but magic under another name? If the good St William could hang his cloak absentmindedly on a sunbeam, or the ikon of St Agnes extend a finger so that a monk could place his ring on it, what are these but demonstrations that the new religion was just as able to make magic as the old? And the duality of body and soul explains how the later witch could leave her body in her husband's bed and fly off to the Sabbath without being missed.

Next we must understand that the magician acquired his power as magicians had always done, by the interaction of his animistic nature with that of plants. If there were no vegetable potions to be had, a hazel twig would do and he would use it as a wand. Equally important, the sorcerer, who incidentally cast no shadow because he *was* a shadow, did magic only in particular places, in marshes, in woodland glades, at crossroads and in graveyards, for these are where both ghosts and demons live—at such places, but also at thresholds or on hearths, in other words at spots sanctified either by spirits of the dead or by the presence of household gods and demons. If no suitable place could be found the sorcerer might simply draw a circle in the dust, "weave a circle round him thrice," and make the shape of the Sanskrit mandala.

Times were important—midnight, sunrise, sunset, under a waning or a waxing moon. And magical rites, being either symbolic or sympathetic all over the world, always had to be introduced by some purifying ceremony. That is why in all magic, in all religions, virginity has been so important, and why conversely the destruction of virginity (as in the later Black Mass) has such magical powers. In almost all societies temple prostitution was a form of cleansing or lustration by the voluntary sacrifice to the god of what the initiate most valued. The divine daughter of Cheops is said to have earned enough by her religious prostitution to build one of the largest of the pyramids.

Now in Merlin we have such a mélange of magic and nature worship, of wars, sieges and revenges, such a mingling of Christian purity and high-born adultery that it cannot possibly have originated in the mind of a single storyteller, or even at any one time. It is in fact an accumulation of myths superimposed on the history or the songs of the obscure Welsh Myrddin. But whether the Merlin of story can be taken to have been this man, or Merlin Wyllt, who lived about 570, or the Merlin who moved the boulders to Stonehenge, or Merlin Ambrosius, or Merlin Sylvester who prophesied to Edward the Confessor, or even the Merlin who went to sea in a glass vessel and vanished for ever, at least he was part of every peasant's preconscious mind, and of the archetypal, confused but diabolic magic with which the early Christian church was at war.

With or on behalf of Arthur he roamed western Europe and beyond. He travelled to Jerusalem and there interpreted the dream of King Fluelis, who sounds suspiciously like a Welshman. He appeared before Julius Caesar and prophesied to him. He invented weapons of fire with which to overwhelm a French stronghold Arthur was besieging. In the Lake of Lausanne, as I mentioned earlier, he caught a great cat who turned out to be the devil, and with whom Arthur had later to do battle. Once while wooing the fair Nimiane who was to prove his downfall— a prototype of *la belle dame sans merci*—he conjured up a whole company of ghostly dancing knights and ladies, as well as an orchard with trees and flowers, to show her an example of his skill. And because there had to be a touch of realism to the story, of the life all men remembered, throughout the history he and Arthur are perpetually at war with Saxon armies that have been plundering England from one end to the other.

If ever this hodgepodge of history and fairy tale could be unravelled, a Jungian might deduce a great deal about peasants who exist otherwise only in the record of what was done to them. In Merlin's story lie all the familiar trappings of mythic sorcery, of myth at its most primitive and fragmented. But chiefly he was the miraculously born young god who killed the old one, the divine priest who will slay the slayer and must himself be slain.

We saw that the "little people" are the remnants of neolithic man, of those who lived in the forest, feared iron and could do magic. In the story of Merlin we find little people, elves and fairies in abundance, magic at every turn, and in the hero himself a clairvoyant mind that sees the beginning and the end of all things. Above all, he was the devil's son. The devil was a god, and as someone once said, "How is it possible to believe that the devil who can raise tempests, transport his servants with incredible speed through the air and perform other miracles equal almost to those of God, cannot at least now and then cure a cow?"

There were Anglo-Saxon charms to heal wounds, to protect against wild animals, to shield one from witches and elves, to bring down a swarm of bees, to help in childbirth, to calm storms, to find thieves and for a host of other purposes. And when last year I tore the three-hundred-year-old ivy off the front of my house, I found engraved in the underlying plaster a hexagram in a circle, a Pythagorean symbol used long after the time of Pythagoras to ward off evil spirits.

Richard Coeur de Lion had a demon mother who is said by Giraldus Cambrensis to have flown off through a church roof at the moment the host was being elevated. The king boasted of it himself. Richard III not only had a hump on his back, but was obviously a sorcerer because he had grown a full set of teeth before he was six months old. Even Gervase of Tilbury, who saw a young girl burn because she would not sleep with him, remarks characteristically,that copulation between women and demons was common among his contemporaries; and there may actually be a perverse truth in this, for elves and goblins frequently abducted girls who took their fancy and carried them off to their subterranean houses. Many a country wench wore vervain or St John's Wort at her breast because if her lover turned out to be the devil in disguise the plants would frighten him away. As late as 1625 the President of Corpus Christi in Oxford recalled hearing the verse sung when he was a boy:

> *If thou hope to be leman mine,*
> *Lay aside the St John's grass and vervine.*

According to him, it was sung to a country girl who liked the devil's love-making, but could not hope to be satisfied until she threw away the flower.

As early as the sixth century Gregory of Tours writes of a holy man (the devil in disguise) who carried a sack full of herbs, moles' teeth and the bones of mice with which to manufacture charms. Many a modern American boy keeps a rabbit's foot in his pocket to work he hardly knows what magic.

But the laws passed over and over again during that first thousand years would be enough evidence if we lacked any other that the early church tried on numerous occasions to put down this subversive magic. As early as 506 the Council of Agde in Languedoc found it necessary to excommunicate vampires, sorcerers and poisoners. And excommunication was a terrible penalty, for in a complicatedly interdependent community it barred the excommunicated from almost all social intercourse. In 541 the Council at Orléans forbade divination. In 589 the Council in Narbonne ordered that sorcerers be sold as slaves for the benefit of the poor and that people who had been caught making love to incubi or succubi should be whipped in public. An edict of Louis the Pious, son of Charlemagne, forbade "sylphs" to show themselves on pain of very heavy penalties.

By sylphs he presumably meant the "undines," the "salamanders" and the gnomes who according to the Cabalists are supposed to have reigned in Paradise with Adam, and who remained forever after images of the miraculous. By forbidding them to appear, Louis was presumably forbidding people to see them—whereupon they were no longer seen. But other miracles, Durandal, the magic sword of Roland, and the horn he had wound in Roncevaux when the Saracens attacked, these still lived on in the popular imagination. Indeed, Charlemagne's world of faerie, almost contemporaneous with that of Arthur in Britain, has not died in France even today.

Even the papacy under Leo III was not ignorant of magic, for the pope sent his manuscript *Enchiridion* to Charlemagne because it contained certain prayers which were said to possess mysterious powers.

In England, for all Augustine's assurance, it was no better, and for all Gregory's faith that the English tribes were eagerly awaiting conversion. As early as 685 Theodore, Archbishop of Canterbury, laid down in the *Liber Poenitentialis* that it was a sin to sacrifice to demons, a sin to eat or drink in a heathen temple or to go about dressed as a stag or a bull. In 690 Wihtraed, King of Kent, imposed fines on whatever subjects were found making offerings to demons. About 750 the Archbishop of York once again forbade sacrifices to demons, vows at wells or in front of stones and trees. And even gathering herbs with incantations was forbidden unless the words used were in the form of Christian prayers.

Late in the ninth century King Alfred, echoing the book of Exodus, decreed that witches and wizards must not be suffered to live. Early in the tenth century fines were again levied for heathen sacrifices. In 959 King Edgar once more prohibited worship at wells, casting spells and certain unnamed practices that had to do with elder trees and stones. In this ordinance, wizards, soothsayers, secret murderers and harlots were all lumped together as malefactors; this was because many a petty nobleman kept a sorceress in his house on the pretext that she was actually his mistress. As for "secret murder", that was of course murder done by witchcraft. Heathen songs and what he called the devil's games were forbidden on feast days.

Early in the eleventh century King Canute once more prohibited the worship of heathen gods, or of the sun and moon, or of wells, stones and trees. And Canute was naturally aware of similar practices in Scandinavia, where according to the Dane, Saxo Grammaticus, both men and women brewed poisons, killed with curses, took the shapes of animals, made love philtres and brought mist and foul weather on command. But the interesting thing is that Canute did not call such people witches. He called them *walcyries*, or choosers of the dead. We shall see in a moment how it all interconnects. In 1008 Aethelred forbade magic, and the tenth century *Blickling Homilies* had insisted that wizards and those who practiced incantations were destined to burn in hell.

Yet the Chronicler of Lanercost reports that as late as 1282 a priest of Inverkeithing was brought before his bishop, charged with leading a fertility dance of young girls (he called them *puellelas*) round the phallic figure of a god, and this was only to be expected, for priests had always been closely in touch with magic. So, for different reasons, were barbers, gravediggers, doctors, shepherds and executioners. But almost every living soul relied on magic in one way or another. Kittredge writes of mothers who lifted their children onto rooftops or into the oven to drive away fevers, of wives who tasted their husbands' blood as a medicine, of misguided Christians who burned grain on the spot where a man had died or been buried—a half conscious association with the sacrifice in reverse, the killing to make grain grow. According to Bede in his *Historia Ecclesiastica*, he had had to preach against people who in time of pestilence abandoned the sacraments altogether to try the efficacy of "incantations or amulets or any other secrets of demonic art".

And now I have mentioned the Venerable Bede, a story about him would not be amiss, for it demonstrates not only what a gentle soul he was, but how the old, magical animism could even be mingled with Christianity when it was being superseded. Bede died in 735, but when he was old and blind he still travelled from town to town and from castle to castle, preaching the word of God, and according to the *Alphabet* he now and then employed a man to act as his eyes.

One day, the guide grew tired of steering the old priest through a stony valley miles from any town, so he stopped to rest. When Bede asked why they had halted, he told him that they had reached a vast public square where a crowd stood waiting breathlessly to hear him. So Bede propped himself on his staff, lifted up one hand in blessing and launched into a sermon. For a long time, standing there with only that one companion in the sun, he spoke with joy and sweetness about the goodness of God. "And when he was done," the storyteller says, "and concluded his sermon with *per secula seculorum*, at once the stones with a great voice cried out and said, '*Amen, venerabilis pater*'."

The church was perfectly aware not only of the confusion, but of the fact that conversion when it came was rarely permanent. In the ninth century the Christianized Guthrun conquered East Anglia for the Danes, and in the eleventh, four hundred years after Augustine, Canute had to do it all over again.[1] And we cannot really wonder at this, for if sorcerers still worked with the uneducated, to the literate the names of the great magicians were as familiar as their own—Simon Magus, who turned wine into coagulating blood at the sacrament; Ostanes, the alchemist, some of whose work has survived in certain Byzantine collections, Geber, the Arab, Comarius, Morien, Aristeius. In the thirteenth century the terrible and secret Vehmic courts with their masked judges and swift sentences were instituted in Germany to put down heathen idolaters with their own savage weapons.

William of Normandy, a hardheaded man if ever there was one, is said to have called in a sorceress when he despaired of taking the Isle of Ely. She performed various incantations at a well, but they failed and William had to retire. As late as 1410 the Bishop of Hereford complained that people from his diocese

[1] Incidentally, it is probably fairly well known by now that when Canute commanded the tide to retreat he was demonstrating to his followers that he was not a god and that therefore the tide would not obey his orders.

were travelling in great numbers to a spring and stone in the parish of Turnaston in the golden valley.

I said there were basic differences in Europe between north and south. The Briton, the German and the Scandinavian filled their magic with savagery, with a rough, practical blend of sexuality and murder, and they died laughing. To Mediterranean man this would have seemed barbarous. The hero in Apuleius was merely turned into an ass and suffered a number of comic disasters. To be sure, Actaeon was torn apart by his own hounds for having spied on Artemis at her bath. But when Circe transformed men into swine and Zeus became a swan and a bull it was because these animals represented what the lovers or the god had become. In the north the devil remained the old, horned hunter. He was as terrible and hard as a fist in the mouth, and his brutality and laughter were part of the very texture of northern superstition.

"That the Anglo-Saxons believed in murderous witches who could fly through the air," Kittredge wrote, "would be probable anyhow, since their Germanic kin on the continent lived in fear of such creatures in the sixth, seventh and eighth centuries, and even charged them with cannibalism, as their laws demonstrate."[1] Grünhütl, the green huntsman who hunted with his wolves, appeared in one of Jung's dreams after his mother had died. The wearer of the little green hat, he told himself, had carried her soul away. And who is this but a cousin of Robin Hood, and by extension of Robin Goodfellow?

Now a good deal of conjecture has been passed back and forth about Robin Hood and Maid Marian as leader and maiden of a witches' coven. He was, to be sure, an antagonist of the church. Indeed it was a nun who in the end betrayed him. But although Professor Murray suggested the contrary, there is no evidence that he was a witch. He was more likely a heroic representative, a prototype of peasant opposition to authority, to sheriffs, to clerics, to the nobility, and if he lived in the forest and wore green he was surely more a symbol of the old magic than of what were to become the diabolic rites of the seventeenth

[1] Kittredge, op. cit.

century. Indeed this is borne out by the phallic maypole and the dancing of young girls round it in his honour, and it is brought a step nearer confirmation by the fact that a similar figure, the original Rob Roy, wore goatskin and was said to have looked like a highland satyr. On the other hand, genuinely diabolic figures existed in every mediaeval mythology. The French fairy, Melusine, the joyous, lovely and despairing bride of the eleventh century Lord of Lusignan, was one of them. She was a singer, a maker of harmonies who, being the devil's child and thus a symbol of eternal change, was forced once every seven nights to walk on serpents' legs. She was not only the devil's daughter, but also daughter to the far-off King of Albania. Gallic Dusius was another, for he was both fertility god and devil, though it depended entirely on one's point of view. Our fathers, when they said "Deuce take it!" were perhaps still swearing by or at him.

Primitive man, we remember, both feared and worshipped his ancestors, so it was only natural that Saxon churchyards should be places both for necromancy and magic. The cavalcade of the dead is common to the folklore of every part of the world. That cavalcade became in time the fairy revels, and the revels were allied to the wild hunt, the ghost-chase led in the north by Wotan, by Herla, in Germany by a Walküre, perhaps Holda or Herlechin, in England by Herne, the hunter, who strode as a malevolent spirit about Windsor Forest (Herne's oak fell down in Shakespeare's time), and who is perhaps another incarnation of the horned Cernunnos.

Herla, Hertha, sometimes known as Velleda, was a high priestess of the Druids, a Gaulic Isis, queen of heaven, a virgin who will one day bring forth a child. She held the distaff of the fates wound with white and black thread. She was a siren too, half woman, half fish or serpent, and in this shape was also known as Melusine, whom we have already met. And here we have come full circle, back to Canute's edict against *walcyries*. For we can go further. Holda or Hertha is identifiable with Nerthus, the earth mother, and if this be true we have established continuity between tenth-century Anglo-Saxons and the

Danes of a thousand years before who had sacrificed priests and virgins to that same goddess in the bogs of Jutland.

Fritz Lander writes in his *Intellektualmythologie* about the horseman in popular superstition, wherein a man is ridden by the devil. And Grimm's *Mythologie* says much the same thing. "The devil has heard you; he rides you as Satan. You are ridden by the nightmare, the hobgoblin." And the very word nightmare indicates how deep in popular consciousness the image lies.

> *Wer reitet so spät durch Nacht und Wind?*
> *Es ist der Vater mit seinem Kind.*

And during the ride in Schiller's verse the frightened child is killed by the dark spirit, the devil in the air.

Now I mentioned an Abbot of Prüm, a monk who had had his wine barrels emptied by the devil in the shape of a little black boy, and more has been written about one Regino, who was actually an earlier Abbot of Prüm, than the good man probably deserves. For about the year 906 he copied or had copied down a document which became known in time as the *Canon Episcopi*, and therein certain women are castigated, not for anything they have done, but for their too vivid imaginations.

"Certain wicked women won over by the devil," he wrote, "and seduced by the illusions and hallucinations of demons, believe and indeed state openly that they ride out at night with Diana, the pagan goddess. Countless numbers of these women travel vast distances in the dark, though it is only on certain nights that they are called out to do this service. Many, misled by false ideas, accept such stories as the plain truth, and in this way deviate from the faith. For they believe that a thing divine both in nature and in power can exist apart from the one true God. The clergy ought to preach that these are only demonic fancies put into their heads, not by God, but by the evil spirit. In this way Satan, who can take the shape of an angel, once he has tangled up some woman's wits, leads her astray in her dreams, so that the victim believes that what happened only in her imagination actually took place in the body."

The exorcism of people 'possessed by devils' was much described and depicted in the Middle Ages and even later, suggesting that the possession itself was by no means uncommon—or at least thought to be so. (*Radio Times Hulton Picture Library*)

Below, a cross-section of a witch's house, presumably for the instruction of the ignorant (1579). The conventions of witches' behaviour were firmly fixed in people's minds. (*Radio Times Hulton Picture Library*)

Above, the trial by water of a suspected witch; the devil often resided in the body of a pig—as in the Gadarene Swine. (*Mansell Collection*)

Below, a seventeenth-century Dutch print of witches. The artist seems more interested in his own drawing than in the subject he is depicting—as though he no longer believed in it. (*Radio Times Hulton Picture Library*)

Above, a renaissance Italian view of Hell from Orvieto Cathedral. (*Mansell Collection*)

Below, a witches' sabbath by Gillot. (*Radio Times Picture Library*)

Two of the devil's many guises. Above, Herne the Hunter is only the English version of a very general legend of malicious woodland demons—an image both widespread and powerful, perhaps owing much to the frightening darkness of northern forests. (*Radio Times Picture Library*). Below, Le Lupeux, a night-phantom of Norman marshes; though it is described as having bird-like aspects, the artist has still felt constrained to give it horns. (*Mansell Collection*)

The pattern of witchcraft continued into the eighteenth century; all these drawings of the interiors of witches' houses are worth studying for their detail (*Mansell Collection*) . . .

. . . but Poussin's age increasingly romanticised Pan and his followers, who in an earlier time would have been seen as the devil and his witches, and, earlier still, the god and his priests and priestesses. (*Mansell Collection*)

This pacified, sophisticated Pan is a long remove from the fierce horned god of the old religion—and yet Burne-Jones's image retains elements that have shown a most particular durability. (*Mansell Collection*)

Almost entirely on the basis of this paragraph the church held for six hundred years thereafter that women rode out at night on certain beasts or on dildo broomsticks to meet their master, Satan. And what is more, it deluded certain women into believing that they had actually done so. On this canon the whole paraphernalia of seventeenth-century persecution of witchcraft was originally based. But there is no mention of witchcraft in Regino's document. It simply states that women sometimes confuse dreams with reality, that they ride out at night in their imaginations and travel through the air on equally imaginary beasts to unspecified destinations for a purpose that is never revealed.

But no matter what they were doing, they were certainly not reverting, as Regino implied, to a classic paganism, but (and even this only in their dreams) to a primitive rite more magical in nature than religious. But why Diana? Why not Herla or Hertha? Much has been made of this, though I think the answer stares one in the face. The leader of that dream-rout was a Nordic goddess emblematic both of the horned beast and the moon under which she rode. Diana had been a huntress, a moon goddess, and the learned Abbot simply called the pagan leader what his classical education would have taught him to call such a figure. My supposition is that Regino, knowing perfectly well what the women were reputed to be worshipping, simply supplied the name of the goddess that seemed to him most fitting and familiar.

Margaret Murray has quoted Regino's text as evidence that the seventeenth-century rites of witchcraft had been practiced continuously, perhaps for as long as a millennium. I do not believe this to be true, for later witchcraft was by no means a confusion of dreams with reality. It was among much else a deliberate perversion of Christian rite. The *vecchia religione* was not. Regino's night riders were simply an evidence that animistic magic had not died.

Individuals, said Marcel Mauss, become magicians in three ways—by revelation, by consecration and by tradition—and we can only presume that ninth-century magicians belong in the

third of these categories. Doctrine, revealed or not, seems unlikely to have been readily transmitted over long periods of time
except by the written word, and in this instance, revelation
would either imply the handing down of arcane theory or be
akin to demonic possession. As we shall see later, such possession is largely hysterical in origin and therefore in all probability
not pertinent here. And it is highly doubtful that a Welsh necro-
mancer knew anything about the Cabala. Consecration is of
course possible, but no evidence exists either for or against it.
As for tradition, we know little about just how it was handed
down, except that it often relied on investment through ordeal.

Now it has repeatedly been noted that myths and fairy tales
are similar in many parts of the world in that they all embody
certain motifs, what Jung called archetypal ideas, which im-
press, influence and indeed fascinate us. These archetypes are
irrepressible, unconscious, pre-existent forms that seem to be
part of the inherited structure of the psyche and can therefore
manifest themselves anywhere and at any time.[1] But here we can
adduce evidence from an unexpected source.

Grimm's fairy tales and the brothers' voluminous studies in
Germanic myth and law have supplied almost innumerable illus-
trations of such traditional magic and such archetypes, not only
in the shape of the expected witches and enchantments, but also
in the many evidences they supply of pre-Christian thought at
work. People invented and told these stories for centuries
because they were accurate reflections of the workings of their
minds.

Thus to take a few simple examples, it behoves every young
man to go out into the wide world, not only to become independent of his parents, but to discover the wonders of which
the world is made. Out in the wild he finds not only that animals
can talk and that forests are peopled with dwarfs and spirits, but,
more important, that the world is full of unexpected enchantments, and that one must undergo an ordeal of some sort before
they can be understood and used. The eventual way to happiness
is to marry the beautiful princess (she is a possible bride even for

[1] C. G. Jung, *Civilization in Transition*—Coll. Works, Vol. 10.

simple farm lads), but she can rarely be won until the hero—who hardly changes from story to story—has performed several all-but-impossible tasks.

These only the young and the innocent can perform, and then only with the help of a charm that has to be learned, or by the assistance of a small, mysterious figure that does the work in return for some future reward. One thinks in this connection of Rumpelstilzchen. In other words, it is by ordeal and by the help of magic and the fairy people that the princess is won, and she is invariably as innocent and unsullied as the boy who wins her. *The Magic Flute*, for all the seeming nonsense of its libretto, is in this context fundamentally sound.

Sometimes an evil spirit, the work of a step-sister, a step-mother or a jealous rival (never a blood relative) will change the princess into an animal or make her seem to die. The only cure for this is to outwit the demon sister, or else to undergo further ordeals by sheer pertinacity and love. In all these adventures one is governed by a varying number of both charms, or amulets, or taboos. Cross the lake, but no matter how he tempts you do not speak to the oarsman. He is death or failure. If you lose the chain round your neck or forget the word you are to repeat you are lost. Whether your mentor is Grimm or Sir Richard Burton, only "sesame" will open the cave.

And here is the very stuff of pre-Christian magic, of *la vecchia religione*, and I can do no more than suggest how vast a field for analysis it really is. One of the most evocative phrases in all story-telling is "Once upon a time". Repetition only makes it more powerful, and who of us does not know the child that asks for the same story over and over again, the story that evokes the archetype and satisfies by its inevitable rightness? Legends introduced by "Once upon a time" are never simply exercises in imagination. That is why they stand repeating so well. They are truths buried in the unconscious, part of that collective *a priori* which is our half remembered inheritance. That is why Jung maintains that people who know nothing about nature are neurotic. They have not been allowed to adapt to reality, and for this neurosis there are no materialistic solutions.

Whether we like it or not we live by myths, and to remain healthy we have to pursue them. We consist of nothing except where our minds have been and of what we have done. We have done and been chiefly the things I have here been talking about.

Those who maintain that there was no continuity of belief in pre-Christian Europe cannot have taken any of this into account. In that continuity the devil plays the principal role. So the practices, the legends, the inner experience that grew out of a belief in magic, all Merlin's supernatural powers were anathematized by the church as diabolic in origin. If the ecclesiastical courts could have laid hands on Rumpelstilzchen they would have had him hanged.

10

But it is too easy, too gross a simplification to set down the history of the church in blacks and whites. It is far harder to get anywhere near the truth, for to ascribe the rise of sorcery and diabolism to the ignorance of the minor clergy or the venality of bishops or the ruthlessness of the still higher orders is of course both superficial and inaccurate. The story is full of complicating factors; it is like an onion from which we have to take off layer after layer before we can get close to the core.

The Catholic Church was a vast and labyrinthine structure. In some of its institutions there was a real magnificence and in much of its learning an exemplary scholarship. Its buildings, its music, its pomp were visible manifestations of the glory of God on earth, and from the vision here exemplified one did not easily turn away one's eyes. One has to take into account not only the simple devotion of many thousands of contemplatives, of friars and parish priests; one must make a supreme effort of the imagination and try, not simply to understand (in spiritual matters, understanding is never enough), but to feel in one's bones the certainty so many people felt of the truth of Christian revelation.

I am not, nor have ever been, a Catholic. I do not even think myself particularly susceptible to the enchantment of the mysterious. To live in a highly industrialized and traditionally Protestant part of the world, to live in the largely dehumanized twentieth century makes it all the less likely that one will be able to put oneself into the mind of anyone differently orientated.

But I feel particularly fortunate when I try to look into those other minds, for when I was nine or ten my parents took my brother and me to Vienna because my father wanted to do post-graduate work there in medicine. So during a visit that lasted about two years we not only all but forgot our own language, more to the point, we lived for a year in the care of an emotional, superstitious and intensely pious governess, and for much of another (I think because it was cheap) in a monastic boarding school where, except for the luxury of electric light and running water, I am certain very little had changed since the later Middle Ages. So as part of an almost subliminal memory, I inhabited a fair facsimile of the sixteenth century.

And what do I remember? Praying until my kneecaps ached for the intercession of saints on their appointed days, long walks crocodile-fashion on cobbled country roads, talks with one or two of the young Brothers as we paced stone corridors on winter afternoons, discussion (yes, at nine or ten) filled with what seemed to me impressive and learned reference on the monks' part to Holy Writ and the opinions of saintly commentators, an intense discipline, spiritual as well as physical, which seemed not only proper and inevitable, but in a way satisfying and full of exercise for the imagination.

I remember an impression of sanctified and almost savoury dustiness in the air, a sense like that in *Kubla Khan* of mysteries and delights I was simply not fitted to share. I remember cold baths which I dreaded in anticipation, but later felt proud of having undergone, draughty corridors, hard benches, sparse collations (one never threw away so much as an apple core), fingers and toes that stung at lessons in the chill of unheated classrooms.

Not only this. One learned about sanctity, and it acquired a human face. The saints chuckled, argued, shrugged their shoulders in heaven just as they had done on earth. They had been fallible and they understood fallible sinners. The Virgin, having been a mother, knew all about the peccadillos of small boys. She understood dirty knees and that one had forgotten one's prayers. St Hubert himself had thrown many a stone at a squirrel. It was wrong, but he knew why one had done it. This saint had stolen a custard out of the kitchen; that one had told a lie to his superior; a third had been late for lessons. So as soon as one had overcome a natural sense of awe they turned out to be people (friends at court) one could gossip about with an easy and wonderful familiarity. St Teresa had said she feared only for those who feared the devil, and that was comforting. Indeed one learned not even to fear death, for it meant only that after a short pain or illness one could go on forever in the company of those warm, friendly and convivial saints.

As for the devil, he was as real as God, though more easily avoided. He shared the podium with St Nicholas on the 6th of December and handed out birch switches to the handful that deserved them. In fact, if one only knew how to handle him he was nothing but a fool. He had once had the effrontery to give a whole series of lectures at the University of Salamanca in the hope that he would pick up a fair harvest of souls there. But the students had outwitted him by simply handing over their shadows, and he had had to retire without actually winning a single soul.

There were holidays too, and not only saints' days. Every boy on his birthday was given a boiled egg all to himself at breakfast, and in the poverty-stricken Austria of those days an egg was a luxury. How their faces, how one's own face shone! And above all I remember, in spite of the hardship, an acute awareness of being safe, not only because the good and learned monks said I was but because I inhabited a blessed calyx of belief. I more than believed, I *knew* that whether I waked or slept there were two angels that hovered perpetually at my shoulders, and that their sole function was to see that I came to no harm.

Only one thing turned out to be lacking in the world they laid so eagerly before us, and that was a sense of how the world actually worked. For all we were taught, no flower might have blossomed, no cattle brought forth young. God alone knew why the sea was salt or the seasons even existed. Latin we read, but not French. What little history we heard about was of holy Catholic powers fighting bravely against seditious Protestantism. No blood, no life existed anywhere except in learned authority. "Copy twenty lines," they said. "Memorize three maxims. Recite these and these examples."

But to a ten year old it made for a happy life, for the only thing one really had to learn was to be obedient, to do good and to work at precisely what was required. So when now, over forty years afterward, I read in the enchanting *Compendium* of Francesco Guazzo how devils can do this or that, how by the example of Margarita of Essling in 1546 or the nobleman's horse or the priest's concubine in Liège or the false Bernard God's mercy is made manifest, I find it difficult to smile at his credulity. "Good old man," I want to say, "you gossip delightfully and I already half believe you."

For his stories are just like those I heard and believed at school and from my enormously fat governess at nine years old, about men proved to be werewolves because a wolf's wounds were discovered in their chests, or witches who stole children to render their fat for ointments that enabled them to fly, or a corpse that screamed when a dagger was plunged into its heart because it was a vampire's. I can see her now. She had heard the scream. She echoed it over supper in a thin, frightening voice, leaning toward us across the table. And I could still hear it later when I lay safe in bed, safe beyond any question because she had left a crucifix to guard me. All I had to do was lay my hand on that cross and I could defy the devil himself. In a way it was like the savage Tertullian's childhood, clouded with superstition, when amid the difficulty of falling asleep he heard from his nurse about man-eating monsters in towers and the scallops of the sun. He remembered childhood jokes about apples that grew in the sea, and fish that swam in trees.

So if today we read the usual authorities and learn to think of the Holy Office as the sanctimonious murderer of political opponents we shall be seeing things solely through modern eyes.

We shall have forgotten that they had to deal with both magic and mystery, that demons were not simply figures in books; they existed, that the long and learned disquisitions of patristic authorities are not (as they seem to us now) dry bones in folio binding, but the result of the slow grinding of the mills of God, and that the corn has been ground as carefully and fine as a mote in the reader's eye.

So to the faithful, the fact that a bishop had his own daughter for mistress, or that St Bernard was a fanatic and an accessory to murder are of no importance at all. And if the Holy Office found it necessary to tear some poor creature's arms out of their sockets to prove her a witch, that was right and proper. Better men than we have been fallible and yet sure of the truth, and for all I know the devil is as real as he seemed to them or as unreal as death, which most of us believe in, but none of us has ever experienced.

We have to understand who those old and long-dead priests and bishops were who committed what seems to us such a mountain of stupidities. It can be said in a word. Primarily they were men who had learned by rocky experience that the greatest virtue under the sun is prudence.

We have to imagine mediaeval France or England or Germany as mile after mile of unhedged, windblown countryside, with roads that lay wallowing in snow half the winter and turned to muddy quagmires in the spring. January was colder and August hotter than either is today. We have to imagine peasant cottages built of peat and turf, without chimneys, without glass for the windows that were needed to let in light, dark, smoky cubicles whose inhabitants slept no more comfortably than the sow or the ox in the shed next door. We have to put ourselves into the bodies of people whose simplest necessities, water, fuel, food, were only collected by the most arduous and unintermittent labour. It is all very well for Belloc to write about the glories of life in thirteenth-century France, but the vast majority lived worse than prisoners in a Siberian labour camp, for they had no prospect of ever getting out. No pardon, no reprieve. They gulped down black bread and cabbage in summer, dried beans, chestnuts, skim milk in wintertime. If a man had meat or fish four or five times a year it was a feast. To own shoes or a coat was affluence. But if the ox fell ill or died, the work still had to be done. Go yoke yourself into the plough, though the field is ankle deep in mud.

> His wijf walked him with · with a longe gode,
> In a cutted cote · cutted full heghe,
> Wrapped in a wynwe schete · to weren hire fro weders,
> · · · · · · · · · ·
> And at the londes ende laye · a litell crom-bolle,
> And thereon lay a litell childe · lapped in cloutes,
> And tweyne of tweie yeres olde · opon another syde,
> And alle they songen o songe · that sorwe was to heren;
> They crieden alle o cry · a carefull note.
> The sely man sighede sore, & seide · "children beth stille!"[1]

To escape! Any young man with initiative thought of how to escape. Take to the roads? Yes, but that too was a precarious life, with the likelihood of short shrift and a rope at the end of it. To join some army or other? Ah, but the villains stole one's pay, the food was worse than at home; it was long marches with nothing but cut-throats for company and a good chance of a pike in the belly when you got to the end of the road. Trade? Fine if you had a bit of money, but where lay one's fingers on enough coin to jingle in the purse? No, there was only one escape, and that was into the church. If you were fortunate enough to be taken into a seminary or into one of the four great orders, then you had a chance. But the next thing was to employ enough ingenuity both to stay there and to secure advancement. Prudence, submission, an ability to accept without question whatever they told you, these were the qualities you needed.

You had to train yourself never to think, for a man who thinks can easily say something rash. So you had to find out

[1] *Pierce the Ploughmans Crede*, ed. W. W. Skeat, E.E.T.S., London, 1867. ll. 433–442.

precisely what was asked for and no more. Even too thorough a knowledge of Holy Scripture might lead to private judgment, and that would be suspect. Imagination was presumption. You had to walk with lowered eyes, for there was (God knew) nothing on earth worth looking at, and a cautious man must not even seem to look. The only safe thought was a thought based on patristic authority and on the ideas of your superiors. And you must never either love or hate too much. Both could be dangerous. The main thing, in a word, was to be politic, to accept anything and, as one great prelate said, "Be a rod in the pope's hand", or else go back to your wretched hamlet and start dying.

What constituted happiness? Dining warmly and well, because you could so easily remember dining badly. Whom did you respect? The man with a coat of fine cloth, the man with a benefice in his pocket, the man with political power. You and your father had never had any of these. Even as a boy you had learned that a want of care was punished with a want of bread. So never be careless; never be imprudent, and if you watch your step you will dine off capon, butter and eggs. If you learn to be clever as well, you will pay for them not with money, but with indulgences.

Above all, living the clerical life, you will find yourself at the heart of all knowledge, *maestro di color che sanno*, as Dante said, for in the world of your contemporaries, knowledge other than the knowledge of God simply does not exist. But instead of munching beans in some smoky hovel you will dine in a great hall with coloured windows tall as those in a cathedral, with cooks and cellarers to serve you. Unlike your father, who grunts and sweats over his plough from dawn to dark, you will work five pleasant hours a day in the garden or the scriptorium. On earth you will be comfortable and in the heaven to come you will be among the blessed. But above all you will be safe no matter where you go, so you will be utterly ruthless in crushing any tatterdemalion sect, any outlaw, any argumentative heretic who dares to question what you are doing, for these people are attacking the roots of your security. You will be a tyrant in defence of your prerogatives, and as Stendhal said many centuries afterward, the idea most useful in the world to tyrants is the idea of God.

So our peasant boy is turned into a priest. In company with his fellows (and like some of us), he becomes in time so obsessed with what he is taught, with what it is necessary to believe, he grows so used to detecting the occult in what would otherwise be rationally explainable that if any act or happening is ascribed to natural causes it makes him positively angry. He has had enough of nature. Nature is unruly, and like the primitive he simply cannot believe that a tree fell because the wind blew it down.

And aside from its long practice in detecting heresy, this is the basis of the Holy Inquisition. There was nothing new in it, no fresh doctrine, no idea, no fresh discovery, simply the sense of outrage authority has always felt at the sight of ingratitude and rebellion. But to explain the Inquisition would be to wander away from the point. We are concerned, not with the ecclesiastical courts, but with their victims. To paraphrase Macchiavelli, the church sowed hemlock and expected to harvest corn.

For a hundred years English armies had burned their way back and forth across a countryside where nobody wanted war except the plunderers. And where could the plundered have turned for help except to the church? But the church ignored them. It was often in league with their plunderers. It refused even to preach its gospel in a language they understood. So at last they fled in great numbers to the devil, who offered present comfort.

It is no accident that the fourteenth century, the century of the Jacquerie and the Black Death, produced demons as virulent in France as did the seventeenth in Germany, when during the Thirty Years' War the devastation was so terrible that it was said there were only wolves for wolves to feed on. Except that in times of hunger wolves will eat mice. What earthly, what natural future was there in times like these?

But the inquisitors acted as though they were unaware. Famine, sickness, war, death, these were acts of God. What was there to understand? No, they sat in their dim libraries and sifted authorities. They turned the pages that had been copied and recopied for centuries of the *Corpus Juris Canonici*, or the opinions of St Thomas, or of the Blessed Albert and St Bonaventura. And it would never have crossed their minds that they were cruel or despotic. They simply ignored, they disallowed the irrepressible face of nature. Tenderness they understood, but only as a facet of Christ's charity to the humbled. It had nothing to do with the recalcitrant or with human relationships, for if it had, their whole laboriously built structure of doctrine would have had to be reinterpreted. And nevertheless on many occasions they went to endless trouble to act humanely, to rescue, if not their victims' bodies, then at least their souls.

In other words, they tried to be just. There was almost no rigging of evidence. There were few wholesale condemnations, few easy evasions of the fact that some of their suspects had been tormented to the point when they were no longer either sane or responsible. And if they tortured bodies with remarkable ingenuity, they were well aware that confessions procured under torture were suspect. Kramer and Sprenger point this out in the *Malleus*, but they point out too that it is better a dozen innocents be twisted on the rack than that one heretical spirit go uncaught. Whatever it cost, the spirit had to be cleaned. The body had no importance at all.

On the 9th of December, 1484 Pope Innocent VIII issued his famous Bull, *Summis desiderantes affectibus*, wherein he appointed two Dominicans, Heinrich Kramer and Jacobus Sprenger, inquisitors throughout northern and western Germany to hunt out and punish witches. And within two years the highly learned Dominicans had published their *Malleus Maleficarum*, The Hammer of Witches, wherein they spent a quarter of a million words describing exhaustively the aspects of diabolism they had encountered, and explaining in meticulous detail how these ought to be dealt with. "There is hardly a problem," says the Reverend Montague Summers, "a complex, a difficulty they have not foreseen and discussed and resolved. . . . For nearly three centuries the *Malleus* lay on the bench of every judge, on the desk of every magistrate. It was the ultimate, the irrefutable, unarguable authority."[1]

And according to Summers' own lights he was right, though for most of the rest of us it is all but impossible to put ourselves into the minds of those meticulous men whose enormous learning was compounded of hearsay, of ideas now long discarded, of authorities ignorant in the extreme and of a prurience remarkable for its ingenuity.

But let us look at that Bull of Innocent VIII. Therein the pope complains of people who have "abandoned themselves to devils, incubi and succubi, and by their incantations, spells, conjurations and other accursed charms and crafts, enormities and horrid offences, have slain infants yet in the mother's womb, as also the offspring of cattle, have blasted the produce of the earth, the grapes of the vine, the fruits of trees, nay, men and women, beasts of burthen, herd-beasts as well as animals of other kinds, vineyards, orchards, meadows, pastureland, corn, wheat and all other cereals: these wretches, furthermore afflict and torment men and women, as well as animals of other kinds, with terrible and piteous pains and sore diseases, both internal and external; they hinder men from performing the sexual act and women from conceiving, whence husbands cannot know their wives nor wives receive their husbands; over and above this, they blasphemously renounce that Faith which is theirs by the sacrament of baptism, and at the instigation of the Enemy of Mankind they do not shrink from committing and perpetrating the foulest excesses to the deadly peril of their own souls, whereby they outrage the Divine Majesty and are a cause of scandal and danger to very many."

There is the charge. And how did Innocent's inquisitors set about driving it home and dealing with offenders? Women are chiefly to blame, they tell us. Indeed, the word *femina* is derived from *fe* and *minus,* because a woman is less capable of faith than a man. Or they discuss with ponderous references to the opinions of church fathers the question of copulation with devils,

[1] See Summers' introduction to his own translation of the *Malleus Maleficarum,* London, 1928.

and enquire of what elements the devil's body is composed, whether he can in fact conceive or cause conception, whether the act is accompanied by the ejaculation of semen, whether the act is visible to anyone who may be standing by, why the devil's penis is so often reported to be cold and painful, and lastly "whether the actual delectation is of a weaker sort".

They investigate tales that witches have turned men into beasts, and there are records worthy of the self-delusion of an Aleister Crowley that describe men and women who have become cats, dogs, wolves, toads and many strange things besides. In 1278 in Switzerland a woman had given birth to a lion. Another in Augsburg brought forth at one birth a human head covered with a caul, a two-legged serpent and at last, miraculously, a complete and living pig.

They investigate cases of incubus and succubus devils, and indeed anti-heretical literature is preoccupied to a remarkable degree with sexual fantasies. In Bamberg there was a certain Peter Stumpf who had committed fornication with a succubus over a period lasting twenty-eight years. Johann Dobeneck (1489–1552) affirms that Martin Luther himself was fathered (like Merlin) by an incubus, and one supposes that this was in a way confirmed by the fact that when the pope's astrologer published Luther's horoscope it foretold plainly that he was destined to burn in hell. The Huns, according to Jordanus in *de rebus Gothicis*, were descended from a union of fauns with Gothic witches, and if a serpent can fecundate a woman in the temple of Asclepios, why not a faun, who is a little god of field and herd, a Pan-god with horns and tiny pointed ears?

They tell us how witches can fly. Quite simply, it is by means of an unguent made out of the fat of slaughtered children. Whoever doubts it is guilty of heresy. Witches can substitute children too, and so great an authority as William of Paris states that such changelings can usually be identified, for they are perpetually crying. That sorcerers fly there can be no real question. "One of us has very often seen and known such men." And one ought to note the logic with which they confirm this. "For there is a man," they write, "who was once a scholar and is now believed to be a priest in the diocese of Freising, who used to say that at one time he had been bodily carried through the air by a devil, and taken to the most remote parts."[1] We shall learn later when we come to the seventeenth-century tales of witchcraft how the illusion of flying was probably induced.

They enquire how witches manage to procure abortions and make people ill, how they possess men, murder children, bring about hailstorms, fires, tempests and bewitch even farmyard animals. They are able, we are told, to make a man impotent by taking away his power of erection and even on rare occasions by making the penis itself disappear. Indeed "the figure of the witch who eats children and who threatens the virility of the male occurs in such a variety of guises all over the world that it is obvious that she is an expression of an archetypal fantasy which is common to all mankind".[2] In a word, the demons whom Iron Age man had placated in a score of different ways had become the devil, the enemy of God, and since no one could lay hands on the devil, one had to be content, like primitive man, with finding and destroying his instruments.

Whether Hindu women make an aphrodisiac by frying the genitalia of male tortoises I do not know, though I have read as much. But mediaeval witches used similar materials, mostly of an associative nature. "Nose of Turk" or "finger of birth-strangled babe" speak for themselves as ingredients likely to arouse horror. By the same token, however, the testicles of a hare would increase a man's potency, and even today hundreds of pounds of ground rhinocerous horn are exported annually from Africa, simply because that single horn is shaped like a rather ambitious phallus.

But aphrodisiacs or no, one can only note with a certain astonishment that married women seem to have left their husbands sound asleep in bed to go flying off to dinners where the food was generally abominable—they were given no salt—and to orgies where the sex was unpleasant in the extreme. Indeed, a strong case can be made for the supposition that at least some of

[1] *Malleus Maleficarum*, Pt. II, Qn. 1.
[2] Storr, Anthony, *Human Aggression*. London, 1968.

176

the later witchcraft, the anti-Christian ceremonial, even the orgies with which meetings ended were suggested and therefore in a sense invented by the Inquisition itself.

For the Holy Office had a very clear idea what it wanted to find, and Inquisitors tried to discover, not what people's religion was, but what it was not. So questioning was conducted not so much to dredge up the truth as to elicit the expected answers. By the time Kramer and Sprenger published their massive document the procedure had become very much cut and dried, and its rules of interrogation would have taken any modern lawyer's breath away.

We have to start by putting ourselves in the position of the poor devil (and there were many hundreds of thousands) who was brought before the courts. Perhaps he had been accused by a spiteful neighbour or a debtor trying to avoid payment or a relative who, for any one of a multitude of reasons, wanted him out of the way. Perhaps in a careless moment he had boasted or made some idle threat. Perhaps he hated the priest or stayed away from mass too often, or perhaps he was one of the dwindling number who still felt in his bones that the old magic of wells and trees made better sense than whatever the church taught. We have to accept this, or else that he was guilty as charged—of raising hailstorms, plaguing his enemies with fevers or now and then causing some woman to give birth to a monster.

At worst he may have wished he could do these things. But whatever the cause, he had been seized and brought before the court, and he stood there, unable to read what was set before him, unable to understand the Latin that learned clerks and court officials were jabbering, not perhaps even knowing at first which men were advocates, who the judge, or even what they suspected. But from now on the law would follow its inexorable course, and the best practical hope he had was to spend the rest of his life on bread and water in a cell. He was three parts lost before he had even learned the rules of the game.

According to the *Malleus*, as soon as a suspect had been arrested his house had to be searched and any articles usable for witchcraft taken away. A cat, a powderbox, a pot of salve, thread, bits of wax, hair collected in a comb, nail parings, these were evidence of evil intent. In 1599 a certain Antide Collas was burned at Dole because her vaginal passage was twisted, and thus she had obviously had intercourse with the devil. A certain judge of Saint-Claude had a woman tortured as a sorceress because there was a piece missing out of the cross of her rosary. One prisoner, put to the torture, confessed everything and was dragged dying to the fire. But a thunderstorm broke out, extinguishing the flames, and instead of considering this a judgment of God, the Inquisitor, Boguet, was delighted, and affirmed that here indeed was proof that his victim enjoyed the devil's protection.

The accused had to be asked first of all if his parents were alive or if they had been burned at the stake. Had he ever heard talk of witchcraft, and did he believe it existed? To say that he did was dangerous. To say that he did not was heretical. Why did he—or she—touch such and such a child before it fell ill? What was he or she doing in the fields at the time of a thunderstorm? Why, with only two or three cows, has she more milk than her neighbour who owns four or five? Does she live in adultery or concubinage? "Whatever we do in word or deed," says the *Malleus*, "let all be done in the name of the Lord, Jesus Christ."

What kind of defence was allowed? To begin with, the accused might not choose an advocate. It was up to the judge to appoint one who was neither litigious nor evil-minded. And the advocate, once chosen, had to be warned not to endanger his own soul by defending heresy. In fact, if he thought the case hopeless, he must retire and return his fee. Indeed, if at any time during the trial the judge thought him objectionable he could be dismissed.

The names of witnesses were to be kept secret from the accused, else they might be exposed to sorcery. "It is more dangerous," the authors declare, "to make known the names of the witnesses to an accused person who is poor, because such a person has many evil accomplices, such as outlaws and homicides . . . which is not the case with anyone who is nobly born and rich."[1] So the defendent was not allowed to know who had accused him, but even so, the scales were weighted against him, for a heretic, or the prisoner's wife or children might give evidence to convict him, but not in his favour. According to Bodin, an honest man cannot smell out a witch, so even perjurors, criminals, men of bad repute might be called as witnesses, though only if they had seriously repented of their crimes. Beyond that, no witnesses were to be called whom the Inquisitors thought superfluous, and as a matter of fact, the authors assert, a trial ought ideally to be conducted without advocates, for only in that way can appeals and obstructions be avoided.

On the other hand the case for the prosecution was easily sustained, for an accused was *prima facie* a witch or a heretic unless he could demonstrate the contrary. If, for example, the accused argued that his enemy's illness had stemmed from natural causes, the judge might confound him by asking why, if that were so, it had not been cured by natural remedies. If he argued that his accusers were enemies, the judge could simply disregard the argument. Every decent individual was the enemy of a witch.

As for the judge, his duty was plain. It was to extort the truth, for only then could a sentence of death be passed. And the accused had to do more than answer questions. He had to confirm that truth, for as the *Malleus* points out, "Common justice demands that a witch should not be condemned to death unless she is convicted by her own confession".[2] One had to beware, however, for the devil was shrewd and might make a prisoner insensible to torture. Even so, torture ought not be neglected. Sometimes as luck would have it, even the devil slept.

"You admit," the judge might say, "that you made certain threats. Now you say that you did not intend to carry them out. But this answer positively offends my ears, so you will have to be put to the question and the rack." Or he might lock the prisoner in a cell and send in her friends to induce a confession. Of course people would be stationed where they could overhear. Or he

[1] *Malleus Maleficarum*, Pt. III, Qn. 9.
[2] *Malleus Maleficarum*, Pt. III, Qn. 13.

might keep postponing the day when she was to be tortured. She would screw up her courage once, twice, half a dozen times, but in the end she might break down. Or he could perhaps have her stripped naked by the gaolers and tortured just a little. Then someone could be prompted to plead that the torture be stopped. Let the prisoner be taken aside again by this friend. Promise her her life for a confession, but only if it will incriminate others. And let the promise actually be kept for a while. But in the end of course she must be burned.

These are some of the precepts to Inquisitors that Kramer and Sprenger laid down. If in spite of all kindness the prisoner did not confess, why then, there was nothing for it, the torture had to start. If the first day left him or her obdurate, then there must be a second and a third. There were many methods—the *tormento de loco*, wherein water is poured drop by drop onto a particular part of the body. Or one thrust a gauze bag into the throat and began filling it with water. This gradually forced the gauze down into the stomach, and the gauze kept the prisoner from vomiting. For a woman one might use the thumbscrew. This pressed her thumbs into a vice until eventually they were crushed. But if all else failed, there was the rack, and this machine to which the victim was tied hand and foot, was turned by a wheel as slowly as one liked, and gradually broke muscles, sinews and even the bones.

When at last the prisoner confessed, she had to be taken into another room at once and made to confess again, so that the confession could not be said to have been extracted under torture. Canon Law forbade it, and this not because of any particular gentleness in Canon Law. But in Rome the master of a slave tortured as the result of a false accusation had been allowed to reclaim double his value, and the church had originally adopted Roman Law. So in 384 a synod in Rome had agreed that the torture even of heretics must be left to secular tribunals, and a Bull of Innocent IV in 1282 directed that heretics be tortured, but only by the civil power as "robbers and murderers of souls, and thus thieves of the sacraments of God".

Witches are dangerous, Kramer and Sprenger tell us, even in

captivity, so the judge is warned never to allow a prisoner to touch him or even to look at him. She must be led in backwards. And he will be safest if he crosses himself at frequent intervals and carries about his person a bit of salt consecrated on Palm Sunday, or a few herbs that have been blessed. Above all, he must not forget to have the hair shaved off every part of the prisoner's body. "The Inquisitor of Como," the authors write, "informed us that last year, that is in 1485, he ordered forty-one witches to be burned after they had been shaved all over".[1]

But if in spite of every effort no evidence has been found, if in spite of repeated torture no confession has been extracted, the judge must never state that the prisoner is innocent, simply that nothing has been proved, and with the hinges of her body broken she may leave.

If, on the other hand, the prisoner is found to be guilty, the judgment ought to be handed down according to a certain formula. "We . . . order," the judge will say, "that you put on a grey-blue garment, and we sentence and condemn you to perpetual imprisonment, there to be punished with the bread of affliction and the water of distress." The prisoner shall then be exhibited in grey-blue at the altar of the church, and afterwards taken away. A sentence of death will follow, but the judge must not pass it himself, lest, having nothing to hope for, the heretic express her impenitence in front of the very cross. After she has been led out of the building, however, a different official must take her aside and tell her that she has been sentenced to the stake.

Roman law had recognized that torture could not be relied on, for it depended for its efficacy on the victim's power of endurance, and indeed even the Inquisition stopped torturing prisoners long before its own suppression. But it kept on at the work of killing its antagonists. Cagliostro, the sorcerer, was condemned to death as late as 1795, but he was eventually reprieved and died in prison, immured *in pace,* at peace, as Michelet has it. Four walls contained as many bodies as the judges found dissident souls. In 1816 a papal Bull finally decreed

[1] *Malleus Maleficarum*, Pt. III, Qn. 15.

that people might no longer be tortured, and that the accused should at last be confronted with his accusers.

Processes like these had never been known in the classical world. But as soon as the devil was invented they were instigated over and over again. The great uneasy theory was formulated of guilt by association. Thus, "If people are found to be meeting secretly for the purpose of worship, or differing in their manner of life and behaviour from the usual habits of the faithful, or if they meet together in sheds and barns," they are under suspicion of heresy and may be brought before the courts.[1] There, unless further evidence is forthcoming, they must at least undergo a solemn adjuration. If afterward they relapse they may be judged impenitent and burned.

But if there is nothing else we learn from history, we learn that in the long run the roots of individual desire always dig deeper than those of established authority. During the next two hundred years (until the scientific revolution) people of all social orders—from the cottager to the king's lady—were to take up arms against doctrine, and if they would not like Jan Hus or Martin Luther actually overcome what oppressed them, they would cling to the living devil, to an actual figure with horns and hoofs, for refuge.

In spite of 1,500 years of Christian teaching, in spite of a holocaust of punitive fires, the devil came into his own, the old animistic magic asserted itself, and to this day among authoritarian Catholics, just as the word *cholera* is used as a term of opprobrium in eastern Europe, so is *Luther,* like a black cat or some nameless viciousness, all the way to the Rhine.

[1] *Malleus Maleficarum*, Pt. III, Qn. 19.

II

Elspeth Reoch of Orkney, confessing in 1616: that when she was a young lass of twelve years of age or thereabouts, and had wandered out of Caithness where she was born to Lochaber, she came to Allan McKeldowie's wife who was her aunt. That one day being away from the loch in the country, and returning and being at the loch side waiting for the boat to fetch her, that there came two men to her, one dressed in black, and the other with a green tartan plaid about him. And that the man with the plaid said to her she was a pretty one, and he would teach her to know and see whatever she should desire. And thereafter within two years she bore her first child. And being delivered in her sister's house, the black man came to her that had first come to her in Lochaber, and called himself a fairy man. On yule day she confessed that the devil she calls the fairy man lay with her, and which time he bade her leave Orkney.

1597. Isobel Strathaquhin and her daughter of Aberdeen. They depone that herself confesses that what skill soever she has, she had it of her mother, and her mother learned it of an elf man that lay with her.

Accusation against Marian Grant of Aberdeen, 1596: The devil whom thou calls thy god, causes thee to worship him on thy knees . . . Margaret Johnson, 1633: there appeared unto her a spirit or devil in the similitude and proportion of a man. And the said devil or spirit bid her call him by the name Mamillion. She saith that in all her talk and conference she calleth the said devil Mamillion, "my god". Isobel Gowdie: he made us believe that there was no god beside him. We call him "our Lord," and each time when we would meet with him, it behoves us to rise and make our curtsey, and we would say, "You are welcome, my lord," and "How do ye, my lord?"

Alice Huson, 1664: the devil appeared like a black man upon a black horse, with cloven feet, and then I fell down and did worship him upon my knees. Northumberland, 1673: the said Ann Baites hath several times danced with the devil at the places aforesaid, calling him sometimes her protector, sometimes her blessed saviour. She saw Forster, Dryden and Thompson and the rest, and their protector, which they called their god, sitting at the head of the table.

Elizabeth Clarke of Essex, 1645: he appeared in the shape of a proper gentleman with a laced band, having the whole proportion of a man. Oftentimes he had knocked on her door at night, and she did arise, open the door and let him in. Rebecca West (elsewhere reported to have "died very stubborn"): the devil appeared in the likeness of a proper young man. Rebecca Jones: the devil was a very handsome young man who came to the door and asked how she did. At Eyemouth in 1634 Bessie Bathgate was seen at twelve at night standing barelegged in her sark valicot at the back of her yard, conferring with the devil who was in green clothes.[1]

Margaret Hamilton conversed with him at the town well, and several times in her own house and drank several choppens (quart measures) of ale with him. Elizabeth Anderson saw a black, grim man go into her grandmother's house, and little Thomas Lindsay's grandmother waked him one night out of his bed and made him take a black, grim gentleman by the hand.

[1] In my ignorance I have not, in spite of considerable hunting, been able to discover the meaning of the word "valicot". If any reader can enlighten me I should be grateful.

To Bessie Henderson he was a bonny young lad with a blue bonnet, to Marie Lamont a black man who sang to them and they danced. Joan Willimott served one William Berry for three years in Rutlandshire, and he blew into her mouth. In Devon in 1662 he wore a blue bonnet again. In 1670 he was a black man in black clothes with a hat on his head, sitting at a table in Betty Laing's house. In Sweden and in Massachusetts he was sometimes dressed as a clergyman. Mary Green's devil in Somerset was a little man who put his hand to his hat and said, "How do ye?" speaking low, but big. One Suffolk devil wore black and had a voice rough but gusty. In Windsor in 1579 he seems to have been the local priest, for Elizabeth Stile "confesseth herself often times to have gone to Father Rosimond's house where she found him sitting in a wood not far from thence, under the body of a tree, sometimes in the shape of an ape, and otherwhiles like a horse". A certain Abbé Guibourg was at one time head of the Paris witches, for he celebrated a black mass and is said to have sacrificed a child.

The devil was not always a man. William Barton was tried at Edinburgh about 1655. "One day, says he, going from my own house in Kirkliston to the Queen's Ferry, I overtook in Dalmeny Muire a young Gentlewoman, as to appearance beautiful and comely. I drew near to her, but she shunned my company, and when I insisted, she became angry and very nice. Said I, we are both going one way, be pleased to accept of a convoy. At last after much entreaty she grew better natured, and at length came to that familiarity that she suffered me to embrace her, and to do that which Christian ears ought not to hear of. At this time I parted with her very joyful." The next night she appeared to him in the very same place, and after that which should not be named, he became sensible that it was the Devil. Here he renounced his Baptism and gave up himself to her service, and she called him her beloved, and gave him this new name of John Baptist, and received the Mark.[1]

Sometimes the devil wears green or grey, but mostly he is dressed in black, and always in the fashion of the time. Some-

[1] Sinclair, George, *Satan's Invisible World Discovered.* Edinburgh, 1871.

times he is a bonny young man, but sometimes old with a grey beard. Sometimes he has a cloven foot (which was probably a thonged sandal). Sometimes he rides a horse. But always they describe his hat, in Belgium his plumes, and almost invariably the deponent has made love with him.

"He came to her (Rebecca West) as she was going to bed and told her he would marry her and she could not deny him. She said he kissed her but was as cold as clay." Antoinette Bourignon writes of a twelve-year-old girl who said the devil was a boy a little bigger than she. He was her love and lay with her every night. Anne Ashby, Anne Martyn and another confessed at Maidstone in 1652 that they were pregnant, not by any man, but by the devil. Nevertheless they were hanged. In Pitcairn's *Criminal Trials*, Isobel Gowdie gives evidence in 1662 that the devil was "a big, black, rich man, very cold; I found his nature as cold within me as spring water. He is abler for us that way than any man can be, only he was heavy—like a malt sack." And later, "His member is exceeding great and long. No man's members are so long and big."

Once he was a great, black goat with a candle between his horns, and had carnal knowledge of the same Isobel which caused great pain. Anne Martyn said the devil had known her carnally, but it had caused her no hurt at all. Sylvine de la Plaine, on the other hand, according to Boguet, said that "qu'il a le membre faict comme un cheval, en entrant est froid comme glace, jette la semence fort froide, et en sortant le brusle comme si c'estoit du feu".

The devil's concubines were of all ages. Elspeth Reoch was a little over twelve. Elizabeth Francis, tried at Chelmsford in 1566 was about the same age when she "first gave her blood to Satan". Kinloch tells us of little Jonet Howat who was only seven, that the devil said of her, "What shall I do with such a little bairn as she?" He called her "his bonny bird". Elizabeth Anderson was seven, and Annabil Stuart fourteen, when, persuaded by her mother, she vowed herself to the devil. In general, a child seems to have been accepted, but not asked to renounce God and marry her new master until she had reached the age of puberty.

Above all, it is clear that the demons bound women to them so firmly that in most cases they allowed themselves to be hanged or burned at the stake rather than betray him. Mme Bourignon's girls, orphans under her care, had daily copulation with the devil, and as one of them said, "I would not be other than I am. I am too content in my condition. I am always caressed". De Lancre examined a woman of twenty-nine who told him the Sabbath was the true paradise, and that there was more joy in its observance than she could express. Because of the pleasure and happiness it gave her it seemed far too short, so she invariably went home with deep regret and longed for the time when she could go again. Another, whom the Inquisitor acknowledged to be very pretty, told him that she took more pleasure in the Sabbath than in the Mass. The devil so had hold of her heart that there was hardly room for anything else to enter it.[1]

To our modern eye the story seems reasonably clear. All over Britain and western Europe there existed young men and old, wearing black or grey or green, with blue bonnets or black, living mostly (but not always) in country districts, who attracted young women by the exercise of a certain animal attraction and by claiming to be practitioners of a fashionable mystery. At any time in history a wicked man has attracted more women than a good; debauchery is more tantalizing than virtue. A murderer about to be hanged used to be able to count on proposals from any number of young women. In 1934, when he was nearly sixty years old, raddled with alcohol and heroin and known as "the wickedest man in the world", Aleister Crowley was approached by a girl of nineteen in the street who asked, almost with tears in her eyes, if she might be the mother of his child. Crowley accepted the offer.[2]

One need not go so far. A matinée idol of the years before the first war, a film star in the 1930's, a pop musician today—any of them has been offered his pick of young girls, because a drab life needs only a minor devil to give it excitement. And to the

[1] De Lancre, Pierre, *L'Incredulité et Mescréance du Sortilege*. Paris, 1622.
[2] Symonds, John, *The Great Beast*. London, 1951.

seventeenth-century housewife or country wench, these men in green and black who spoke so kindly but in such deep or gusty voices, offered not only illicit excitement, but a promise of power over her less fortunate neighbours.

He would show her how to make wax images to the torment of some gossip she hated, to make cows barren or to cause hailstorms in this or that particular field. On the coasts of Scotland she would cause shipwrecks that might cast a treasure ashore. She would cure the sick, make her own hens lay and her own cow give more milk. If she were Alice Perrers she would cast spells to win the love of Edward III. If she were a Madame de Montespan she would employ learned Abbés to rekindle a passion in Louis XIV. But whoever she was she would acquire a not always enviable reputation for being both wise and dangerous. Above all, she could leave her husband snoring in bed at night, go out to eat, drink, dance, and know that before the night was out she would be the lover of a god.

And this of course accounts for "the nature as cold within me as spring water". For not even a devil would be capable of serving the whole of his coven without an artificial member. It is described as having scales like a fish, as being rough as leather and almost always larger than life.

In a traditional society the individual is rarely allowed a separate existence. These women—and sometimes men—were making one for themselves. And as most secret societies have a sign by which members can know each other, or as in religions there is a laying on of hands, so was it here. The devil touched or pricked or in some way marked his servants so that they could for ever after be identified.

A witch in Yarmouth testified at her trial in 1644 that she saw a tall black man standing at her door in the moonlight. He asked to look at her hand, and taking out a tiny knife, gave it a scratch. Rebecca Jones, tried in Essex the following year, reported that "there came one morning one to the door and knocked . . . and she saw there a very handsome young man . . . who asked this examinant how she did and desired to see her left wrist, which she then showed to him, and he took a pin from the examinant's own sleeve and pricked her wrist twice, and there came out a drop of blood which he took off with the top of his finger and so departed".

The child-witch of Forfar, Jonet Howat, said "the devil kissed her and nipped her upon one of her shoulders", but afterward he called her "his bonny bird, did kiss her and stroked her shoulder which was nipped with his hand, and that presently after that she was eased of her pain".

Sometimes the spots became insensitive. In the *Highland Papers* it is reported at the trial of one Kate Moore that a white, insensible spot was found underneath her right shoulder. On Mary Sykes a wart was discovered that pulled out the length of half a finger, and Margaret Morton (marvellous to relate), had two black spots between her thigh and her body. Reginald Scot states that if a witch have any privy mark under her armpits, under her hair, under her lip, on her buttock or in her private parts it is a presumption sufficient for a judge to proceed to give sentence of death upon her. Many a suspect is reported to have been stripped, blindfolded and then pricked with needles in various parts of her body to see if an anaesthetized spot could be found.

Indeed a body of men known as "witch finders" claimed to be able to hunt witches down almost by a species of intuition. Pennethorne Hughes tells of a Scotsman active in Newcastle-on-Tyne in 1649. He "knew whether they were witches or not by their looks". A certain "personable and good like woman, in front of a crowd had her body laid naked to the waist, with her cloathes over her head, by which fright and shame all her blood contracted into one part of her body, and then he ran a pin into her thigh, and then suddenly let her coats fall, and then demanded whether she had nothing of his in her body but did not bleed, but she being amazed replied little, then he put his hand up her coats and pulled out the pin and set her aside as a guilty person and child of the Devil, and fell to try others whom he made guilty."

To be sure, the prurient bullies did not always have it their own way. In this case, one "Lt. Colonel Hobson, perceiving the alteration of the aforesaid woman by her blood settling in her right parts, caused that woman to be brought again, and her cloathes pulled up to her thigh, and required the Scot to run the pin into the same place, and then it gushed out of blood and the said Scot cleared her, and said she was not a child of the Devil".

But we have to make plain just what these women did, why they were so widely feared, and in this context one of the most familiar of Freud's case histories comes to mind. A girl of fifteen, lying in bed under the watchful eye of a strict grandmother, suddenly cried out. She had dreamed she felt a penetrating pain in her forehead, and before she finally sought psychiatric help that pain recurred sharply but intermittently for almost thirty years. During analysis, she was eventually able to tell Freud that the grandmother had given her a look so intense that she imagined at the time that it had gone straight into her skull.

The inference need not be laboured. Many an evil eye contained no more evil intent than the grandmother's glance. Nor need we elaborate on the obvious village jealousies and feuds that would make one accuse another, or the innumerable accidents that would lend these accusations credibility. But guilty or innocent, 30,000 witches were executed in France during the fifteen years reign of Henry III. In 1627 a hundred and fifty seven were burned in Würzburg alone. It almost passes comprehension that any madness could have been so long continued.

Now of course a great deal has been written about witchcraft, perhaps more than about any other aspect of demonology, and a good deal of it either passes the bounds of credulity or contradicts much of the rest. The Rev. Montague Summers wrote a number of volumes and proved himself almost as credulous as the mediaeval chroniclers. G. L. Kittredge, on the other hand, looked at the evidence for witchcraft in England and set down what he found with careful and scholarly accuracy. Margaret Murray tried to prove (with a certain limited success) that witchcraft was derived from the magical practices of *la vecchia religione*, Chadwick Hansen wrote a serious treatise on witchcraft in seventeenth-century Massachusetts, and Remigius,

Guazzo, Scot and Glanvil compiled several hundred stories between them, some of them ludicrous, some of them very moving. In most of this material a great deal is made of Sabbath feasts and dances, of copulation with the devil and of the fact that women often paid homage by kissing the devil's arse.

But in plain fact, once you have described a single set of witches you have more or less described them all. Not one of the historians has done more than hazard a guess about the *why* of it, for in fact nobody knows. Michelet draws a horrifying picture of poor countrywomen made desperate by poverty and oppression until they sell their souls to Satan for a temporary relief. And vivid as his picture is, we cannot really believe it applies to the bonny bird, Jonet Howat or to Mme Bourignon's girls or to anyone like them. Professor Murray insisted that witches were putting into practise their preconscious memories of magical practice. But this too seems only part of the truth. For witch-craft—what we know of it—is divisible into various, sometimes contradictory categories.

The first was that which relied on the old sympathetic magic. In its simplest form one made a figure of wax or clay or wood and then either pierced it or burned it so that the person it represented might suffer corresponding torments. A Bishop of Troyes was accused in 1308 of murdering Philip IV's queen in this way. He had had a wax image made and baptized in her name, for if his magic was primitive he had superimposed on it a certain amount of Christian doctrine. The image was pierced in head and belly with a needle, and at once, we are told, the queen fell ill. Again and again he attacked the little sculpture, but still the queen lingered. So at last he broke its legs, stamped on it and threw it into the fire. "Will the woman live for ever?" he cried. And very soon afterward she died.

Alice Perrers is said to have made images, as I suggested earlier, to cause the king to fall in love with her. Henry V prosecuted his stepmother for trying to kill him by sorcery, and her confessor, one Friar Randolf, confessed his part in the plot, was imprisoned and eventually murdered by having his head bashed in with a stone. Ten years later seven witches were committed to the Fleet for plotting the death of Henry VI, and that was the year a Frenchwoman was taken armed in the field, "a false witch called Pucelle de Dieux". Edward IV is said to have been seduced into marriage with Elizabeth Grey by sorcery, and only a few years afterward one Johanna Benet was charged with sorcery by means of a candle. "As the candle is consumed," the formula ran, "so will a man waste away." According to Kittredge, a similar candle magic is practiced even today in some parts of the British Isles to torment a faithless lover.

Witchcraft sometimes employed animals for its purposes, and in rites reminiscent of primitive sacrifice. As late as 1861 in Durham—this also from Kittredge—"When a woman was thought to be suffering from witchcraft, pins were run into a live pigeon by each member of her family and the bird was roasted." There is a record dating from 1920 of a cockerel tortured to death with pins in Devon, and at the same time a spell was recited: with this pin I thee prick; my enemy's heart I hope to stick. And a tablet was dug out of the ruins of Carthage with an inscription reading: this cock's tongue I have torn out while he was alive. . . . So may the tongues of my enemies be made dumb against me.

Grimm informs us that the Germans had been accustomed to bury an animal alive to cure the cattle plague, and Gregor in a study of Scottish folklore writes that it was not unknown for a black cock to be buried under the bed to cure epilepsy. In Devon they buried a puppy in a field to eradicate weeds, and gravediggers have now and then turned up bottles buried after having been filled with pins, nail parings and human hair, which had originally been thrust into coffins to destroy some witch's power.

But witchcraft could be benevolent too. There were of course love potions. Chapuys reported in 1536 that Henry VIII had been forced by such a philtre to marry Anne Boleyn, and many a woman was charged before the courts either with making "love drinks" or with extracting money from the gullible for promising to do so. Not only the court records, the ballads are full of such sorcery, of potions, curses, magic rings. On another Carthaginian tablet a wife is cursed by a mistress in love with the woman's husband. There are others still in Greek, in Latin, in Hebrew. Let her not sleep until she comes and satisfies my longing. Make her come to me full of love. One Felix conjures Vettia in Carthage that she neither eat nor sleep, that she forget parents, relatives, friends and all other men. There also was found the earliest carving of two hearts transfixed—to avow, or perhaps to ensure eternal love.

We saw that according to the *Malleus Maleficarum* witchcraft could cause impotence, and accusations before the courts are practically innumerable. But witches eased—or arrested—childbirth also, it seems, by sympathetic magic, for they could do it either by locking or unlocking a door.

Now we saw that even in pre-Christian Europe, that is, long before incubi and succubi existed, children were sometimes conceived by the actions of spirits, and that such conception was often necessary before the child could be thought of as divine. In the early Middle Ages the doctrine was established as an article of faith, except that the spirit was now no longer divine, but diabolic. We read that one woman in the thirteenth century fought so hard for her honour that the enraged incubus killed her husband, one of her children, and as for the woman herself, it struck her blind. A certain Joan, living near Winchester in 1337, walked into a little copse one afternoon with her lover, William, only to meet him on her way home and learn that he had not left his house all day. The shock killed her. According to Giraldus, a certain Meilerius actually went mad when his beautiful mistress was suddenly transformed into a fiend.

For witches could drive one mad. We have seen how Christina von Stommeln's very thighs were lacerated by demons that hid under her clothing. But the same thing could be made to happen with spells, or by a vividness in the "devil", a sheer spiritual energy his victims were not able to cope with. At least three of Aleister Crowley's mistresses killed themselves, and as we shall see in a moment, there were dozens of perplexed little nuns in seventeenth-century France driven to raving lunacy by a witchcraft, or what they thought of as witchcraft, that was simply too potent for their poor brains to assimilate. The devil in human form could be very powerful indeed. In 1493 one Elena Dalok was brought to trial for claiming, perhaps with some justice, that whoever she cursed was sure to die. She cared nothing for any heaven to come, she told the court. All she wanted was heaven on earth. In fact, she hoped actively to go to hell, for there was a certain John Gybbys down there already burning with whom she had an account or two to settle.

If witches poisoned souls, they poisoned bodies too. Thucydides, writing of the plague that struck Athens in 430 BC, says that it was supposed the Peloponnesians had poisoned the cisterns, no conduits having as yet been made there. By the same token my Viennese governess assured me that after the first world war Americans had sent over poisoned bacon to kill whatever Austrians they had not already killed on the battlefield.

In Reginald Scot's *Discoverie of Witchcraft* we read that in 1536 there were forty *veneficae* in Italy who smeared doors and doorposts with ointment to infect people with the plague. Charms and incantations, he assures us, can do the same thing as well as poisons. And it ought to be mentioned that one of the most famous murders in English history had its origin in witchcraft. In 1477 George, Duke of Clarence, had two people hanged for allegedly poisoning his wife and son, and then, being accused of "having noised abroad . . . that the King, our Sovereign Lord wrought by necromancie and used craft to poison his subjects", and having stated that "the King intended to consume him, Clarence, in like wise as a candle consumeth by burning", he was imprisoned in the Tower and shortly afterward drowned by the king's order in the proverbial butt of Malmsey.

But let us look at some of the evidence which to the local courts must have seemed worrying in the extreme. By the middle of the seventeenth century there was already a great deal of scepticism about anything that smacked of the supernatural.

"On Sunday, the 15th of November, 1657," Glanvill writes, "about Three of the Clock in the Afternoon, Richard Jones, then a sprightly youth about twelve years old, Son of Henry Jones of Shepton Mallet in the County of *Somerset*, being in his

Father's House alone, and perceiving one looking in at the Windows, went to the Door, where one *Jane Brooks* of the same Town (but then by name unknown to this Boy) came to him. She desired him to give her a piece of close Bread, and gave him an Apple. After which she also stroked him down on the right side, shook him by the hand and so bid him good night."

What then befell Richard Jones is too long here to set down. In brief, he fell into fits, and for the next four months, whenever, as an experiment ordered by his father, Jane Brooks came and touched him he fainted and lost the power of speech. On several occasions he was found suspended from the rafters to which he said the woman had lifted him, and once at least, being at the house of one Richard Isles of Shepton Mallet, he was seen by Mrs Isles to rise into the air and fly some thirty yards over the garden wall. When he recovered consciousness he said that Jane Brooks had carried him there by the arm.

On another occasion he started out of bed and cried that he could see her standing by the wall. A certain Mr Gibson struck the place with a knife and the boy shouted that he had wounded Jane in the hand. Gibson and the boy's father fetched a constable, went with him to the woman's house and found her nursing a hand she said she had cut with a pin.

On three separate occasions victim and suspect were examined before the Justices, but on the 10th of March, when Jane and her sister (who had once said to the boy, "How do ye, my honey?") were committed to prison the fits and illnesses ceased. Jane Brooks was sentenced to death at Chard assizes and hanged on the 26th of March, 1658.

On the 26th of January, 1664, William Parsons, rector of Trister in Somerset, was examined before Robert Hunt about one Richard Hill's daughter who had been bewitched. On a Monday night before Christmas he had come into a room while Elizabeth was in a fit, many of his parishioners being present, and there had seen the child being held in a chair, foaming at the mouth and biting at her arms and clothing. This had gone on for about half an hour. After some time she had pointed a finger at the left side of her head, next to her left arm, then to her left hand. At each place he perceived a red spot with a bit of black in the middle of it like a thorn. The next day he had seen thorns in these places.

On the same day one Elizabeth Styles was brought before the justice and confessed that about ten years previously the devil had appeared to her in the shape of a handsome man. On another occasion he became a black dog. He promised that for twelve years she should have money, live gallantly and enjoy the pleasures of the world if she would sign a contract in her own blood, agreeing to give him her soul and observe his laws. This after four separate solicitations the examinant acceded to. So he had pricked the fourth finger of her right hand (the scar was still visible), and with a drop or two of blood she had signed the paper with an O. Upon this, the devil had given her sixpence and disappeared.

When she wishes to do harm, she calls him, using the name Robin, and says, "Oh, Satan, give me my purpose". It was in this way that she had asked him to torment Elizabeth Hill and stick thorns into her flesh. About a month before, at nine at night she had been with Alice Duke, Anne Bishop and Mary Penny in the common near Trister Gate, when they "met a man in black clothes . . . to whom they curtseyed, and Alice Duke had brought a wax image of Elizabeth Hill. The man in black . . . anointed its forehead and said, 'I baptize thee with this oil'. They called it Elizabeth and stuck thorns into several parts of the neck, hand, wrists, fingers and other parts of the image. After which they had wine, cakes and roast meat (all brought by the man in black) which they did eat and drink. They danced and were merry, were bodily there and in their clothes. Before they are carried to their meetings they anoint their foreheads and wrists with an oil which smells raw, and then they are carried in a very short time. At their meetings they have wine or beer, cakes or the like. The man in black sits at the upper end of the table and uses certain words before meat, but none after. His voice is audible, but very low. The reason she caused Elizabeth Hill to be tormented was because her father had said she was a witch."

Seven other witnesses gave evidence. Thus Alice Duke deposed that "they all make very low obeisance to the devil, who appears in black clothes and a little band. He bids them welcome and brings wine or beer, cakes, meat and the like. He sits at the upper end, and Anne Bishop next to him. They eat, drink, dance and have music. At their parting they say 'Merry meet, merry part'. They anoint their foreheads with a greenish oil which smells raw and are for the most part carried to meetings through the air."

There are so many depositions from many periods and many places, all in substantial agreement, that we cannot really doubt these things took place. The devil spoke in a deep, quiet voice and almost invariably women flew—or imagined they flew—through the air just as Regino's women had dreamed seven hundred years earlier.

Sometimes they travelled in the normal way, on horseback. One girl of fifteen in Lille declared that her mother had carried her to meetings in her arms when she was small. The Lancashire witches in 1613 rode on foals of various colours. But at the Crook of Devon Bessie Henderson claimed that she flew to a meeting. Swedish witches in 1669 stated that they flew high over steeples. "He gives us a horn with a salve in it, wherewith we do anoint ourselves, and then he gives us a Saddle with a Hammer and a wooden nail, thereby to fix the saddle; whereupon we call the devil and away we go."[1] Isobel Gowdie, for whom the devil was as heavy as a malt sack, "had a little horse and would say 'Horse and hattock in the devil's name'. And then we would fly away where we would, even as straws would fly upon a highway. We would fly like straws when we pleased. Wild straws and corn straws will be horses to us if we put them betwixt our feet and say 'Horse and hattock, in the devil's name'." Glanvil quotes the witch, Julian Cox, telling how one evening she walked out about a mile from her own house, and there came riding towards her three persons borne up about a

---

[1] Anthony Hornbeck in the appendix to Glanvill, Joseph, *Saducismus triumphatus*. London, 1689.

yard and a half from the ground. Two of them she had formerly known as a witch and a wizard. The third person she knew not. He came in the shape of a black man.

In New England Goody Foster was carried by the devil on a pole, but the pole broke and she fell, hurting herself badly, but Mrs Osgood of Andover travelled quite safely on a pole to Five Mile Pond.

Now, they all refer to a greenish oil that smells raw. Elizabeth Styles anointed her wrists and forehead. Alice Duke anointed her forehead, and this same oil or ointment appears in Sweden, in Germany and in France. What could it have been made of, one wonders.

Well, it seems there were three formulae. The first was purely herbal, and except for the addition of soot to render one invisible, would seem unlikely to have had any effect. To be sure, it did contain aconite, which is a poison and would induce irregularity in the heartbeat. But that would hardly make one fly. The second added hemlock, and this would cause nervous excitement and a gradual motor paralysis. The third is the most interesting, for it was made of baby's fat (presumably as an emollient), water parsnip (which may be cowbane or hemlock), aconite, cinquefoil (which is harmless) bats' blood (for levitation by sympathetic magic), soot again and deadly nightshade. Deadly nightshade is belladonna. Fourteen berries are known to have been enough to cause death, and smaller amounts would produce a delirious excitement. So the whole compound would cause a partial paralysis, excitability and a certain delirium. These might very well induce a sensation of flying, and what the poisons partly accomplished, autosuggestion would complete.

Cotton Mather[1] writes that "the witches do say that they form themselves much after the manner of Congregational Churches, and that they have a Baptism, and a Supper and Officers among them abominably resembling those of our Lord". And De Lancre[2] adds that there are two sorts of witches, one, who having

[1] Mather, Cotton, *Wonders of the Invisible World*. London, 1862.
[2] De Lancre, op. cit.

abandoned God, hunt for drugs and poisons, the other who have expressly renounced Christ and the faith. These are the sort who work wonders.

So if they abjured their faith in Christ, they cannot, as Margaret Murray asserts, have simply been carrying on the practises of a *vecchia religione*. There had been a break in the tradition, and these were rebels reverting to something they no longer understood. They had waited, as I said earlier, for a second coming that never came, for miracles that were never performed, and had turned finally to the devil and to small, sad miracles of their own. If the old gods could cause thunderstorms, so could they. If the Walkyrie rode through the air, their ointments enabled them to do the same. If the priest's God could kill or cure, theirs had similar powers, and if the church, the bodiless, prying authorities, believed they enjoyed a wild sexual felicity denied to other people, they would have that too, make a heaven of earth and forget their hopes of heaven. The rebellion grew. It became a positive fever that was never abated until the scientific revolution taught people to believe in nothing that they could not see.

If Rebecca West "died stubborn" as Arnold's little mistress in Cologne had done, if Mary Phillips and Elinor Shaw, two of the Northamptonshire witches, laughed aloud as they were about to be hanged, and called on the devil to help them, it was not because they had dreamed or imagined anything. It was because their devil-god had appeared to them in the flesh as had Joan of Arc's angels, because he was *here,* because there had never been any question of blind faith, because they had seen with their own eyes the working of miracles, because instead of ritual being performed on their behalf by a priest, they had performed it themselves, because their ceremonies were full of dancing and music, because they had eaten, drunk, copulated and still seen god. And beside this, whatever the church could offer looked very pale indeed.

But no coven's records (if they kept any) have survived, so what actually happened we cannot know with certainty. The only evidence is of depositions at the trials. It is as if the history of the Russian church were known only through the writers of the Communist Manifesto.

Three hundred years of persecution did not suffice to destroy these people, but at the end of the seventeenth century organized witchcraft died in the course of a generation, and of its own accord. It had offered an illusion of power to many tens or perhaps hundreds of thousands. It had expressed their affinity with a half-remembered paradise, with gods in trees and running water, with a magic that grew out of the elements with which they were surrounded. Like the Jews they had been a chosen people, marked out by visible gods for a visible salvation. Like the pythoness at Delphi, they had had cloudy and uncertain visions of the future. Like the Bacchae, they had released inhibitions, and like half-civilized peoples everywhere they had played at mumbo-jumbo and called it magic. But they seem to have been happy, and if they often wished to do evil, then they were burned and hanged for wishing. But there is no real evidence that they ever did very much to justify being put down.

Above all, they would never have got anywhere without the existence of credulous neighbours. African witch doctors can kill, but only if the victim believes. Witchcraft in Europe worked in a world dominated by an increasing scepticism. It was nothing but a shadow of the primitive magic on which it had been based. No doubt it exists today, but today it has more to do with commercialism than with the devil. In the 20th century the old horned god has moved out of the country into the suburbs and there died.

12

If we believe in demons, if they exist everywhere in the air around us, it is only natural that we can sometimes communicate with or be possessed by them. Perhaps some kinds of possession are even the origin of myth. But whether or no, it has certainly caused a number of phenomena unusual in the extreme.

The Marshal Trivulce died of terror while protecting himself with a sword against demons swarming about him in his room. Demons destroyed so suave a priest as Urbain Grandier of Loudun in what someone has called "a totally unexpected and preposterous trap". They killed any number of highly intelligent and learned exorcists, and they produced in some victims what must be regarded as unquestionable evidence of clairvoyance and precognition. Over two hundred years ago, J. S. Semler, who was an astute German theologian, said that "If I wished to collect the thousands upon thousands of stories of possessed persons and their cure, it would be a vast labour, but it would constitute a history of the devil in the Middle Ages".

One could tell about Edwin, the young monk of Ely, who went mad at compline. A holy man from Winchester saw a creature like a black boy clutching the sufferer's cowl. Or one might read in the *Knighton Chronicle*, the annals of Worcester, about how in 1355 people went mad all over the country. They hid in the woods like animals, or ran from the woods into the streets, and had to be tied up and taken into the churches before they could be cured. Or, reading Sir Thomas More, one can meet Anne, the daughter of Sir Richard Wentworth, "a fair young gentlewoman of twelve years of age", who was "in a marvellous manner vexed and tormented by our ghostly enemy, the devil".

Now we have already seen how frightening a phenomenon such possession can be, notably in the Siberian shaman and the prophetesses of Delphi and Dodona. Demons did not by any means come into the world with Christianity, but the sickness had grown out of all bounds in the classical world just when that world was in process of dying, and Christians, drawn mostly from among the lower classes, felt the power of demons more than most, for possession has almost always been a disease of the poor and the illiterate.

"All over the world," Harnack wrote, "Christians became exorcists . . . and they exorcised not only the devils that lived in men. They purged them out of the air and even from public life. For the whole second century was under the dominion of the spirit of darkness. The world and the air around it was peopled with devils; all the formalities of daily living, not merely the worship of idols, were governed by them. They sat on thrones and hovered round children's cots. The earth, God's creation though it may be, now and for ever, became in fact a hell."[1]

We have already seen how vividly mediaeval men could imagine the devil. A perfect illustration (though of much later date) may be found in the *Iconographie de la Salpêtrière*.

There was a female patient in the hospital known as the Lariboisière. After one of her attacks (she suffered from fits) the almoner came to see her and told her it was Satan that had caused her sickness. Under the influence of this suggestion her illness became far more intense, and at last in the delirium of one of her convulsive fits she actually saw the devil. He was tall, she

[1] Harnack, A., *Die Mission und Ausbreitung des Christentums in den ersten drei Jahrhunderten*. Leipzig, 1915.

said, and covered in scales. His legs ended in claws. "He stretched out his arms as though to take hold of me. His eyes were fiery red and his body ended in a great tail with tufts of hair at the end like a lion's. . . ."

A nun and the almoner had told her she was possessed because she did not pray enough, and that she was going to die. So she had Masses said, and paid a franc or one franc fifty a time. She made her confession; she went to communion. The almoner sprinkled her as often as possible with holy water and kept making the sign of the cross over her.

Sometimes the patient even saw the devil in more lucid moments. If she happened to be in bed she at once buried her head in the bedclothes, but still she could see him. The more they talked to her of the devil the clearer he became, and the more violent and frequent her attacks. Even after she had been admitted to the Salpêtrière in Paris she kept having diabolic visions. But then she began going to church less frequently, and when nobody talked to her about devils any more she gradually regained her peace of mind, and at last she quite got rid of the idea that the devil possessed her.

In the *Historia Francorum*, written in the sixth century by Gregory of Tours, we read that: "On feast days in the churches these demoniacs go positively mad. To the terror of the parishioners around them they even smash the lamps. But if they happen to be splashed by the oil the demon leaves them and they return to their senses."

Cyril of Jerusalem, writing his *Catechisms* two hundred years earlier, says that: "The unclean devil comes upon the soul of a man like a wolf on a sheep, lusting for blood. His presence is terribly cruel . . . the mind grows black, and indeed the attack is unjust too, for like a tyrant the devil is using another's body as his own. He twists the tongue and tortures the lips. Instead of using words the victim foams at the mouth and is filled with darkness. The eyes remain open, but his soul cannot see out through them."

A beautiful description of an epileptic seizure, and of course Gregory's demoniacs were schizophrenics, but other cases turned out to be far more complicated. Twelve hundred years afterward in Loudun, where one of the most famous outbreaks of mass hysteria sometimes drew audience of seven thousand spectators at a time—at Loudun, where the devil was said actually to have caused the deaths of exorcists, Asmodeus "shook the girl back and forth a number of times and made her positively throb like a trip-hammer, and so rapidly that her teeth rattled while groans were forced out of her throat. . . . Her face became quite unrecognizable, her tongue terribly long and furry, lolling out of her mouth".[1]

Sister Jeanne des Anges of Loudun wrote in her autobiography that "I felt for God a constant aversion. . . . In my mind I kept working out ways to displease him and to make others trespass against him. . . . Sometimes I tore all my veils and those of any of my sisters I could lay hands on. I trampled them, I bit them and cursed the hour when I took my vows. . . . When I received the host at communion, when I had half wet it between my lips, the devil took it and flung it back into the priest's face."

The Abbé Surin, who seems to have been not only a mystic but a highly intelligent old man, was one of the exorcists who had been sent down to cure the plague. "In the exercise of my ministry," he writes, "the devil passes out of the body of the possessed woman and enters into mine. He attacks and confuses me . . . possessing me for hours on end as though I were a demoniac. I cannot explain what happens, except by saying that the spirit becomes like another me, as if I had two souls . . . one of which is watching the other. Two spirits fight in one battle-field which is my body. I . . . feel that the cries coming out of my mouth come from both souls. When I try to make the sign of the cross in front of my lips, the other soul knocks away my hand or grips it in my teeth to bite me in its fury. When the other possessed victims see me in this condition, how they triumph, how the devils mock at me and cry, 'Physician, heal thyself! What a spectacle to watch him preaching after he has just been rolling on the gound!' " He ends his long account by saying, "I do not know if our Lord will soon take away my

[1] *Histoire des diables de Loudun.* Amsterdam, 1716.

life . . . but it seems that the devil, by cursing me with so many bodily ills, wants to exercise his power and gradually wear me out."

Any of us, looking at himself impartially, knows how open to suggestion he is. A young girl is quite unreasonably convinced that she is in love. A mob is incited into a lust for loot and murder. The examples are too commonplace even to need listing. But demoniacal possession went beyond this, for it drove vast numbers of its victims into states that were more than self-hypnotic and hallucinatory. People did things which they would not have permitted under hypnosis, which in a normal waking state would have seemed physically impossible. They spoke in languages they had never learned, foretold the future, sometimes with startling accuracy, and displayed a clairvoyance like that of the primitive, but which in our present state of knowledge we simply cannot explain.

Of course prophecy tends to be self-fulfilling and faith works wonders. But there remains in the history of demoniacal possession a residue of the incomprehensible, for as when looking at primitive magic or the pythoness at Delphi, we see only symptoms and not causes. Perhaps the growth of science has been the destruction of life, and as J. H. Plumb once wrote in another context, "An epoch that started ten thousand years ago is ending".

The infamous Ursuline, Jeanne des Anges, spoke in seven different diabolic voices, and when we read her autobiographical description of how the devil arched her body until her head all but touched her heels, and shouted obscenities out of her mouth that it shocked her to hear, when we are told of a fat old priest, clumsy and short of breath, who danced when in a state of possession with a wild and beautiful abandon so that onlookers did not believe him capable of making the movements, it reminds us of nothing so much as of the Dionysia and the corybantic revellers who danced when they were out of their minds, and the Bacchic maidens who, Plato said, could draw milk and honey out of the rivers, but not when they were sane.

Kerner, in his *Nachricht von dem Vorkommen des Besessenseins*, writes of an eight-year-old girl who, when in a state of possession, spoke in the deep, coarse voice of a man. Or there was the child called Caroline[1] whose subconscious must have been capable of a quite extraordinary imagination, for she described hell not only as loathsome and full of a quite unbearable stench. If she had added that the damned copulated there one might have thought her merely precocious. But she went further. The devil, she said, forced men to make love perpetually with whatever women they had enjoyed while they were alive.

Maury, Janet and Eginhard have all quoted the case wherein "the evil spirit talked through the mouth of the sick woman, and it was extraordinary to hear the sound alternatively of a masculine voice and a feminine one, but each so distinct and separate that we could not believe only the woman was speaking. It was as if two excited people were quarrelling and hurling abuse at each other."

The famous Maid of Orlach was possessed by the diabolical spirit of a monk who wore black. "I am now going into you in spite of everything you can do", he tells her, and then approaches (always from the left). She feels an icy hand on the back of her neck and then suddenly he has entered her body. At once she is no longer herself. She speaks in a bass voice. Her face is contorted and vulgarized. And the point is that this little Magdalena saw the spirit come up to her from the left, just as her remotest ancestors had done.

The stories are all but innumerable. Lemaitre tells of a twelve-year-old boy who seems to have been caught masturbating, so he fell into a trance wherein he was possessed by, of all people, a man who spoke quite intelligible Armenian, though the patient had never, so far as anyone knew, heard the language before in his life.

Of course it was not only devils that inhabited the possessed. St Paula, who died in 404 heard men in Samaria that howled like wolves, and of course werewolves, both real and mythological, reappeared long afterward in Anglo-Saxon England and

[1] These cases are quoted in Oesterreich, T. K., *Possession, Demoniacal and Other*, trans. D. Ibberson. New York, 1966.

in Germany, where they roamed the forests, let their hair and nails grow, and sometimes attacked, killed and devoured children.

Sometimes it was not devils that possessed men, but the demon spirits of the dead, and there are many remarkable accounts in the literature of people so possessed. Here again we can go back in time to the very beginnings, for we saw how palaeolithic man probably worshipped and feared the dead who flitted like demon spirits on every side.

Now the church's attitude to these painful happenings was both consistent and sensible. Strangely enough, its exorcism of possessing demons seems to have been effective for reasons of which it was not usually aware. Justin Martyr in his *Apology* claims that "Numberless demoniacs throughout the whole world, and in your city (Rome) many of our Christian men ... have healed and do heal, rendering helpless and driving the possessing devils out of the men, though they could not be cured by all the other exorcists and those who used incantations and drugs".

And this was actually so, for early Christians possessed just those qualities most helpful in exorcism; a certainty of success and a profound purity that inspired trust in the victims. To be in the company, not of a sanctimonious, but of a really good man gives one even today a sense of peace not easily attainable on one's own, and the men of the first and second centuries were filled with a calm, lucid understanding of what they believed.

Even as he lay dying St Augustine is said in the *Acta Sanctorum* to have expelled demons by a laying on of hands. In the twelfth century Giraldus Cambrensis saw prophets in Wales who were "agitated and tortured like men possessed. Revelations came to them in dreams when as they said they tasted milk and honey in their mouths". And again we are forced to remember Plato's Bacchic maidens. St Bernard had a vast reputation as an exorcist, and it was probably justified, for he must have been a man of compelling spiritual strength.

The *Acta Sanctorum* is full of stories about the curing of

demoniacs. In the Church of St Ambrose in Milan when St Bernard was sitting near the altar between Masses while the clerks were singing, they "pointed out to him a little girl who was greatly tormented by the devil and begged him to help the poor little thing". He saw how she "ground her teeth and cried out so that she was an object of horror to all those who beheld her. He had pity on her youth and suffered with her suffering. So he picked up the paten of the chalice in which he meant to celebrate the divine mysteries, spilt some wine from it onto his fingers, praying silently but with great intentness, and touched the liquid to the child's lips, letting fall some drops upon her body. And all at once Satan, quite scalded, could no longer endure this holy goodness. Suddenly all quivering he came out in a stinking vomit. . . . In front of them all the girl who had been saved was taken home by her family, and the man of God, being much jostled by the crowd, reached the place where he was staying with great difficulty."

In Pavia he cured a married woman, but as soon as they took her home the devil returned. "The miserable husband did not know which way to turn. What was he to do? It seemed to him dangerous to live with a demoniac and impious to abandon her. He therefore arose, and taking his wife with him, returned to Pavia. There, as he did not meet the man of God, he pushed on to Cremona where he told him what had occurred and begged him with tears to lend his aid. The clemency of the Abbot did not repulse this pious request, but he commanded them to go into the church of the town and (before the body of confessors) to engage in prayer until he himself should come. Remembering then his promise, he went to the church with a single companion at the hour of twilight when others were going to bed, and passing the whole night in prayers, he obtained from God that which he asked, and health having been restored to the woman, he commanded her to return without anxiety to her house. But as he feared what had already occurred, the re-entry of the devil into her, he commanded that there should be fastened round her neck a notice bearing these words: In the name of our Lord Jesus Christ I command thee, demon, to dare to touch this woman no more. This command frightened the devil who was never afterwards minded to approach the woman after her return home."[1]

Bernard was a warrior priest, and achieved what contemporaries thought his miracles of exorcism by sheer hypnotic determination. But the gentle St Francis exercised a different sort of power. At Città di Castello a woman possessed by the devil was brought to the house where Father Francis was staying. She stood outside in the street, roaring and gnashing her teeth, so Francis sent a Brother out to her to find out if it was really a devil as she said. But "when the woman saw the Brother she laughed and mocked him, knowing it was not St Francis. The holy father was praying within, and when he had finished his prayer he came out; and then the woman began to tremble and to roll on the ground, unable to stand his power. St Francis called her to him and said, 'In virtue of obedience I bid thee go out of her, thou unclean spirit', and straightaway it left her, doing her no hurt, and departed very full of wrath."[2]

St Francis seems to have had a sense of humour too. In the *Fioretti* we read about a certain demoniac who ran away for miles across country, pursued by his anxious relatives. When they caught him and asked him why, he told them he had met a certain Brother Juniper whom he could not stand the sight of. Thereafter St Francis "when they brought to him those who were possessed to be healed, if the devils departed not straightaway at his command, would say, 'If thou come not out of this creature of God I will send for Brother Juniper to deal with thee'. And thereat the demon, fearing the presence of Brother Juniper and not being able to endure the virtue and humility of St Francis, would depart".[3]

But the devil was very often a match for sanctity, as innumerable stories remind us. There was Jeanne Pothierre, for example, the nun of Le Quesnoy, a middle-aged woman, but susceptible.

[1] Ernaldus, *Vita Bernardi Abbatis Claravallensis.* Paris, 1690.
[2] Thomas of Celano, *The Lives of St Francis of Assissi,* trans. A. G. Ferrers Howell. London, 1908.
[3] *The Little Flowers of St Francis,* trans. T. W. Arnold. London, 1899.

She fell in love with her confessor who, when she confessed her passion, promptly had himself moved to the next diocese. But according to the chroniclers of Hainault, the devil took the holy father's shape, returned to Le Quesnoy, climbed the convent wall and possessed her—she seems to have kept a journal—on four hundred and thirty-four separate occasions.

In other words people either dreaded demons or they desired them, but whichever they did the demons almost invariably appeared. In the sixteenth and seventeenth centuries, it has been computed, a nun could generally stand about ten years of incarceration before it killed her. By the end of that time the lack of exercise and sunlight, the gloom, the damp walls, the loneliness, the monotony and the sheer boredom of a life without any hope of change had planted in her the tuberculosis, the dysentery or one of the various fevers that carried her off. Many of the poor creatures actually went mad, and from being obsessed by hallucinations or dread of demons to falling in love was a very small step. But who was there to love? The gardener? The porter? The old man who carried in wood to the kitchens? Surely the young priest who came to hold Mass or hear confessions was far more suitable.

Of course if the nun was young and the priest virile and careless of consequences, then nature often ran its course with erotic pleasures heightened by a sense of shared perils and perhaps pangs of conscience which time and the confessional would eventually assuage. But it was different with the Provençal priest, Louis Gauffridi. Traveller, mystic, mountaineer and most agreeable preacher, he seems to have been a considerable success with women too. And this was all very well until about 1605, when a pretty, fair-haired girl of twelve, a certain Madeleine de la Palud, was confided to his care. She was the child of a distinguished family, and the worldly and extremely vulnerable Gauffridi lost his head.

It happened, I said, in Provence, and Provence is a country of hot summers and pale skies. The air shimmers. The very shadows are unsteady in the dusty roads. The ladies fan themselves in the arbours, and the young priest stands talking to them so wisely he might almost be a saint, and such a charming saint. But the affectionate little Madeleine, having given herself to him, already feels terrible moments of depression. She is ruined; she can never hope to marry.

So Gauffridi tells her that if he cannot marry her in the sight of God he will marry her in the sight of the devil. What he actually did we do not know. But he seems to have taken her to a witches' Sabbath, for years afterward she professed a fear of being carried off bodily to hell. Some sort of ceremony there was. He acquired a silver ring engraved with cabalistic signs and placed it on her finger. Then, perhaps to keep her quiet, he introduced her into a convent, an Ursuline convent to which he was confessor in the little town of Sainte-Baume.

Whether Gauffridi was caught there *in flagrante delicto* with his little mistress, or whether he became the lover of others too, whether the love-sick girl boasted or simply confided in one or two that she was the devil's concubine, has never been found out. But in a very short time indeed the convent was possessed by what Michelet very aptly called sheer midsummer madness. Madeleine was reputed to be the mistress of Beelzebub himself. Then a certain Louise Capeau turned out to have three devils. But that was not enough. Such a jealousy overcame her, such hatred of her fair-haired sister that, consciously or unconsciously, she determined to destroy them all.

Now enters an exorcist from Flanders, a certain Dr Dompt; but by this time the redoubtable Louise is quite out of her mind. She rates, she rebukes, she rages—twice every day in front of an audience, shouting, slandering, confessing to positive mon-strosities with never a stop for breath until Madeleine falls into convulsions, Louise attacks her and people have to drag the two women apart.

But Louise has not even started. In front of the exorcist and the Inquisitor, one Michaëlis, she calls on Gauffridi to repent and be converted. In the body of the church she shouts out that her lover must be arrested. He must be bound. He must be sent for trial and burned. Wherever she looks she can see sorcerers, devils—there—and there—all in priestly clothing. And the audience begins to be afraid of her.

The politics of it was all too complex to be set down here. Down in Marseilles the Capuchins banded together to get their errant brother out of his scrape. But it was hopeless. Gauffridi appeared at Sainte-Baume. Louise, already three parts out of her mind, alternated between begging God to save him and interrogating him in public, interrogating in cogent, damning inquisitorial fashion. And Gauffridi had no real defence. He was guilty.

Poor little Madeleine made it worse. Six hundred and sixty-six devils were exorcised out of her. She danced for her interrogators; she flaunted herself. She told them her dreams, how she stood naked at the Sabbath and the sorcerers adored her pretty body. Gauffridi turned up in her dreams with a rope around his neck.

One day a door was inadvertently left open and she fled to rejoin her lover. But she was recaptured, the silver ring taken from her and broken into pieces. She herself was trussed up, taken to Aix and thrown into a cellar full of old bones in a hope that they would bring her to her senses. And that finally tamed her.

The result of Gauffridi's trial at Aix was a foregone conclusion. Its most dramatic moment came when the still venomous and stridently dramatic Louise was asked what had happened to a devil in the shape of a toad that had been dragged out of Madeleine's body.

She turned, looked confusedly round the court, and there was a momentary silence. Suddenly, as though the motion were quite involuntary, her arm shot out and she pointed straight at Gauffridi. "There!" she screamed. "There it is, on his shoulder."

Madeleine herself, (still only nineteen, still pretty though they had cut off her hair, but by now not so much possessed as unbeloved), gave witness that "the accursed magician Lewes did first invent the saying of Masse at the Sabbaths and did really consecrate and present the sacrifice to Lucifer. The said magician did sprinkle the consecrated wine upon all the company, at which time everyone cryeth, *Sanguis eius super nos et filios nostros.*"

On the 30th of April, 1611 Gauffridi was burned at the stake in Aix. As for Madeleine, she, was immured on papal territory lest she confess more that might do damage to others. Her family cast her off. She was employed cutting wood to be sold for charity until in 1653 the Parliament of Aix condemned her to perpetual seclusion. Louise Capeau, she ranted on, accusing now one, now another of sorcery until she was able to see a second victim burned, a blind girl known to us only as Honorée.

In almost the same way the poor creatures at Loudun, driven out of their minds by loneliness, fear and bodily desire, killed Urbain Grandier and caused the deaths of three exorcists from terror and exhaustion. Hysteria is almost infinitely contagious. Freud believed that its origins lay in sexuality, and indeed these nuns, lacerated by the devils they could feel in their bodies danced, howled, writhed on the ground and shouted marvellously inventive obscenities to satisfy their audiences.

Gauffridi was guilty. Whether Grandier was guilty or innocent nobody knows to this day. He wrote to his mother from prison, "I bear my affliction with patience, and pity yours more than my own. I am very unwell, having no bed. Try to have mine brought me, for if the body does not rest the mind gives way. Send me also a breviary, my Bible and St Thomas for my consolation. For the rest, do not grieve. I hope that God will vindicate my innocence."

Chiefly one is struck by the rage, the blind hatred many of his accusers felt for him, a hatred inspired, one feels, not so much by his diabolism (if such it was) as by envy. "The Confessor whose authority was menaced", Michelet wrote, "the husband whose honour was attacked, the father whose feelings were outraged", all these united their jealousy and indignation at the wrong done to family life. One of these accusers actually walled up the room in which Grandier was held in the hope that he would be suffocated. And before he was at last dragged to the stake (he could not walk, for his legs had been broken) they made a bargain with him. If he would hold his tongue and not implicate others they would have him strangled before anyone lighted the faggots. And he agreed. But at the last moment when the wood was piled round him, his own confessor, not waiting for the executioner, set the sticks afire. "You have cheated me", Grandier shouted out. Then the smoke and the flame crackling drowned out anything else he might have wanted to say. That was on the 18th of August, 1634.

The story of another nun, Madeleine Bavent, would put to shame the most lurid of Gothic novels. An orphan girl of Rouen, she was early apprenticed to a clothmaker, a woman who made habits for nuns and who thus depended entirely on the good will of the church for her livelihood. The confessor of the house was a Franciscan. Before Madeleine arrived he had already seduced the three other girls working there, convincing them in some way or other that he would take them to a witches' Sabbath. When she was fourteen Madeleine became the fourth.

One has to imagine the no doubt attractive but illiterate girl, half frightened, half in awe at being paid attention by so important a man, shivering at the thought of having been given to the devil, but at the same time aware of her new dignity as a woman. She became filled with a confused, but intense piety.

No doubt with the friar's help, she was admitted as a novice in a newly established convent at Louviers. It was a small place, gloomy, secluded and superintended by a certain Father David, a priest already well past middle age and possessed of rather unusual ideas. Years earlier he had written a book attacking the abuses practiced in various religious houses. *Fouet des Paillards* it was called, A Whip for Wantons. At the same time he was an Adamite, a descendent of those old Brethren of the Free Spirit who believed that only in nakedness could one re-discover Adam's original innocence.

So novices were forced not only to take their daily exercise, but to go to chapel in the nude, and Madeleine first incurred the Lady Superior's displeasure by trying to hide her breasts with the altar cloth during communion. Perhaps it was because of this chiding that she refused any longer to make her confession to the Abbess. Instead she chose the good old priest, Father David. She was now sixteen.

The story is almost too vulgarly predictable. It simply has the virtue of being true. The other nuns, infected no doubt by the atmosphere of sanctified prurience, confronted for hours each day with each other's nakedness, began quite openly to engage in mutual masturbation and lesbian affairs. Old as he was, Father David made advances to the little novice. "The body cannot contaminate the soul," he assured her. "Sin only makes us humble and thus conquers sin." Madeleine kept as much out of the way of the others as she could. Then when she was eighteen Father David died.

His successor was a certain Picart, and by this time she was forbidden any other confessor, for nuns and Abbess alike were afraid of what she might disclose. Picart, assuring her that he possessed diabolic talismans inherited from his predecessor, introduced her to certain Sabbatical rites wherein she said later she had been "both altar and victim". And at last inevitably he seduced her and made her pregnant. What happened to the child she bore we do not know.

It was not original. It was not even particularly reprehensible. Cardinal Tencin, their contemporary, was living openly with a wife who was his sister. The Canons of Pignan in Provence, according to the *Histoire* of Renoux, had by tacit understanding a right to any nuns in Provence. There were sixteen of these Canons, and in the course of one particular year there were sixteen confessions of pregnancy made in neighbouring convents.

By this time Picart too was getting on in years, and he was terrified lest he lose the girl. He made her swear that she would kill herself when he died. He played on her fears of hellfire and the devil. He held little private orgies with her, introducing another nun and his vicar, a man called Boullé, for variety. He dipped the holy wafer in her blood, used it as a talisman and buried it in the convent garden. And at last Madeleine was possessed by the devil. Devils hemmed her in on every side. Other sisters began to catch the infection, and the Lady Abbess was pleased. Urbain Grandier had just been burned. Her convent was poor, and she was well aware what notoriety and increase of income just such happenings had recently brought to Loudun.

Then Picart died too and a certain Anne, another sister, swore she could see the devil standing naked at Madeleine's shoulder. Madeleine replied by swearing that she had seen Anne at a witches' Sabbath. The Lady Abbess had been there too.

So Madeleine was arrested, stripped, her body shaved and pricked to find the devil's mark (they found none), and she was sentenced to life imprisonment in a cellar dungeon in Rouen. But her removal did not stop the growing hysteria in Louviers. By now there were eighteen or twenty infected women there.

So Madeleine was moved farther away to the episcopal prison at Evreux and immured in an underground cell. Hoping to kill herself, she found spiders and ate them; she only vomited. She fought a never-ending battle against rats. With two stones for mortar and pestle she ground up a bottle and swallowed the powder. Nothing happened. She found a blunt knife, cut her belly open and tried to cut her throat, but the blade was not sharp enough. She stopped eating and began to see the devil in her dreams. The whole story is nothing but *grand guignol*. The gaolers, servants of the bishop's household, came down into her dungeon and, filthy as she was, turned her into their private whore. One of them gave her some poison for the rats, and she decided to take it herself, but her long dormant eagerness to live re-awoke and prevented her.

Instead, after having dreamed of the devil for weeks, suddenly she began praying for his help. She called to her gaolers, demanded to see the bishop and when she was brought before him, not only wrote out and signed numerous lists of her own crimes, but denounced others for having been her helpers. There were political opponents the authorities wanted to be rid of. She was told how to identify them and, brought face to face, she duly pointed them out as having been with her at the witches' Sabbath. They were burned.

Madeleine herself they no longer thought worth burning.

They left her door open. She could come and go as she pleased, but there was nowhere to go. Instead she confessed; she denounced. She developed an imagination of such wonderful ingenuity that whenever the authorities wanted evidence against this one or that they went to Madeleine and the evidence was duly supplied. Old Picart's body was dug up out of its grave and burned. The vicar, Boullé, was brought to trial, condemned, drawn on a hurdle to the fish market, and there on the 21st of August, 1647, put to the stake. The convent of Louviers was broken up and whatever young women still lived there were sent back to their homes. The last record we have of Madeleine Bavent lists her as still living in the prison at Rouen.

There are enough similar accounts of demoniac possession to fill several volumes. But I shall end with a different kind of story, one particularly vivid and not without humour, taken from the autobiography of a Polish Jew who lived in the early nineteenth century.[1] It is quoted in Oesterreich, and since I have not been able to lay hands on the book in its original German, I am using Ibberson's translation as printed in Oesterreich's *Possession.*

"... A crowd assembled. 'The dibbuk is coming.' A big strong girl with disordered hair and an agitated face was rather dragged than led in by men and women. She begged to be taken back to the house and reiterated incessantly, 'I feel better already.'

"Sights like this were not new to me. I had already often seen possessed persons at home and knew their fate. . . .

"The present case interested me very particularly. I had as a matter of fact learned that the spirit inhabiting this girl was a *bachour* of great Talmudic learning. Having become an Epicurean through reading heretical works, he had fled secretly from Bethamidrasch and succeeded in reaching Germany. There his co-religionists cared for him and enabled him to study. But in the course of time he revealed himself as so profound a heretic that it became too much for the German Jews and his protectors withdrew from him. He struggled for some time in the bitterest

[1] Fromer, Jacob, *Ghetto Dämmerung.* Leipzig, 1812.

distress and was finally obliged to give up his studies. He took to drink, frequented dubious society, and was finally imprisoned. After that he was packed off to his own home. His parents would have nothing to do with a son who spoke German and dressed in European style. His co-religionists insulted, despised and stoned him. In despair he went to the local clergyman and was baptized. But neither could or would the Christians do anything for him. Sunk in depravity and a physical and moral wreck through alcohol, suffering and privations, he was incapable of sustained work. The only help given to him took the form of permission to sit before the church among the beggars and eke out his miserable existence with alms. In the end he was unable to endure this life of shame; he drowned himself.

"When I heard the story of this unfortunate man related I was seized with a painful feeling which first became clear to me much later through the knowledge of the Buddhist saying: *Tat twam asi* (so art thou thyself). I knew that this girl was sick, deranged in mind, and that she had nothing to do with the dead man's destiny. Nevertheless mass-suggestion had so wrought upon me that I was anxious to learn by her mouth something about the poor wretch's fate.

"The wide and spacious room where the girl had been brought and seated on a chair in the middle was filled with the serried ranks of the crowd. I had a good place from which I could see and hear everything. She sat down, languid and exhausted, with haggard, fearful eyes, and from time to time lamented, begging to be taken back to the house because she was afraid of the wonder-rabbi. Her voice, weak and beseeching, inspired sympathy and compassion. Suddenly she sprang up and made efforts to remain standing.

" '*Silentium strictissimum!*'

"I could not believe my ears. It was a real man's voice, harsh and rough, and the onlookers affirmed that it was exactly the voice of the *meshoummed*, the baptized man. Not one of us knew the meaning of these words. We only knew that it was a strange language which the sick woman understood as little as ourselves. 'Ladies and gentlemen,' continued she. . . . Then she pronounced a long, confused discourse with High German turns of phrase, of which I understood only that it greeted a festive gathering and wished to draw attention to the meaning of the feast.

"She broke off in the middle of this speech and burst into a frightful laugh which made us shudder to the marrow. . . . I was as if thunderstruck.

"A murmur arose: 'the rabbi is coming.'

"The crowd drew aside respectfully to make room for the new arrival. A short, rotund little man came in sight, dressed from head to foot in white. Around the long white *talar* which fell to his feet was swathed a wide white sash, and his head was covered with a white *streimel* [a fur trimmed hat]. The full cheeks hung like peaches in his face with its complexion of mingled blood and milk, while long and bushy eyebrows overhung his eyes. In one hand he held a *shofar* (a horn) and in the other a *loulaf* (a frond of palm). He entered at a run, chanting Hebrew verses, and followed by a secretary and servants, until arrived in front of the girl, he handed the *loulaf* and the *shofar* to the secretary and lifted up his eyebrows with his hands. From his coal-black eyes shone a light like the sparkle of a diamond; the girl was unable to sustain his look and lowered her eyes in confusion. Two lighted tapers were brought and the rabbi began his address. 'In the name of the forty-two letters of the God with long sight which has indeed no end, in the name of the lesser and greater celestial families, in the name of the chiefs of the bodyguard: Sandolfon, Uriel, Akatriel and Usiel, in the name of the potent Metateron surrounded with strength, awe-inspiring, vouchsafing salvation or damnation, I adjure thee, abject spirit, outcast from hell, to reply to my words and obey all my commands.'

"Stifling heat prevailed in the room. Through the wide, high windows fell the rays of a burning August sun which flooded the rapt faces of the crowd.

" 'What is thy name?' the rabbi asked the sick woman in a loud, harsh voice. 'Esther,' replied the girl softly and faintly, trembling all over.

" 'Silence, thou *chazufe*' (impudent woman), cried the rabbi. 'I asked not thee, but the dibbuk.'

"'There was a long silence.

" 'Wilt thou or wilt thou not reply?' resumed the rabbi, making as if to strike the girl with the *loulaf*.

" 'Do not strike me,' implored the man's voice. 'I will reply.' 'What is they name?' 'Christian Davidovitch.' '*Jemach shemo*' (may his name be blotted out), spat the rabbi, stopping his ears. 'I would know thy Jewish name.' 'Chaim.' 'And what was thy mother's name?' 'Sarah.' 'Chaim ben Sarah,' commanded the rabbi, 'relate what occurred after thy death.'

"The dibbuk told a long story. After death he had been cast out of hell with insults and approbrium. He wandered for a long time, but could no longer remain without habitation and finally entered into a pig.

" 'How like a *meshoummed!*' murmured the entranced on-lookers.

"That was not too bad. When the pig was slaughtered he passed into a horse, where he had a very poor time. It was a draughthorse which had to work hard, receive many blows and never eat his fill. At length he decided to try man. The occasion was propitious. He knew that Esther had illicit relations with a young man, and watched for the moment when she abandoned herself to his embraces; at that instant he was permitted to enter into her. He ended his narrative by begging not to be driven out; in life and after death he had suffered so greatly that they should have pity on him and grant him a little rest.

"This prayer appeared to make no impression on the rabbi. With an air of asperity he took the *shofar* from the hand of his secretary and put it to his mouth. But what is this? In spite of all his efforts he was unable to make any sound. Some minutes passed in anxious waiting. The rabbi put forth all his strength, sweat poured from his brow and still no sound was heard. He gave up the attempt and remained for some instants plunged in deep meditation. Suddenly his face cleared; an inspiration of genius appeared to flash across his brow; he whispered something in his secretary's ear, and the latter went away quietly and returned with a piece of wax. The rabbi snatched it from his hands and stopped the two openings of the refractory instrument. He tested carefully whether the closure was complete, then burst into a triumphant laugh, saying, 'Now see, accursed Satan, how thou canst get out!'

"He raised the *shofar* to his mouth. Now everything went beautifully.

"*Tekio!* and a clear, forthright blast rang out.

"*Teruo!* A resounding noise rent the air.

"*Shevorim!* The notes gushed forth in rapid succession.

"*Tekio gedolo!* This time it was a sound and piercing sound.

"*Abbela Srallok!* burst forth the man's voice suddenly with the same strident laughter as before.

"Abbela was the rabbi's name. *Srallok* is a coarse insult. The rabbi changed colour and shook with rage and excitement. He had never yet encountered such impudence. But he recovered his self-control rapidly, seized the *loulaf* and struck the girl violently in the face with it. Then an incredible thing happened; the girl had freed her hands with lightning speed and before anyone could prevent her she dealt the rabbi two resounding blows on the ears.

"A panic followed. The frightened crowd uttered cries and oaths, storming and weeping with excitement. Never had the like been seen. Nevertheless strong arms had seized the sick girl, the rabbi struck her so furiously with the *loulaf* that her face streamed with blood; she collapsed with a terrible cry and became unconscious. At this moment a noise was heard at the window as if it had been struck by a small stone. Everyone rushed towards it and discovered in one pane a hole the size of a pea, through which aperture the spirit had fled. The girl was carried out.

"After this scene I was as if transformed. I had come there as an unbeliever, an atheist, ostensibly to study on the spot superstition, religious dementia. The experience of an hour had sufficed to overthrow like a house of cards the independent ideas which I had acquired by years of study, trial and struggles. In vain I told myself a thousand times that the girl was ill, that she had been in touch with the dead man in his lifetime and might have imitated his voice and manner of speech. In vain I asserted that the rabbi had executed an illusion with involuntary comic effect. Before me were thousands of men, older, more experienced, wiser than I. They all believed in the existence of the dibbuk, they had seen the spirit come out, they had heard the impact on the window and seen the hole in the pane. They all attested that the rabbi had times without number cured incurable sicknesses, recalled the dead to life, and brought to light inscrutable mysteries.

"Now that I am committing these thoughts to writing I can, if I wish, call these men fools. What is there to prevent me? I am sitting alone in my room, have paper and pen and can think and write what I please. But at that moment I found myself like a single and tiny intelligence amongst thousands of stronger ones which weighed me down, absorbed me and carried me away. My brain had almost ceased to work. I gave myself up entirely to the sensations and emotions which assailed me so powerfully."

Oesterreich comments that the account offers us no unusual psychological information and is insufficient to make us admit the presence of parapsychological phenomena. Of course he is right. But the audience believed, and that is the real point. For it is with what people have believed that I am primarily concerned. The first thing the hysterical girl said was that she wanted to go home. She was feeling better already, and the most obvious psychiatric theory would be that the dibbuk had entered her body when she developed a neurosis because of her illicit affair, that here in public she went through a process of self-analysis, became aware of the trauma and brought about the abreaction necessary for cure. Madeleine de la Palud and Madeleine Bavent had had exactly the same experience. The devil had possessed them when they had done a thing they had been taught was wrong.

But in this case the rabbi had been perfectly right, and through his good offices the devil had been expelled.

13

As Europe and then America moved like unwieldy hulks into what seemed at last a calm and rational tide, it looked as though the devil had disappeared into thin air. Empires of the spirit began to be turned by sleight of hand into empires piled up in warehouses. We stopped killing witches—the last was a poor girl called Anna Maria Schwägel, decapitated in Kempten in 1775. Instead we locked them up in madhouses. We made Sunday outings to point and laugh and jabber at them sitting in the straw.

We no longer fought wars because we were on the side of God, but because we were on the side of civilization, and civilization, we told ourselves, was exemplified by clear, crisp thinking and the acquisition of material goods. On several occasions we tore down and built the world again, and that was good. The terrible devil of St Bernard was turned into the rational devil of Bernard Shaw, and hobgoblins to frighten children into funny little figures that amused them. We tamed whatever we could see. The natural world that had once been full of demons became no more than a tank full of iron and oil, and everything around us could be explained in material terms. That also was good.

But before one could accept the material as the only and indeed the best of all possible worlds, one had to account for three annoying bits of contradictory evidence. The first was simply a banal sense that would not go away of something being wrong. The second was that in a rational society there were people amongst us who possessed such an intense vitality that they actually wanted to destroy what they had had a share in making. They searched out the devil as an irrational counterpoise to arithmetic. And thirdly, with increasing frequency, certain teasing phenomena appeared that physics and chemistry simply could not explain.

The mind, for example (the whole thing had started in the mind), was still largely unexplored. More important, it looked to be largely unexplorable, and I shall explain this seeming heresy in a moment. But to start on the simplest level, we accept as a fact the existence of psychosomatic disease. A man falls ill or dies when there is apparently nothing wrong with him. The primitive said his death was caused by a demon, but demons cannot be called up in the laboratory. More pertinently, the "demon" originating in the brain could bring about physical effects out of nonphysical causes. By the end of the nineteenth century there had been some 321 saints psychically marked with physical stigmata that imitated Christ's wounds. Rybolkin produced blisters by touching a patient's hand to a cold surface which the patient had been told was hot.

Our minds can cause us to "see" and "hear" things which do not exist. We accept this as a fact and call such phenomena hallucinations. Perhaps—we postulate—they are like dreams or are caused telepathically. The dying mother speaks to her child and he "hears" her a hundred miles away. The wife "appears" to her husband, wearing clothes she bought in his absence, and informs him of some fact which otherwise he had no way of knowing. Soal and Bowden worked with two young Welsh boys, subjected them to the most careful scrutiny, and under laboratory conditions that ruled out any possibility of fraud, saw one of the boys—twenty-five times in a row—"read" a card that the other had looked at.[1] The chances against their doing this by accident are several million millions to one.

We are forced to accept such evidence, for this was not hallucination. So there presumably exist certain electrical waves we cannot yet describe. But what shall we say then of a hallucination that appears to two or more people at the same time? There seems to be "a complete machinery in the personality for producing visual imagery exactly like that of normal perception up to the range of a complete environment."[2]

H. H. Price, Professor of Logic at the University of Oxford, adds in his introduction to the same volume that there have even been a few experimental cases "where person A by a deliberate effort of the will, has succeeded in causing another person B to experience an apparition of him at a distance". And "the very existence of collective cases is on the face of it a grave difficulty for any telepathic theory of apparitions. Surely a telepathic hallucination ought to be a purely private phenomenon . . . but in fact it is sometimes experienced by indifferent bystanders as well. The notion of a public hallucination is a very strange one, almost as strange as the notion of a public dream."

These are embarrassing facts. It makes one wonder if Christ's reincarnation might not have been such a collective hallucination, for according to the Gospels he appeared and disappeared in just the way that apparitions are said to do. It may be that Simon Magus did indeed seem to rise in the air in front of Nero as he had said he would, and that we have no need to imagine a complicated set of wires that helped him do it.

But we are not done. Telepathically-induced hallucination may yet be explained and demonstrated in the laboratory. Telekinetic phenomena, on the other hand, are something else, and the evidence for these is simply inexplicable by any rational means. One is aware of the possibility, indeed of the frequent likelihood of fraud. But the phenomena have been reported by so many diverse witnesses, corroborated on many occasions by

[1] Soal, S. G. and Bowden, H. T., *The Mind Readers, Some Recent Experiments in Telepathy.* London, 1959.
[2] Tyrrell, G. N. M., *Apparitions.* London, 1953.

people of such integrity and intelligence that in the end it becomes almost impossible to doubt them. Here, for example, is a statement made by one William Higgs, a London police constable, who on the night of the 2nd of March, 1883, was sent for to the house of a man called White, a horse dealer in Worksop.

"I went round to the kitchen at 11.55 p.m. as near as I can judge, and found Joe White in the kitchen of his house. There was one candle lighted in the room, and a good fire burning, so that one could see things pretty clearly. The cupboard doors were open, and White went and shut them and then came and stood against the chest of drawers. I stood near the outer door. No one else was in the room at the time. White had hardly shut the cupboard doors when they flew open and a large glass jar came out past me and pitched in the yard outside, smashing itself. I didn't see the jar leave the cupboard or fly through the air; it went too quick. But I am quite sure it wasn't thrown by White or anyone else. White couldn't have done it without my seeing him. The jar couldn't go in a straight line from the cupboard out of the door, but it certainly did go.

"Then White asked me to see the things which had been smashed in the inner room. He led the way and I followed. As I passed the chest of drawers in the kitchen I noticed a tumbler standing on it. Just after I passed I heard a crash, and looking round I saw that the tumbler had fallen on the ground in the direction of the fireplace and was broken. I don't know how it happened. There was no one else in the room.

"I went into the inner room and saw the bits of pots and things on the floor, and then I came back with White into the kitchen. The girl, Rose, had come into the kitchen during our absence. She was standing with her back against the bin near the fire. There was a cup standing on the bin, rather nearer the door. She said to me, 'Cup'll soon go; it's been down three times already'. She then pushed it a little farther on the bin and turned round and stood talking to me by the fire. She had hardly done so when the cup jumped up suddenly about four or five feet into the air and then fell on the floor and smashed itself. White was sitting on the other side of the fire."

A doctor had been called, and he now joined them. So did three other people who were neighbours. The constable writes: "Suddenly a basin which stood on the end of the bin near the door got up into the air, turning over and over as it went. It went up not very quickly, not as quickly as if it had been thrown. When it reached the ceiling it fell plump and smashed. I called Dr Lloyd's attention to it, and we all saw it. No one was near it, and I don't know how it happened. I stayed about ten minutes more, but saw nothing else. I don't know what to make of it all. I don't think White or the girl could possibly have done the things which I saw."

The case was investigated by Frank Podmore for the Society for Psychical Research. He searched the house thoroughly, but "could discern no holes in the walls or ceilings, nor any trace of the extensive and elaborate machinery which would have been required to produce the movements by ordinary mechanical means".[1]

White himself had stated that: "Dr Lloyd came in with my wife, and Higgs showed him what had happened in the inner room. Then when we had got into the kitchen again, and were all standing near the door of the inner room—Higgs, my wife, and Tom and Wass, and Lloyd—who was about six feet from the bin, and the nearest to it of our party—we all saw a basin which was lying on the bin near the door, get up two or three times in the air, rising slowly a few inches or perhaps a foot and then falling plump. Then it got up higher, and went slowly, wobbling as it went up to the ceiling, and when it had reached the ceiling, it fell down all at once and broke itself. Dr Lloyd then looked in the bin, saying the devil must be in the house, and then left."

Arthur Currass, a coal miner, whom Podmore describes as "a Methodist and apparently a very steady, respectable man," stated that: "The girl Rose was coming out of the kitchen toward the inner door, but had not got quite up to it. She seemed to be much frightened. White said to me, 'It doesn't matter a damn where that lass goes, there's something smashes'.

[1] Report by Frank Podmore in the *Proceedings* of the Society for Psychical Research, Vol. XII. June, 1896.

The clock [which had fallen] was taken right away into the yard and placed on an empty cask, and there it stayed. White and I were alone in the front room when the clock fell. White and I then went into the back kitchen, and I remained about four feet from the outer door, with my face toward the fireplace. I then saw a pot dog leap from the mantelpiece and come within five feet of the pantry door and break, passing close to me. There was nothing attached to it and there was no one near it."

This was not trickery. Nor was it anyone's hallucination. When the girl, Rose, was sent away the manifestations ceased. In most of the reported cases—and for whatever inexplicable reason—there is a young girl at the heart of the trouble. Sometimes the disturbances follow her from house to house, yet she is invariably found to be physically innocent, and sometimes incapable of having caused whatever trouble occurred.

As I said earlier, "*Il n'y a que le premier pas qui coûte.*" It looks as though whether we believe it or not we are billeted in a world full of invisible lunatics. All we can do is lie in the dark and listen to the clockwork of that world of which, in spite of the scientific revolution, we understand hardly anything at all.

Whether the Poltergeist has anything to do with the devil I cannot say, except that it gives the lie to our notions of a purely material universe. Lighted matches drop off a naked ceiling. A horse is found in a hayroom, the door of which is too small even to admit a man. Furniture, sometimes too heavy for all the people in the house to have lifted, is piled into the middle of a room. Objects move through the air too slowly to have been thrown. A stone weighing ten pounds comes flying up out of a well. A woman in her sixties lying in a suburban bed is burned to death, but there is no fire in the house and her sheets and blankets are found not even to have been scorched. Doors to empty rooms are locked from the inside. Noises are heard, thumpings, bangings, loud, regular and unmistakable, quite without visible cause, but repeated over and over again. The phenomena continue for days, weeks, sometimes even years. They are perceived by dozens of witnesses. Things even move about in a house when nobody is there.

This is not the levitation of a St Francis, reported by some disciple, perhaps under the influence of a self-induced hypnosis. This is not Daniel Dunglas Home, the spiritualist, who one night in London in front of several witnesses floated out of a third-storey window in Victoria Street and back in through another. He was very probably a fraud. This is not even the witch doctor who purports to see things happening at a distance (and very likely does), but who may be playing on the gullibility of his audience. It is not a faith healer curing hysterically-induced illnesses.

As far as one can judge, certain telekinetic forces seem to exist for which no one has found any reasonable explanation. Sir William Barrett, FRS goes over to Ireland to unmask a young carpenter who keeps being pulled out of bed at night. The bedroom is examined with a meticulous attention to detail. The bed is dragged away from the wall, searched and remade. In front of three witnesses the young man gets into bed and twice in full view of them all is pulled out with the sheet still under him and a sweat of pure terror on his face. He finds new lodgings and is never heard from again.

Young Hetty Wesley was turned out of her bed too, in her father's parsonage. Years afterward her brother John set down an account of what had happened. He mentioned his sister Molly who said, "It signifies nothing to run away, for whatever it is can run faster than me".

"Till this time," he wrote, "my father had never heard the least disturbance in his study. But the next evening, as he attempted to go into his study (of which none had any key but himself) when he opened the door, it was thrust back with such violence as had like to have thrown him down. However he thrust the door open and went in. Presently there was knocking, first on one side, then on the other, and after a time in the next room wherein my sister Nancy was. He went into that room and (the noise continuing) adjured it to speak, but in vain. He then said, 'These spirits love darkness; put out the candle and perhaps it will speak'. She did so, and he repeated his adjuration, but still there was only knocking and no articulate sound. Upon this he said, 'Nancy, two Christians are an overmatch for the devil. Go all of you downstairs. It may be when I am alone, he will have courage to speak'. When she was gone a thought came in and he said, 'If thou art the spirit of my son Samuel, I pray, knock three knocks and no more'. Immediately all was silence, and there was no more knocking at all that night.

"I asked my sister Nancy (then about fifteen years old) whether she was not afraid when my father used that adjuration. She answered she was sadly afraid it would speak when she put out the candle. But she was not at all afraid in the day time when it walked after her as she swept the chambers, as it constantly did, and seemed to sweep after her. Only she thought it might have done it *for her* and saved her the trouble."

I have brought the ghost in by the heels simply to demonstrate that, while much of what I have set down in this devil's history is a record of subjectively induced phenomena, there is a residue that neither I nor anyone else can rationally explain. If the physical world is the only reality, if nothing exists except what can be shown in a laboratory to exist, then our equipment is inadequate and our methodology somewhere at fault. And we are left with a little Welsh boy who can "read" the faces of twenty-five invisible cards in a row.

Hellfire faded in the light of reason, but Satan remained no less intriguing a figure than he had always been, for most of us enjoy a certain irrational wickedness. In the early eighteenth century there were gangs of well-to-do young men roaming the streets of London who called themselves Mohocks. They were the only devils left, for as Dr Burney said years afterward in a letter still unpublished, they sallied out and "cut people's noses with a sniggersnee, for 'twas a way they had".

At about the same time or a few years afterward Bubb Dodington, John Wilkes and Sir Francis Dashwood founded their Hellfire Club at Medmenham Abbey in Buckinghamshire. They and their friends are said to have brought girls down from London, celebrated Black Masses, drunk, copulated, invoked Satan and no doubt enjoyed themselves enormously. *Fay ce que voudras*, do what you will, they inscribed over the doorway, for

Rabelais had written that that was the motto of his Abbey of Thelema in *Gargantua*. Dashwood became Chancellor of the Exchequer, Dodington, Treasurer of the Navy, and Wilkes, among many other things, Fellow of the Royal Society and Lord Mayor of London.

Satanism had, in short, degenerated into a love for the macabre or an excuse for the venting of high spirits. A generation after the Hellfire Club had been disbanded and when Dashwood was bumbling about as a septuagenarian Postmaster General, bands of young German noblemen terrorized the peasantry by riding the roads at night in death's head masks, tumbling the occasional peasant girl in a haycock and now and then celebrating a Black Mass in some barnyard by the light of a dozen or so guttering candles.

Rasputin was said to have been in league with the devil. At least he seems to have possessed all the devil's virility, and like Rebecca West, when it came time for him to be murdered, died very hard. Aleister Crowley, on the other hand, the best known of twentieth-century Satanists, died gently, and according to John Symonds his last words were a whispered, "I am perplexed".

"Do what thou wilt shall be the whole of the law", had been his watchword. He had ranted and plunged like a stallion from Nepal to New York. And he too had founded an Abbey of Thelema—on the island of Cefalu off Sicily. It seems to have been a miserable ramshackle place, but Crowley had lived there with his mistresses and followers, alternately bickering and offering sacrifices to whatever primitive spirits he could conjure up either out of his voluminous reading or out of his paranoid imagination.

At the age of twelve he had crucified a toad as an experiment in the invocation of occult powers. At fifty on Cefalu he had had one naked mistress mounted by a goat whose throat he cut at the moment of orgasm so that its blood would gush out over her back. He had called down curses on the heads of those who offended him. He had attracted women who clung to him, but who then killed themselves or went mad or simply ran away. He had been for many years a heroin addict, and injected himself with as much as eleven grains a day. He had fathered several children, two of whom died of neglect. He had written innumerable pamphlets, poems, plays, magical treatises, stories and experiments in erotica. And when he finally lay dying, a frail old man in a boarding house in Hastings, the tears kept rolling down his cheeks and he did not know the "truth" any more. He was "perplexed".

So that devil died, not with a bang, but with a whimper, and the few devils left amongst us are like commercial travellers scrabbling to make a maximum of pennies from a minimum of sins. One is the pastor of a Satanic Church in California. Another wrote about her diabolism and retired to Florida on the earnings. A third leads housewifely covens through drab little rituals in Sussex. Still others keep shops where ointments can be bought to help one fly, or charms acquired that are guaranteed to turn one's antagonists into frogs.

Plato's Bacchic maidens or the pythoness at Delphi would weep to see what we have made of them. Jacob wrestling with the angel, St Bernard with his conscience, Jesus in Gethsemane with the fate that was about to befall him, Luther with a devil as real as his own right hand, the flagellants, the young girl drowning, breathless with divinity, in Jutland, St Asella with the cartilagenous lumps on her knees, St Brigit who would not bathe, Brother Michael who died singing *Te Deum* in the square in Florence, the small slave, Blandina, hanging on the cross in Lyons, Arnold's mistress who fled into the bonfire in Cologne— they simply would not be able to understand so great a waste of spirit. For very few of us, after all that suffering in the name of the spirit, wonder more than idly about an infinite that lies close around us like a shroud.

In our own lifetimes we are watching the disintegration of social structures older than written history. Ten thousand years have taught us that individuals can not exist for long except as members of a social and spiritual organism. But we aspire to what we call progress and measure our rates of growth arithmetically, as though economics were the be-all and the end-all.

God and the devil have turned big business. But as Herbert Read wrote in *Art and Industry*, "Between functional thinking and imaginative thinking there can be no compromise. One mode of thought is based on the principle of causality, and its method is logical; the other is based on symbolic discourse and its method is creative. One relies on the accumulation of knowledge; the other is an extension of consciousness."

It sounds simplistic to say that the only evil we cannot comprehend is that there is a mysterious innocence always in the process of being lost. Our yesterdays are frightening and momentous. They lie out beyond the gate I can see from my window as I write, for I live on the edge of a hamlet wherein there are only six small cottages, a church and a fistful of farms. My neighbours have been in turn pagan, Catholic, nonconformist and certain only of one thing, that perpetual regeneration is the one real function of the world.

Last winter a child was born at the post office. Last month a farmer died and was buried. At this moment I can hear new lambs bleating in Lower Field. The sun rises like a burnished little kettle over the hills; buds burst in the orchard; the bull bellows in Church House meadow. A neighbour walks past outside the gate with a forkful of hay on his shoulder, and then the Vicar strides up the road, cassock billowing like a sail, but the power all spilled out of him, for he and his like are merely episodes. The hamlet, the organism, is older than its church. It will be here when the church has tumbled into a pile of building stone. Delphi lasted three thousand years.

The primordial things are commonplace, frog voices in the pond, crickets, a bull bellowing, the sun climbing up out of the bracken high over Red Hill. If we understand this we have begun to see our ideas of causality in perspective and become part not only of the past, but of both God and devil, for it is in these things that God and the devil were born and where they live.

I end where I began. Even in Birmingham or Pittsburgh people can hear panpipes trilling. And with an uneasy, inward sense they long for some lost paradise where under green boughs both the devil and God stand laughing. I do not mean that either of these creatures is here or there or anywhere. They are within us, but to identify them is the whole purpose of life.

In a moment a new Pandora will look, a new Eve will pluck and eat. At some one time for each individual it starts all over again, and whatever hinders awareness of this important episode is simply a distraction. Without awareness we are like Plato's spectators that sat with their backs to the light, looking their whole lives long at shadows that passed for reality.

Glascwm,
Radnorshire.
15 March, 1973.

Bibliography

Anon., *Ophiolatreia, an Account of Serpent Worship.* (n.d.).
Apuleius, Lucius, *The Golden Ass*, trans. Robert Graves. Harmonds-
worth, 1950.
Augustine, *De Civitate Dei.* Many editions.
Arnold of Liège, *Alphabetum Narrationum*, a fifteenth-century trans-
lation, ed. Mary MacLeod Banks, 2 vols. EETS. London, 1905.
Bodin, Jean, *De la Démonomanie des Sourciers.* Rouen, 1604.
Boguet, Henri, *Discours des Sourciers.* Lyons, 1608.
Brand, John, *Observations on the Popular Superstitions of Great Britain.*
3 vols. London, 1848.
Briggs, K. N., *Pale Hecate's Team.* London, 1962.
Budge, E. A. Willis, *The Gods of the Egyptians.* London, 1904.
Campbell, John Gregorson, *Superstitions of the Highlands.* Glasgow,
1902.
Castiglione, Arturo, *Adventures of the Mind.* London, 1947.
Caesarius Heisterbacensis, *Dialogus Miraculorum*, ed. Strange.
Cologne, 1851.
Cohn, Norman, *The Pursuit of the Millennium.* London, 1957.
Coulton, G. G., *Life in the Middle Ages*, 4 vols. Cambridge, 1928–30.
De Lancre, Pierre, *L'Incredulité et Mescréance du Sortilège.* Paris, 1622.
Ewen, C. L'Estrange, *Witchcraft and Demonianism.* London, 1933.
Fisher, G. P., *The History of the Church.* London, 1890.
Forsyth, J. S., *Demonologia.* London, 1827.
Frazer, Sir James, *The Golden Bough*, 13 vols. London, 1932–36.
Geikie, James, *Prehistoric Europe.* London, 1881.
Gibbon, Edward, *The Decline and Fall of the Roman Empire*, 7 vols.
London, 1853.
Glanvill, Joseph, *Saducismus triumphatus.* London, 1689.
Glob, P. V., *The Bog People.* London, 1969.
Glover, T. R., *The Conflict of Religions in the Early Roman Empire.*
London, 1909.
Gomme, George Lawrence, *Folklore Relics of Early Village Life.*
London, 1877.
Graves, Robert, *The White Goddess.* London, 1962.
Grimm, Jacob, *Deutsche Mythologie.* Göttingen, 1835.
Guazzo, Francesco Maria, *Compendium Maleficarum*, trans. E. A.
Ashwin. London, 1929.

Gwatkin, H. N., *Early Church History to AD 313,* 2 vols. London, 1912.

Hansen, Chadwick, *Witchcraft at Salem.* London, 1970.

Harnack, A., *Die Mission und Ausbreitung des Christentums in den ersten drei Jahrhunderten.* Leipzig, 1915.

Harrison, W., *Description of England,* ed. F. J. Furnivall. London, 1877.

Hughes, Pennethorne, *Witchcraft.* London, 1952.

James, William, *The Varieties of Religious Experience.* London, 1968.

Janssens, Paul A., *Palaeopathology.* London, 1970.

Jung, C. G., *Memories, Dreams, Reflections.* London, 1963.

Kittredge, G. L., *Witchcraft in Old and New England.* Harvard, 1929.

Klaatsch, Hermann, *The Evolution and Progress of Mankind,* trans. Joseph McCabe. London, 1923.

Koestler, Arthur, *The Ghost in the Machine.* London, 1967.

Kramer, Heinrich and Sprenger, Jacobus, *Malleus Maleficarum,* trans. Montague Summers. London, 1928.

Lang, Andrew, *The Meaning of Religion.* London, 1898.

Lecky, William, *The Rise and Influence of the Spirit of Rationalism in Europe,* 2 vols. London, 1933.

Lévi, Éliphas (Alphonse Louis Constant), *The History of Magic,* trans. Arthur Edward Waite. London, 1972.

Lévy-Bruhl, Lucien, *Les Fonctions des Sociétés Inférieures.* Paris, 1910.

— *Primitive Mentality,* trans. Lilian A. Clare. London, 1923.

Lissner, Ivar, *Man, God and Magic.* London, 1961.

Mather, Cotton, *Wonders of the Invisible World.* London, 1862.

Mauss, Marcel, *The Gift,* trans. Ian Cunnison. London, 1969.

— *A General Theory of Magic,* trans. Robert Brain. London, 1972.

— (with Henri Hubert), *Sacrifice,* trans. W. D. Halls. London, 1968.

Merivale, Patricia, *Pan the Goat God.* Harvard, 1969.

Michelet, Jules, *La Sourcière.* Paris, 1862.

Murray, Margaret Alice, *The Witch Cult in Western Europe.* Oxford, 1921.

— *The God of the Witches.* London, 1933.

Notestein, Wallace, *History of Witchcraft in England.* Washington, 1911.

Nutt, Alfred, *The Fairy Mythology of Shakespeare.* London, 1900.

Oesterreich, T. K., *Possession, Demoniacal and Other,* trans. D. Ibberson. New York, 1966.

Panofsky, Dora and Erwin, *Pandora's Box.* London, 1956.

Piggott, Stuart, *Ancient Europe.* Edinburgh, 1965.

Pitcairn, Robert, *Criminal Trials.* Edinburgh, 1833.

Remy, Nicholas, *Demonolatry,* trans. E. A. Ashwin, London, 1930.

Robbins, Rossell Hope, *The Encyclopedia of Witchcraft and Demonology.* New York, 1959.

Rohde, Erwin, *Psyche*. Tübingen, 1898.
Rose, Elliot, *Razor for a Goat*. Toronto, 1962.
Scot, Reginald, *Discoverie of Witchcraft*. London, 1584.
Scott, Sir Walter, *Letters on Demonology and Witchcraft*. London, 1884.
Sinclair, George, *Satan's Invisible World Discovered*. Edinburgh, 1871.
Sitwell, Sacheverell, *Poltergeists*. London, 1940.
Soal, S. G. and Bowden, H. T., *The Mind Readers, some Recent Experiments in Telepathy*. London, 1959.
Southey, Robert, *Life of John Wesley*, 2 vols. London, 1925.
Squire, Charles, *The Mythology of the British Islands*. London, 1905.
Stengel, Paul, *Die Griechische Kultusaltertümer*. München, 1898.
Stevenson, H. (ed.) *Chronicon de Lanercost*. Maitland Club. Glasgow, 1839.
Storr, Anthony, *Human Aggression*. London, 1968.
Symonds, John, *The Great Beast*. London, 1951.
Tacitus, Cornelius, *Annales*. Many editions.
— *Germania*. Many editions.
Thomas of Celano, *Lives of St Francis*, trans. A. G. Ferrers Howell. London, 1908.
Underwood, Guy, *The Pattern of the Past*. London, 1969.
Wheatley, Henry B. (ed.) *Merlin*, 3 vols. EETS. London, 1938.
Wind, Edgar, *Pagan Mysteries in the Renaissance*. London, 1968.

Index